JIM REARDEN'S
ALASKA

OTHER BOOKS BY JIM REARDEN INCLUDE:

Alaska's Wolf Man

Koga's Zero

Castner's Cutthroats

In the Shadow of Eagles,
with Rudy Billberg

Shadows on the Koyukuk,
with Sidney Huntington

Tales of Alaska's Big Bears

Arctic Bush Pilot,
with James "Andy" Anderson

Trail of the Eagle, with Bud Conkle

Wind on the Water,
with LeNora Huntley Conkle

White Squaw, with Delores Cline Brown

JIM REARDEN'S ALASKA
Fifty Years
of Frontier Adventure

by Jim Rearden

EPICENTER PRESS
Alaska Book Adventures

Epicenter Press is a regional press founded in Alaska whose interests include but are not limited to the arts, history, environment, and diverse cultures and lifestyles of the Pacific Northwest and high latitudes. We seek both the traditional and innovative in publishing nonfiction tradebooks, and contemporary art and photography giftbooks.

Publisher: Kent Sturgis
Editor: Don Graydon
Proofreader: Sherrill Carlson
Cover: Betty Watson
Text design: Victoria Sturgis
Maps: Marge Mueller, Grey Mouse Graphics
Printer: Transcontinental Printing

Library of Congress Control Number: 2001095784

ISBN: 0-9708493-1-1

To order single copies of JIM REARDEN'S ALASKA: mail $17.95 plus $4.95 for shipping (Washington residents must add $1.60 sales tax) to Epicenter Press, Box 82368, Kenmore, WA 98028; call toll-free 1-800-950-6663; or visit us online at www.EpicenterPress.com.

Booksellers: Retail discounts are available from our distributor, Graphic Arts Center Publishing Company, Box 10306, Portland, OR 97210.
Phone: 1-800-452-3032.

First printing September 2001

10 9 8 7 6 5 4 3 2 1

Printed in Canada

PREFACE: TRAIL OF A WRITER

After half a century of writing about Alaska I decided it was time to publish a representative collection of my work. The pieces I have selected for this volume, principally from the more than five hundred magazine articles I have had published, form a kind of history of my Alaska—the Alaska I have known since I arrived in the Territory in 1947.

I decided I wanted to write for a living when I was in high school in Petaluma, California, where my father was the agriculture teacher. I believe the desire came from reading voraciously before I was ten years old.

Animal stories of any kind attracted me. I loved tales of the Pacific tropical islands and sailing. One book, *Blue Water Vagabond* by Dennis Puleston, especially appealed to me; for a time after reading it I was going to wander among the Pacific islands with my own sailboat and pay my way by writing about my adventures. Weekly, I listened to the wonderful *Hawaii Calls* radio program broadcast from "beneath the spreading banyan tree at the Royal Hawaiian Hotel on Waikiki Beach." I still like Hawaiian music. I was a romantic even then. Writers do have to be romantics if they are to interest readers.

Then I discovered Alaska. I decided I was going to homestead in Alaska and raise beef cattle (not dairy cattle; I had to milk two cows twice a day all through high school). I would also write about my hunting and fishing adventures in the Territory. A high school friend, Louis Eckman, wanted to become a commercial pilot. He agreed to fly the beef meat from my farm to market.

Obviously, Louis and I at sixteen years of age didn't have much of a grasp on life. Strangely, I did make Alaska my life, and Louis learned to fly. He was a pilot in the Navy during World War II. He is gone now—something that seems to be happening more and more frequently to my life's associates as I survive into my late seventies.

I graduated from high school in June 1942 at the age of seventeen and that fall enrolled in the fish and game management course at Oregon State College at Corvallis. My grades were average and below, and I dropped out after a quarter. Most of the male students were in the military and I was uncomfortable attending classes while everyone else was at war.

In March 1943, a month shy of my eighteenth birthday, with my father's permission I enlisted in the Navy, where I was trained to operate underwater sound gear—sonar. I became one of the commissioning crew of 130 for the USS *Lovering*, a destroyer escort.

My dream of visiting a tropical Pacific island came true when the *Lovering* dropped anchor in Pearl Harbor. This wasn't the Hawaii I had envisioned. The military presence was overwhelming. Ships that were bombed and torpedoed during the Japanese attack on December 7, 1941, were still being repaired. The sunken hull of the battleship *Arizona* was marked by the scorched and damaged superstructure that rose above the water.

My juvenile notion that war was a great adventure evaporated about then. We sailed into the Central Pacific war zone. I was the ship's mail orderly, and I went ashore at every port to get the mail. My war memories include viewing hundreds of Japanese bodies on Tarawa a couple days after the battle there, with splintered palm trees and shell craters everywhere, and the unmistakable odor of rotting human remains; hearing the excited voices of our Navy and Marine pilots from the speaker on our ship's bridge as they bombed and strafed the Marshall Islands while we patrolled offshore, a safety ship in event a plane went down; seeing the flame throwers and the fighting infantry on Eniwetok Island from the deck of the *Lovering* as they wiped out dug-in Japanese.

I remember months of boredom as our ship swung around the hook in the lagoons of backwater, palm-tree-waving atolls, and the persistent sound of sonar pinging as I searched for hostile submarines. I watched as three F4U Corsairs returned from a successful raid and buzzed an island airstrip. As they circled for landing, flying close formation over the water, two collided and one splashed into the sea. The pilot's body was never found. I watched a shark pull a coxswain from the *Lovering* under as he swam after a whaleboat that had gone adrift in Tarawa lagoon. Sharks there had learned to eat humans.

There was more, but this is not the place for it.

I was not yet twenty years old.

The war over, I returned to OSC in September 1945 with a wife and, shortly, a daughter. The three-year hiatus from studies, plus my war experience, had made a different person of me. Learning about wildlife management was far more fun than making war, and my grades were good. It was fun to be alive.

At the end of my junior year in 1947 I landed a summer job at Chignik, on the south side of the Alaska Peninsula, as a fishery patrol agent for the U.S. Fish and Wildlife Service. With a thirty-foot patrol boat, I enforced commercial salmon fishing regulations. It was there I first saw silvery salmon swimming into a clear river in what seemed unending numbers. I encountered huge brown bears, saw hundreds of bald eagles, got acquainted with ptarmigan, and even had an encounter with a wolverine. For the first time I saw a land essentially untouched by man. The residents were hardy, friendly Aleuts.

I returned to OSC and graduated in June 1948 with a BS degree in fish and game management. In 1950, after receiving an MS degree in wildlife conservation from the University of Maine, I was hired to organize a new wildlife department and teach wildlife management at the University of Alaska Fairbanks.

With my wife and two daughters I arrived at College, near Fairbanks, in June 1950, after driving a 1941 Buick over the Alaska Highway. I was broke, and worked through the summer as a gandy dancer (track laborer) with the Alaska Railroad, which paid for groceries until classes began in September.

I was given a free hand in organizing classes and requirements for a bachelor of science degree in wildlife management to be offered by the university. I was also a nervous, inexperienced, twenty-five-year-old assistant professor as classes started that fall.

By my third year of teaching I was a full professor. The program had attracted students, and they had no difficulty finding summer jobs in the wildlife field. But I was restless. As I lectured at a classroom in the old Main Building I could look across the wild Tanana Valley to the Alaska Range a hundred miles away, and I often wondered what I was doing in front of a blackboard. I wanted to be out there in that exciting land. I wanted to write stories of Alaska and Alaskans.

It was then I met Frank Glaser, who worked for the Fish and Wildlife Service as a wolf hunter—official title, Predator Control Agent. He was a sourdough who arrived in Alaska in 1915. He had been a market hunter, killing and selling wild game, the only reliable source of meat in the Interior until the Alaska Railroad was completed in 1923. He had owned the Black Rapids Roadhouse on the Richardson Highway where it penetrates the white-peaked Alaska Range, had been a professional dog musher and a big game guide. For more than a decade he had lived at Savage River, trapping valuable fur animals. He had bred and driven a team of wolf-dogs. For sixteen years he had hunted wolves in Alaska for the federal government. In short, he had led an adventurous outdoor life.

Frank Glaser loved to talk. I suspect he was making up for his years of living alone in the wilderness. Some called him Silent Frank. Unlike some incessant talkers, Glaser wasn't a bore; he was a marvelous storyteller with a steel-trap memory.

JIM REARDEN'S ALASKA

In 1953 I recorded Glaser's stories with a tape recorder—a new piece of equipment then. It had glass vacuum tubes, and a foot pedal to stop the machine as I transcribed his words. Over the next couple of years I sold about a dozen Frank Glaser as-told-to Jim Rearden stories, mostly to *Outdoor Life* magazine. This was the start of my writing career. After four years of teaching I resigned my professorship and turned to full-time writing.

Looking back, it wasn't a prudent move; in fact, it was probably foolish, but I was following a dream. Alaska is a land that encourages dreamers and adventurers, and I happily took the plunge. To augment my diminished income I became a registered big game guide and took nonresident hunters into the wilderness after trophies. I added commercial photography to my writing. I soon moved to Homer, on the Kenai Peninsula, to be near the rich North Pacific Ocean, where I still live.

I guided hunters in the arctic Brooks Range, on the Alaska Peninsula, on the Kenai Peninsula, and I wrote and sold stories of some of those hunts. I photographed winter carnival beauty queens, and did portraits as well as passport photos. My articles sold, but there were dry spells, and my family had to make do in many ways. When writing didn't sell, I worked as a clerk, as a bookkeeper and office manager, as a carpenter, even as a seal hunter.

In 1959 I was hired by the Territorial Department of Fisheries to monitor an offshore seismic operation in Cook Inlet to see that the explosives they used did not kill salmon or other valuable species. Statehood came, and this temporary position led to a job with the new Alaska Department of Fish and Game, where after a time I became area biologist in charge of management of the commercial fisheries in Cook Inlet. The steady income was nice, and I still had evenings and weekends to write.

My growing family, which eventually included two sons and three daughters, plus two stepsons and a stepdaughter, needed more room. And I needed space for my magazine work. In my spare time, with my own hands I built a 34-by-45-foot two-story log house with a full basement, so that everyone had a bedroom and I finally had the office and darkroom space I needed.

Strangely, my navy sonar training came to my aid as a fishery management biologist. To properly manage salmon, one must know how many salmon reach their spawning grounds. In clear streams and lakes they can easily be counted. But many of Cook Inlet's major salmon streams are silty. Salmon can't be seen in them.

I remembered my sonar training. Could sonar detect salmon in silty water? No one knew. Could sonar be used to count salmon?

PREFACE: TRAIL OF A WRITER

No one knew.

With backing from Commissioner of Fish and Game Walter Kirkness, I wrote every sonar manufacturer in the United States, expressing interest in the possible development of a sonar salmon counter. Only one company responded. The Bendix company sent Al Menin, an electronics genius, with a machine to determine if sonar could "see" salmon in silty water.

The machine "saw" salmon in the silty Kasilof River, and Menin told me he could develop a salmon counter. The next season he arrived in Alaska with a working machine. Today sonar salmon counters are annually installed in major salmon streams, both clear and silty, from the Yukon drainage south.

Naturally, I sold an article about the salmon sonar counter to *Outdoor Life.* The editors labeled it "Salmon Do Their Own Counting," and it appeared in March 1969.

In the 1950s and 1960s I wrote frequently for *The Alaska Sportsman* magazine. In 1968 owner Bob Henning listed me on his masthead as outdoors editor and started sending me work. My first project was to go through a box that held more than fifty manuscripts, some of which Henning had kept unused for several years. "Accept and edit those that are worth printing; return the others to the authors," he instructed.

I wrote a lot of apologetic letters over the next few months. I knew from experience the frustration of writing an article and waiting for an editor's response.

The publication's name changed to *Alaska* magazine in 1969. While continuing to work as a fishery biologist, evenings and weekends I edited contributors' articles and wrote my own articles for *Alaska.* Bob paid me by the hour. I resigned my fishery position at the end of 1969 and went to work full time as outdoors editor for *Alaska* magazine, a position I held for twenty years, working out of my home office.

At the magazine, I preached scientific management of Alaska's fish and wildlife. Bob Henning assigned me to write a monthly conservation department titled "The Alaska Sportsman," in which I covered natural history, fishery and game management problems, and related subjects. *Alaska* magazine was the only publication reaching into essentially every town and village in Alaska in those years, and I think the constant theme of the need for proper management of fish and game, written in popular style, helped increase a statewide understanding of the value of the resource and why we should take the best of care of it.

I also sold articles and completed assignments for about forty different magazines in the United States, France, Germany, England, Australia, New Zealand, and Canada, including the *National Geographic,* the German and French *Geo, Outdoor Life, Field & Stream, Sports Afield, National Wildlife, International Wildlife, Audubon,* and *Sports Illustrated.* I wrote so many articles for *Outdoor Life* that for twenty years I was listed on the masthead as a field editor, even while working for *Alaska* magazine.

Most of my writing involved Alaska's animals. Thus I have watched with interest the public's attitude change over the years toward some of these animals, especially the wolf and the bear. During my first years in Alaska, wolves were considered "bad" animals: poison, traps, snares, and aerial hunting were used by federal wildlife agents in attempts to eradicate them. After statehood in 1959, Alaskans classified the wolf both as a furbearer and a big game animal and it suddenly became a "good" animal. The public generally embraced this view.

Today many sincere urban residents, most of whom have never seen a wild wolf, regard the animal as a totem that represents wilderness. Even regulated hunting and trapping prompt objections, although the wolf, our most prolific large mammal, is probably as abundant in Alaska today as it has ever been.

Bears were "damned pests" to many Alaskans in the early twentieth century and were often killed simply because they were bears. They could be dangerous; they broke into cabins, tore up camps, and frightened or attacked horses then used for transportation. Even in mid-century, hunting regulations allowed sportsmen to kill as many as four grizzlies a year. In the 1950s a federal fishery biologist proposed killing brown/grizzly bears on Kodiak Island because they were eating salmon on the spawning grounds. One of Alaska's early Territorial governors proposed eradicating Alaska's grizzlies "to allow the country to develop."

Today, Alaska's bears are prized for simply being bears. As with wolves, the bear population, both black bears and brown/grizzly bears, is probably as high as it has ever been. Hunting seasons and bag limits are closely regulated. Many areas have been set aside for viewing the animals. A few grizzlies, and sometimes more than a few black bears, inhabit or invade urban areas, including Anchorage, Alaska's largest city. When wildlife managers ask if the animals should be removed, most residents say no.

PREFACE: TRAIL OF A WRITER

In 1970, Governor Bill Egan appointed me to the Alaska Board of Fish and Game. I served for twelve years—the last seven as a member of the Board of Game after the dual-purpose board was split into two, game and fisheries. In 1976 President Gerald Ford appointed me to the National Advisory Committee on Oceans and Atmosphere, an eighteen-member so-called blue-ribbon committee of primarily scientists from universities and agencies around the nation. Each month for a year and a half I flew to Washington, D.C., for a weeklong meeting and gloried in the excitement of rubbing shoulders with some of the nation's top scientists and having a tiny say in recommendations that went directly to the president.

I've long been attracted by Alaskans who have great stories to tell, and early on I found that editors especially liked such stories if they were told in the first person. As a result I've written many "as-told-to" Jim Rearden stories, including several in this book. I could have written them in the third person, but they would not have been nearly so compelling.

I left my position with *Alaska* magazine in 1988 and turned to writing books. I quickly found that the adventurous careers of Alaskans was a fertile area for books as well as articles. I have written half a dozen "as-told-to" books (of the eighteen books I have written) based on the lives of early 1900s to post-World War II bush pilots, a hunting guide, and rural residents, capturing bits of history that otherwise would likely have been lost.

One of the books, *Alaska's Wolf Man: The 1915-55 Wilderness Adventures of Frank Glaser,* published in 1998, resulted in my being named Historian of the Year 1999 by the Alaska Historical Society. Two books—*Shadows on the Koyukuk*, with Sidney Huntington, and *Cracking the Zero Mystery* (later rewritten and retitled *Koga's Zero*)—have been translated into Japanese and sold in that country.

As one ages, he or she becomes the sum of all of life's experiences. The more experiences, the greater is one's potential as a writer. My wartime service, college courses in journalism and photography, formal training in fisheries and wildlife, years of receiving rejection slips for articles, and field experience in operating boats and in hunting and fishing have all helped me in my work as a journalist. My background served me well in writing about Alaska. I hope the articles in this volume please modern readers who wish to learn more about life in Alaska as I have recorded it over the past fifty years.

Jim Rearden
Homer, Alaska

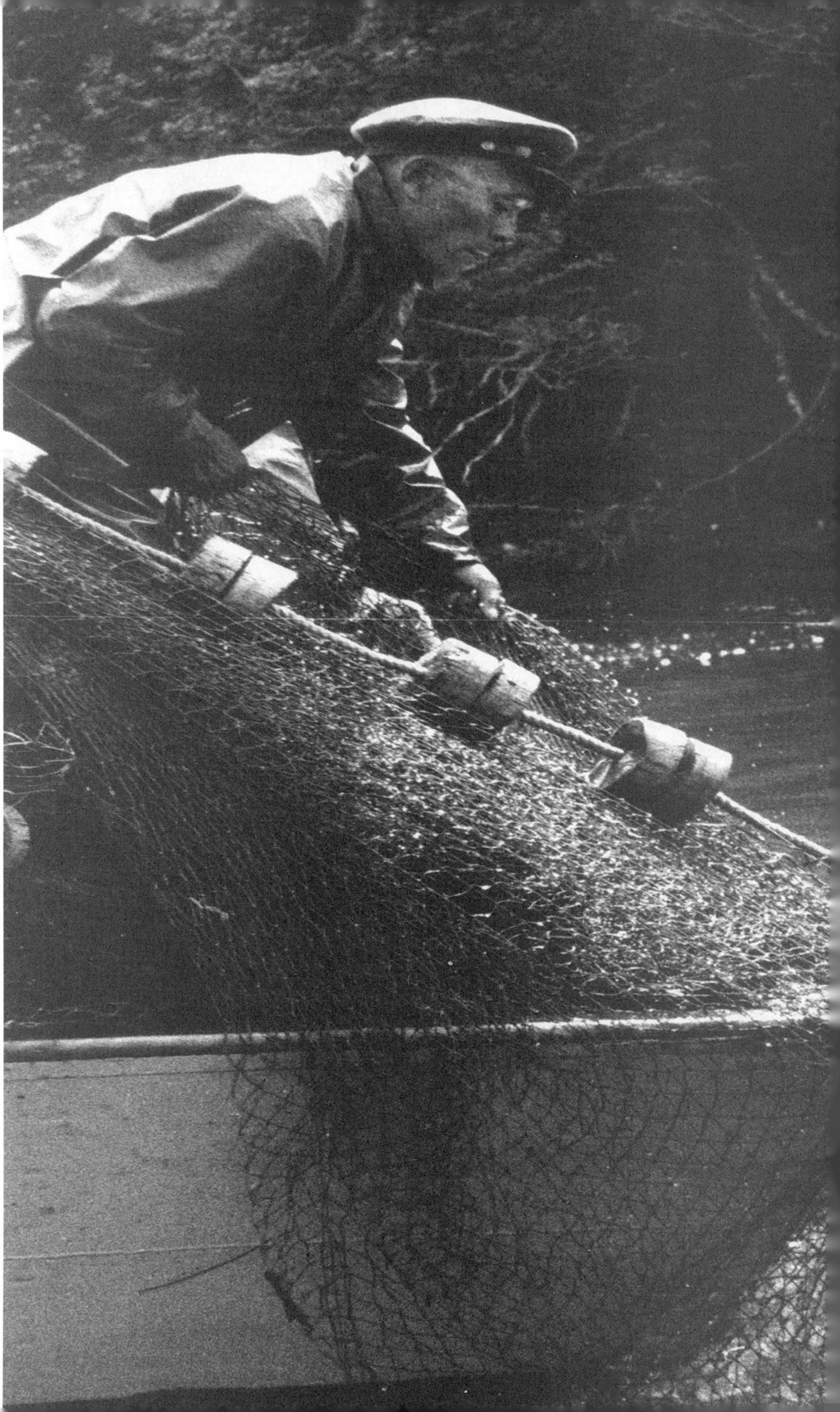

TABLE OF CONTENTS

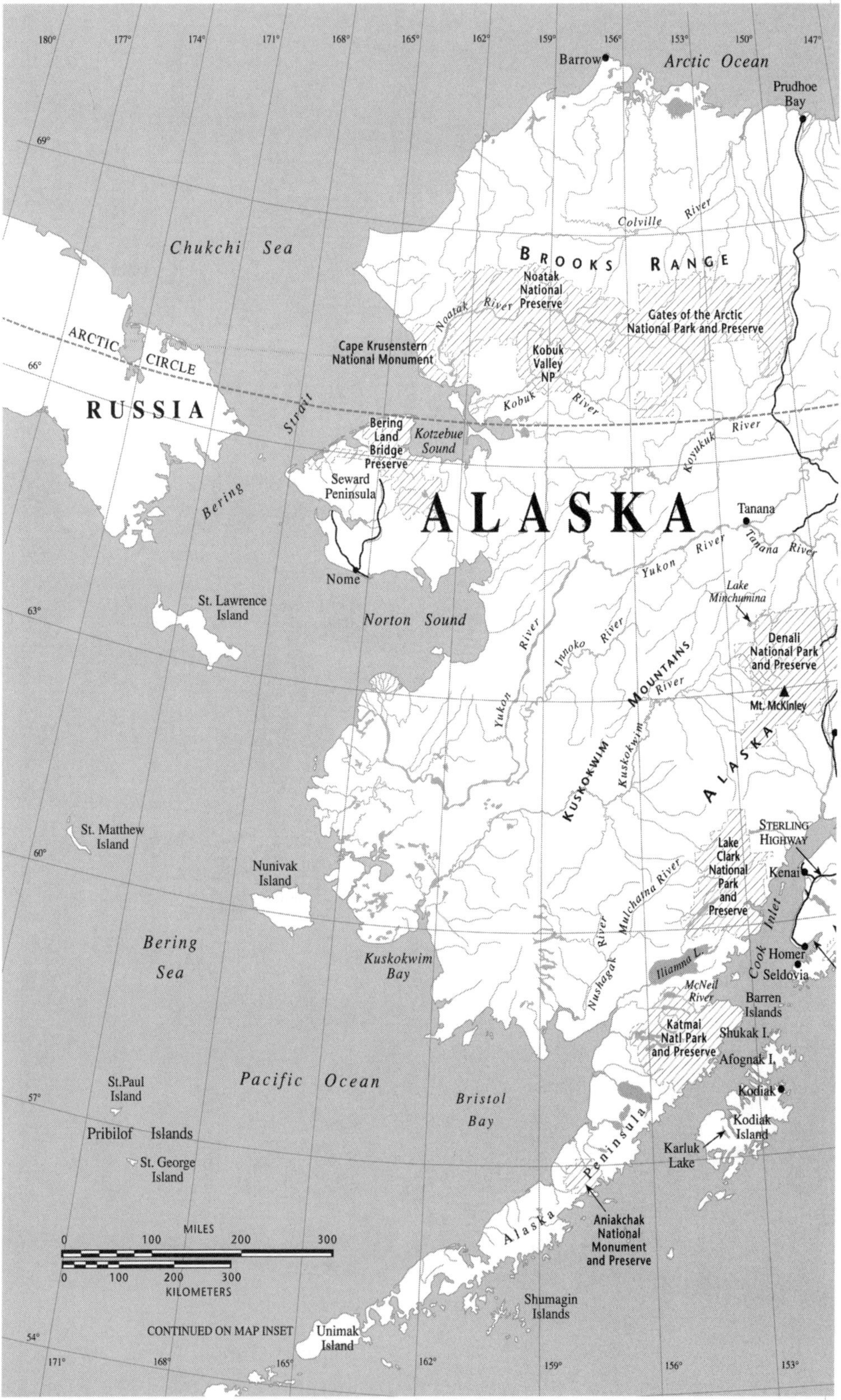

180°
177°
174°
171°
168°
165°
162°
159°
156°
153°
150°
147°
Barrow
Arctic Ocean
Prudhoe Bay
69°
Colville River
Chukchi Sea
BROOKS RANGE
Noatak National Preserve
Noatak River
Gates of the Arctic National Park and Preserve
ARCTIC CIRCLE
Cape Krusenstern National Monument
Kobuk Valley NP
66°
Kobuk River
RUSSIA
Strait
Bering Land Bridge Preserve
Kotzebue Sound
Koyukuk River
Seward Peninsula
Bering
ALASKA
Tanana
Tanana River
Yukon River
Nome
Lake Minchumina
St. Lawrence Island
63°
Norton Sound
Innoko River
Denali National Park and Preserve
Yukon River
KUSKOKWIM MOUNTAINS
River
Mt. McKinley
Kuskokwim
ALASKA
St. Matthew Island
60°
Sterling Highway
Lake Clark National Park and Preserve
Kenai
Nunivak Island
Mulchatna River
Cook Inlet
Bering Sea
Nushagak River
Homer
Seldovia
Kuskokwim Bay
Iliamna L.
McNeil River
Barren Islands
Katmai Natl Park and Preserve
Shukak I.
Afognak I.
Pacific Ocean
St.Paul Island
57°
Bristol Bay
Kodiak
Kodiak Island
Pribilof Islands
Karluk Lake
St. George Island
Alaska Peninsula
Aniakchak National Monument and Preserve
MILES
0
100
200
300
0
100
200
300
KILOMETERS
Shumagin Islands
CONTINUED ON MAP INSET
Unimak Island
54°
171°
168°
165°
162°
159°
156°
153°

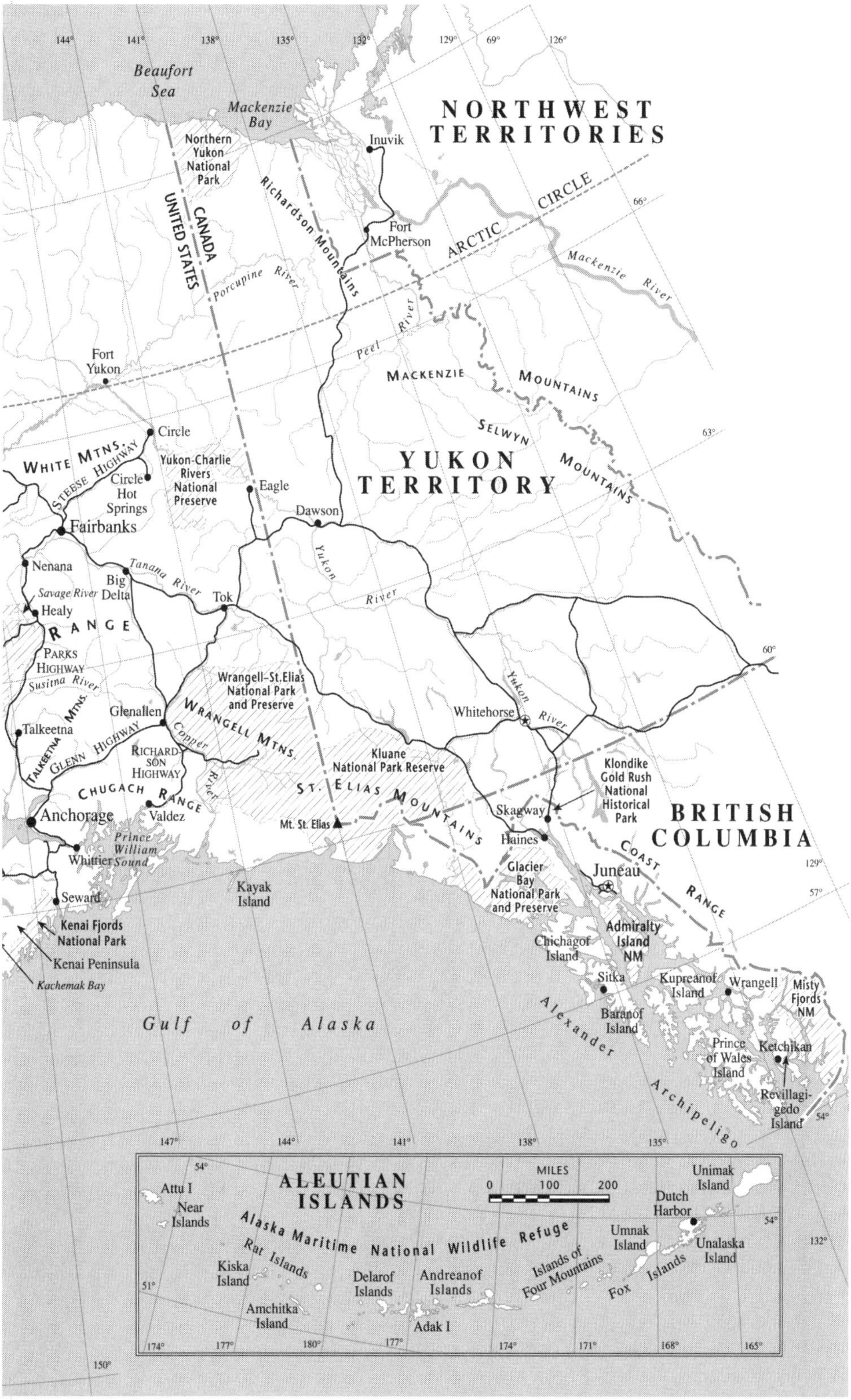

Beaufort Sea
Mackenzie Bay
NORTHWEST TERRITORIES
Northern Yukon National Park
Inuvik
Richardson Mountains
CANADA
UNITED STATES
Fort McPherson
ARCTIC CIRCLE
Mackenzie River
Porcupine River
Peel River
Fort Yukon
MACKENZIE MOUNTAINS
SELWYN MOUNTAINS
Circle
WHITE MTNS.
STEESE HIGHWAY
Yukon-Charlie Rivers National Preserve
Circle Hot Springs
YUKON TERRITORY
Eagle
Dawson
Fairbanks
Nenana
Big Delta
Tanana River
Yukon River
Savage River
Healy
Tok
RANGE
PARKS HIGHWAY
Susitna River
Wrangell-St.Elias National Park and Preserve
Glenallen
WRANGELL MTNS.
Whitehorse
Talkeetna
TALKEETNA MTNS.
GLENN HIGHWAY
Copper River
RICHARDSON HIGHWAY
Kluane National Park Reserve
Klondike Gold Rush National Historical Park
CHUGACH RANGE
ST. ELIAS MOUNTAINS
Anchorage
Valdez
Mt. St. Elias
Skagway
BRITISH COLUMBIA
Haines
Prince William Sound
Whittier
Glacier Bay National Park and Preserve
COAST RANGE
Juneau
Kayak Island
Seward
Kenai Fjords National Park
Kenai Peninsula
Kachemak Bay
Admiralty Island NM
Chichagof Island
Sitka
Kupreanof Island
Wrangell
Misty Fjords NM
Baranof Island
Gulf of Alaska
Alexander Archipelago
Prince of Wales Island
Ketchikan
Revillagigedo Island
ALEUTIAN ISLANDS
MILES
0 100 200
Attu I
Near Islands
Alaska Maritime National Wildlife Refuge
Rat Islands
Kiska Island
Amchitka Island
Delarof Islands
Andreanof Islands
Adak I
Islands of Four Mountains
Fox Islands
Umnak Island
Unalaska Island
Dutch Harbor
Unimak Island

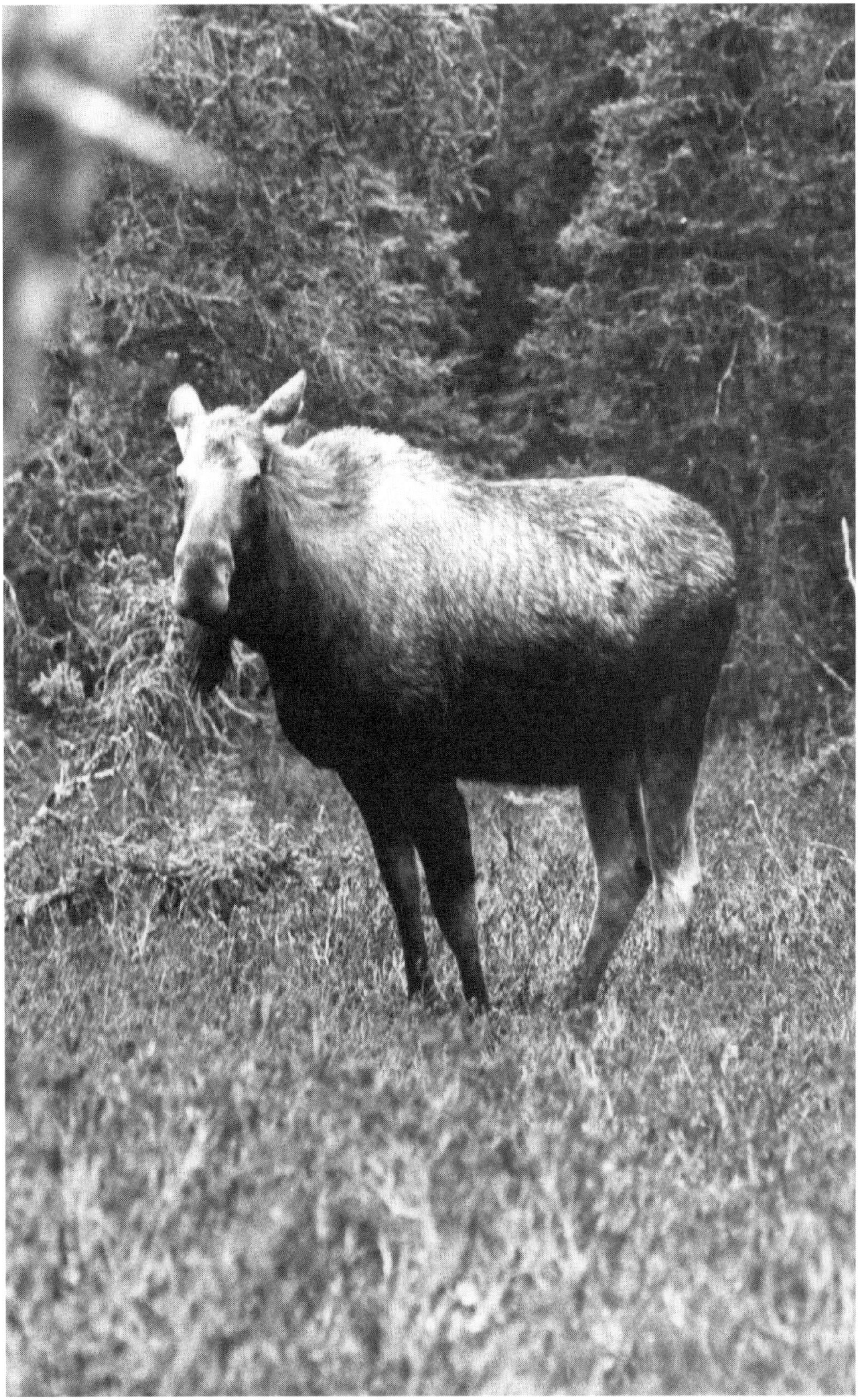

CHAPTER ONE

MOOSE JOHNSON'S YINX

I was on the beach at Homer one day in the late 1950s when I noticed an old man with a big dog wandering along the shore. He was a six-footer, a bit stooped, with a neat white beard. He wore rubber-bottom, leather-top shoepacks, whipcord trousers, and a light whipcord jacket— an outfit we used to call an Alaska tuxedo. His dog must have weighed close to 125 pounds.

As the man neared, I walked to meet him. I knew most Homer residents then, and he was a stranger.

"Hello," I said. "Is that a Mackenzie River husky?"

"Yah. You know about dis kind of dog?" he responded in a strong Swedish accent.

We fell into friendly conversation, and shortly I learned his name was Moose Johnson. I had heard the name be-fore. Curious, I asked if he was the trapper who had had so many troubles with moose away back when.

He grinned, and admitted he was the guy. It had been more than three decades since he had earned his nick-name, he said.

"You still remember the details?" I asked

An unfriendly cow moose. She has a sprinkle of fresh snow on her back, and her ears are about half way down. When a moose's ears lay flat back, look out, it's angry, and may attack. Moose Johnson learned about angry moose the hard way.

JIM REARDEN PHOTO

"Yah. I never forget that winter," he said, shaking his head.

"Would you tell me about it?" I asked.

"Yah. Why not?" he answered.

"Do you mind if I use a tape recorder?"

"OK wit' me."

Moose Johnson and his dog accompanied me home and I recorded his story. He stayed for dinner, and we spent a pleasant evening visiting. After he left town, I never saw him again. But he left me with a wonderful story to tell.

A man without a nickname was a rarity in the Alaska of the first half of the twentieth century. Once a nickname was bestowed, he was known by it forever after, and often his given name was forgotten. Nicknames were usually colorful, often unprintable, at least in the old days of polite print. Generally they were earned. The Malamute Kid freighted with huge dog teams; Laughing Ole could be heard laughing to himself on the trail from a mile away on a quiet day; Ptarmigan Dunbar liked to eat ptarmigan; Hungry Mike was a big eater, and the Diamond Kid decorated himself with big sparklers. Hopalong Hansen, Walking Bill, and Hobo Ed earned their names from their constant travel. Sometimes a name was earned the hard way, as Drunken Mike earned his, and as Moose Johnson earned his.

Knut Johnson, his birth name, was a fiddle-footed, blue-eyed loner who drifted from interior Alaska to the railhead at coastal Seward in July 1922, in search of new trapping grounds. Six-foot tall, blond, and Swedish-born, Johnson had lived in Alaska for about twenty years, most

of which time he spent trapping alone in the high country of the vast Alaska Range. His English was heavily ac-
cented, and, unless he had a few relaxing drinks, he was
shy around people. He was in his seventies when he told
me about his "yinx" and how he earned his nickname.

Knut had decided, after his years in Alaska's subarctic Interior, that coastal Alaska might prove warmer; he
was tired of deep-cold winters. At Seward he yanked his
five big Mackenzie River huskies out of the rickety Alaska
Railroad boxcar, arranged to leave his sled and other gear
with the stationmaster, then walked with his dogs to the
edge of Seward, where he made camp under a dry spruce.
He purchased supplies, and a week later, with his dogs,
boarded a local trading schooner bound for Kenai, where
he planned to head inland.

At Kenai, Knut bought a twenty-foot poling boat from
an Indian, piled into it his dogsled, traps, grub, .405 Winchester, and a few tools, and headed upriver. He let the
dogs run along the bank as he laboriously poled upstream.
When he reached Funny River he eyed the high-country
spruce-covered benches and ridges it drains, and decided
it looked good.

He poled up the Funny as far as he could, pulled the
boat ashore, and turned it over. He found three cottonwood trees growing close together, built a ladder out of
poles, and built a platform cache where he left his sled,
dog harness, traps, and most of his grub. He then packed
about twenty-five pounds on each dog, shouldered a pack
himself, and headed for the plateau that divides the Funny
and Killey Rivers.

He quickly decided, "Lots moose dat country," as he
explained it to me. Within two days, he said, he had seen
more moose than he had seen in a year in interior Alaska.
At least he wouldn't be meat hungry. He kept a sharp eye
on his five huge dogs; though well trained, they occasionally succumbed to the joy of chasing game.

He encountered cow moose with their two-month-old reddish calves, white-legged yearlings, and huge slab-sided bulls with bulbous, half-formed antlers in velvet. Knut was right about there being plenty of moose. What he didn't know was he had accidentally wandered into the midst of what was probably the heaviest concentration of moose in Alaska in that year of 1922. Three great fires had swept the Kenai Peninsula—one in 1871, another in 1891, and a third in 1910. In addition, many small fires had swept a ridge here, a thousand acres of spruce there, eliminating old growth.

Until 1910 there was much down timber from the earlier fires, and travel for moose and man was difficult, but the 1910 fire cleaned out much of this, and thereafter moose increased rapidly, what with all the fine birch, aspen, cottonwood, and willow—favorite moose foods—replacing the old-growth spruce.

He chose a small, well-drained clearing a mile or so below timberline and there built a 10-by-12 dirt-floor cabin of green spruce logs chinked with sphagnum moss.

A few days after he started work on the cabin he was walking with his axe through the timber, circling the cabin site looking for suitable logs, when he came face-to-face with a cow moose with a late-born calf at heel. Knut froze, as did the cow. She made a noise and the calf dropped to its belly in the bushes. The cow laid her big ears back and the hair on her neck stood up.

Knut took an uneasy step backward, looking over his shoulder for the nearest tree. The cow charged, and Knut fled. Her hooves were thudding close when he ducked behind a tree. She skidded to a stop while he scrambled upward through the branches of a prickly spruce, leaving his axe on the ground. Incredibly, as he reached a height he thought safe, the cow stood on hind legs and grasped one of his shoepacks in her mouth and tried to yank him down. He yelled, half in fright, half in surprise, kicked loose, and hoisted himself upward another several feet.

There he remained, scratched and disgusted, waiting for the cow to leave. But she walked around the tree, looking up at him angrily. He stood on one foot, then the other, swatted mosquitoes, and cursed in Swedish and English. Each time he started to descend, the cow charged, ears back, hackles on end, and he hastily retreated upward.

It couldn't last forever. The cow finally wandered out of sight and Knut eased himself to the ground, picked up his axe, and started to sneak away. To his consternation the cow came thundering from behind a near spruce. This time Knut sprinted to two trees that grew close together and eased between them. She followed, poking her head through, but her shoulders stopped her. Knut slammed her with the axe, knocking her off her feet, her head caught like that of a cow in a stanchion. Half a dozen more swings with the axe severed her head.

He dressed the carcass and hung the meat high in a tree. He then searched for and found the calf, still following its mother's orders to lie still. It allowed him to touch it before leaping to its feet to run, but by then Knut had a good grip on it. He soothed the damp-eyed little creature, and within ten minutes it followed wherever he went.

At the cabin Knut fashioned a bottle with a loose rag cover from which the calf could suck evaporated milk, of which he had half a dozen cans.

For a week the calf gamboled about the growing cabin, and even the huskies accepted it and offered it no harm. It slept nights next to Knut and never let him out of sight during the day. But Knut soon ran out of milk, and ten days after he acquired it the calf died. Until the cow's carcass was eaten by himself and the dogs, he felt like a murderer with each bite.

By mid-September he had brushed out two ten-mile traplines. But Knut was worried; he had seen little fur sign. If he had taken the trouble to ask at Kenai, he'd have learned why. In 1890 a group of fifty-two gold seekers, called the Kings County Bunch (for Kings County, New York), arrived on the Kenai. Soon after they arrived a rabies epidemic swept the area, and they scattered strychnine baits across the hills from Homer, at the lower end of the Kenai, to Skilak Lake, north of Knut's trapping grounds. By 1922, when Knut arrived, furbearers had not fully recovered from the lethal effects of rabies and strychnine.

The country was alive with rabbits (snowshoe hares), though, and lynx were abundant. Instead of marten, which Knut had hoped for, it became obvious he would have to depend upon lynx for his trapping efforts.

As mid-September approached, Knut realized he had built his cabin where breeding moose concentrated. Within a mile he often saw as many as a dozen bulls, and even more cows, standing amidst the small scattered spruces or bedded in the timberline willows. At this time of year the bulls' peeled antlers gleamed like gold, and he often saw bulls miles away as their clean antlers flashed in the sun.

Frosts arrived, and the moose started talking; bulls grunted, cows chirped and bawled.

One night two big bulls started to fight near the cabin. Knut opened the door and looked into the brilliant frost-sparkled moonlight to see the antagonists less than a hundred yards away, antler to antler. One bull was huge, slab-sided, the other chunky, heavy set; both carried racks that spread nearly six feet. As he watched, Slabside rammed his huge antlers at the other bull, pushing him back fifty feet or more. Then Chunky got himself set and slammed his three-quarters of a ton into Slabside, nearly knocking him on his rear.

Knut's huskies were strangely silent. All summer when moose had wandered into the cabin clearing the dogs had barked or howled. But tonight they slunk into the moon shadows, and all five sat watching the two bulls intently without so much as a chain clink.

Knut watched from his open door for a few minutes until the chill penetrated his red flannel underwear, then he retreated to his bunk and warm lynx-skin robe. But the clatter of bulls' antlers, their hoarse grunts, the snapping of brush and trees and the rush of pounding hooves made sleep impossible. The fighting bulls sounded ever closer. He decided to watch the show and got up and dressed in the dark.

He opened the door just as Chunky managed to slam his six-foot-wide rack into the belly of Slabside, pick him up, and carry him sideways in a tremendous display of strength and rutting fervor. Knut had stepped out of the door when he saw the black, struggling form of the carried bull surging sideways toward him. He leaped inside as the two fifteen-hundred-pound moose slammed into the door, tearing it from its leather hinges and partially caving in the front wall of the little cabin.

As Slabside hit the cabin he kept to his feet and leaped ahead. The victorious bull followed, prodding his rear. They hit the brush running, a couple of hundred feet from the cabin. Knut recovered from his shock and reached for his .405 Winchester, but it was too late. He listened to them crash out of hearing.

It took half a day for him to fix the door, straighten the front of the caved-in cabin, and replace loosened sod on the roof. It took slightly longer for him to rid himself of the startling vision of the two bulls slamming into the cabin a few feet from where he stood, and he didn't quit saying "Yumpin' yesus," his current favorite curse, for many days.

A day or two later, while splitting firewood, he looked up to see a young bull moose on a high trot heading almost soundlessly toward him, neck hair raised, as if ready to fight. Knut sprinted into the cabin and watched the bull circle the cabin, snorting and tossing antlers. The huskies remained meekly silent, cowering beneath the pole lean-tos he had constructed for them.

Two days later, again splitting firewood, he looked up to see another big yellow-antlered bull on a high trot toward him. He suddenly realized the chopping noise was attracting the bulls, that these critters were rutting, on the prowl, spoiling for a fight. For the next couple of weeks he used the axe sparingly, and when he did use it, he kept his rifle handy.

He continued to lay out trapline trails. During the moose rutting season he noticed that bulls walked with toes spread, and that cows were often in harems of from two to fourteen. The bigger bulls had the biggest harems. The bulls became gaunter and gaunter, for they didn't feed; they were too busy fighting and breeding.

Once the rut was over and temperatures dropped so meat would keep, Knut decided to kill the legal limit of two bulls. Early one morning he found a good-size young bull bedded less than a mile from the cabin. Using the yellow-clean antlers jutting above willows as a guide, he slipped in from above, and when near, he walked openly toward the bull until the animal stood and stared at him. He dumped the animal with 300 grains of .405 lead in the neck. He leaned the rifle against a willow and started to tie a rope to a hind leg to stretch it out so he could more easily dress the animal. He was bent over tying the rope when the bull lunged in a violent death kick and a sharp hoof caught Knut on the side of the head and knocked him about ten feet. He didn't know how long he lay unconscious. His head was sore and swollen for a week.

It was an agonizing job to dress and butcher the bull with his king-size headache and swollen face. He saved as much of the moose blood as he could in coffee cans; he allowed it to sour and later used it for bait for his traps. He built a platform cache about ten feet above ground where three trees grew close together, and piled the moose meat onto it, covering it with the moose's hide. He planned to haul it to his cabin with the dog team when there was enough snow.

A week or so later he killed another bull within a few hundred yards of his cabin. He approached this one warily after it was down; one kick in the head was enough. Before its hide stiffened in death, he rolled the bull on its side and plucked the hair clean from along its backbone, like one plucks a duck. He hung this thick strip— the heaviest hide on a moose—from a tall spruce with a hundred-pound log and when it was well stretched he cut strips of babiche (rawhide) from it, to be used for repairing his dogsled, making snowshoes, and fixing dog harness.

Snow fell in early October and he walked with the dogs to his boat and the cache at Funny River. He piled traps and grub in the sled and mushed back to his cabin.

During October and November he traveled with his dog team, laying out more traplines. He built three tiny, crude overnight shelters and cut firewood at each. Ptarmigan, rabbits, and porcupines were abundant, and when on the trail, he and the dogs often lived on this bounty. He bagged them with his .22 pistol.

Tracking snows confirmed his suspicions that fur was scarce, with few foxes, few mink, and virtually no marten. But there were many lynx ("link," Knut called them).

In his travels, he kept to the high country, near and above timberline, because it was easier going than in the lower-altitude heavy spruce stands. He was constantly amazed at the number of moose. One November day he counted more than a hundred of the big deer in sight at one time where they were scattered above timberline across high, treeless, snow-covered ridges. Most were bulls; cows and calves had headed for lower elevations when the snow came.

Knut had another grim encounter in mid-November. He worked his five dogs two-and-two with a single leader because some of his trails were through timber, and this short-coupled team could turn more easily. That day he broke out of a spruce thicket between two bedded moose, both big bulls. The dogs became confused. The moose were so close Knut had little control over the excited team; the wheel dogs tried to tackle the moose on the left; the other three dogs decided they were going to catch the moose on the right.

The bull to the left was uphill, and when the team suddenly appeared, he leaped to his feet and as he plunged about he skidded down a bank and landed amidst the dogs. A dog yelped as a sharp hoof flattened it into the snow. The remaining four dogs, harness in tangles, swirled about the moose. The stumbling bull lowered his huge antlers at the boiling team, trying to impale one or more of the dogs, but he had difficulty moving because several dogs clung to him with wolflike teeth.

Knut shrieked at the dogs and the moose, without impressing either. His heavy rifle was at his cabin, and his .22 was too light to stop the bull quickly; besides he was afraid of hitting a dog.

He grabbed the nearest weapon, a sharp ice chisel on a five-foot handle that he used for getting water at his camps. He leaped into waist-deep snow beside the team where the bull was plunging, and repeatedly thrust at the animal's neck. The bull lowered his head and tried to charge Knut, but one of the dogs grabbed the nose of the moose, stopping him. The moose tossed his head, throwing the 125-pound husky as far as its harness would allow. Knut again sliced the big neck with the chisel; it bit deeply this time, and the moose's head drooped. Knut continued to slice the neck, and finally the animal fell in his tracks, entangled with towline, harness, and four growling huskies.

The fifth dog lay quietly in the snow, and died within twenty minutes.

In late November, Knut harnessed the remaining dogs and went to haul home the moose he had left on the platform cache. The temperature was near zero, with nearly three feet of snow. When he drove into the timber near the cache the dogs' hackles raised, and they slowed and looked inquiringly back. He looked around, expecting to see a moose. But when near the cache he saw a freshly packed trail filled with huge tracks.

"Bjorn" (bear), he muttered. He turned the dogs with difficulty and returned to the cabin, where he tied them. He walked back to the cache on snowshoes, carrying his .405.

Snow was flattened for twenty feet around the cache, where the bear had patrolled, guarding "his" meat. The platform was pulled down, and trails from it led in several directions.

"Yumpin' yesus, " he mumbled. He took the mitten off his right hand and put the hand inside his parka to keep it warm as he eased toward the cache, step by crunchy step. A huge mound of brush and snow lay beyond the cache, and he decided this was where most of the meat would be.

When he was within fifteen feet of the mound, the bear, a huge brownie, stood on hind legs to his full eight-foot height and peered nearsightedly toward the trapper. Knut had never seen a brownie—his experience was limited to the smaller Interior grizzlies—but he had no time to be awed. He started to pour lead into the huge hairy chest. The bear dropped and lay thrashing. Knut shot repeatedly with the big rifle until the animal moved no more.

A sportsman would have been thrilled at that kill, but to Knut the bear was a nuisance. He had lost his moose meat, for little of it was salvageable, even for dog food, so now he had to turn for food to the moose he had killed with the ice chisel, an animal that had less fat. He skinned the bear, hoping to sell the hide. It squared over nine feet (average of width and length).

That wasn't the end to his winter moose problems. One cold January night when Knut was at his main cabin, he started for his outhouse, which was a simple pole shelter seventy-five feet from the cabin. Halfway there he met a moose standing in the trail. Loose snow was three feet deep on either side of the trail, and Knut didn't have snowshoes on. He stood uncertainly, then yelled at the moose. The hair on the animal's neck promptly stood on end; it laid its ears back and charged. Knut fled to the cabin, slamming the door inches in front of the moose.

The cranky animal kept him inside the cabin for a couple of hours. Each time he tried to go out it drove him back. Again, his huskies remained as silent as ghosts.

Knut began to wonder whether having many moose around was an advantage or a curse. "Damned moose have a yinx on me," he muttered again and again that winter.

That January of 1923 was one of unusually heavy snow on the Kenai, and Knut's trails constantly drifted over. He had to break trail for his dog team almost every mile he traveled. He worked harder than any dog in the team.

Knut followed a routine in his work. He mushed along one of his traplines, piling the carcasses of animals he caught into the sled (mostly lynx that winter) and resetting traps and snares. When dark came he spent the night in one of his tiny overnight shelters. Next night he returned to his main cabin, where he thawed the frozen carcasses so he could skin them next morning.

On those nights he continually scratched flea bites, as the always abundant lynx fleas left the frozen carcasses and found his (relatively) unfrozen one. Next morning he skinned his catch, baked sourdough bread to last a few days, and cooked beans or stew and froze it in small portions for use on the trail; he also repaired dog harness, fur parka, or sled or snowshoes, cut wood, and split kindling. Next day he would run another trapline to repeat the sequence. There was never a time when a job wasn't waiting his attention.

In February he had another moose-dog team tangle. The big bull had shed his antlers, and white circles marked the sides of his head where they had grown. As Knut came around the brow of a hill he saw the animal ahead, walking toward him on one of his packed trapline trails. As the animal neared, Knut yelled and waved his arms, which caused his dogs to run toward the moose. He stood on the sled brake, but it hardly slowed the dogs. The bull was reluctant to leave the hard-packed trail.

Knut was shrieking at both the team and the moose when they came together. The bull plunged a few times, using its slashing front hooves as weapons, then it leaped into deep snow and wallowed off, leaving one dog with a broken leg and two others gashed and bleeding.

Knut put the dog with the broken leg in the sled and wearily returned to his main cabin, where he set and splinted the leg. By next morning the dog had pulled the wrappings and splint off. Knut resplinted it and devised a large collar that kept the dog's teeth away from the injured leg. He left the animal food and water and ran one of his traplines with his three remaining dogs. The injured dog recovered and Knut eventually put him back in the team.

That winter Knut caught more than three hundred lynx, about a dozen foxes, half a dozen mink, and one otter. It was a good catch, considering he was in new country. In early April, while there was still snow, he stored his fur in the cache beside the boat on Funny River and returned to his cabin, planning to wait until the spring breakup of ice, when he would take the fur downriver to sell at Kenai. He could then replenish his supplies and start readying for the next trapping season.

It was early May before snow and river ice was gone and Knut set out on foot with his four dogs following. He carried his rifle, watching warily for moose, for he had learned to expect the unexpected with so many of the huge deer around.

But the rifle didn't help with the next moose crisis. He could scarcely believe his eyes when he arrived at the cache. The three trees he had cut off to make his cache had been cottonwood. Moose frequently strip cottonwood bark to eat, especially when other food is scarce. A cow moose had apparently been peeling bark from one of the cache trees, standing on hind legs, when a front hoof became caught in the platform. There she had hung and died.

When Knut saw the half-rotten moose carcass draped from his cache he hurriedly climbed to the platform and lifted the canvas covering his furs. Sure enough, several shrews scurried out of the warm nests they had made of his fur. They had lived on the dead moose, which they used as a ladder to reach the cache.

Knut figured he was lucky: only about thirty of his lynx skins and two of the mink were ruined.

In Kenai, after selling his remaining good skins, he got a haircut, took a bath, and put on new clothes. Then he bought a couple of jugs of a moonshiner's white mule and headed for the nearby roadhouse, where he shared his booze with the locals. After a few drinks he started talking. "Ah tall yoo, dem moose have me yinxed, gude," he said. Then he carefully recounted every last moose escapade. The more he talked about the moose the angrier he became. The raw whiskey and his Swedish accent, which became more pronounced with each swallow, attracted considerable attention, and it wasn't long before he had a large audience.

After that night Knut might as well have forgotten his given name. He had been known as "that Swede, Johnson," but ever after, in whatever part of Alaska he roamed, he was known as Moose Johnson.

After my friendly encounter with Moose Johnson, I occasionally heard of him from others who ran into him at Fairbanks, at Kenai, and other places. Alaska in the days before the oil boom was a relatively small community, and "moccasin telegraph" carried news of old-timers and their travels fairly efficiently. About ten years after I recorded his story, I read about Moose Johnson's death in the Fairbanks Daily News Miner. *I think it's a shame they inscribed* Knut *instead of* Moose *on his headstone. He earned that name the hard way.*

This story appeared in *Sports Afield* magazine in July 1966.

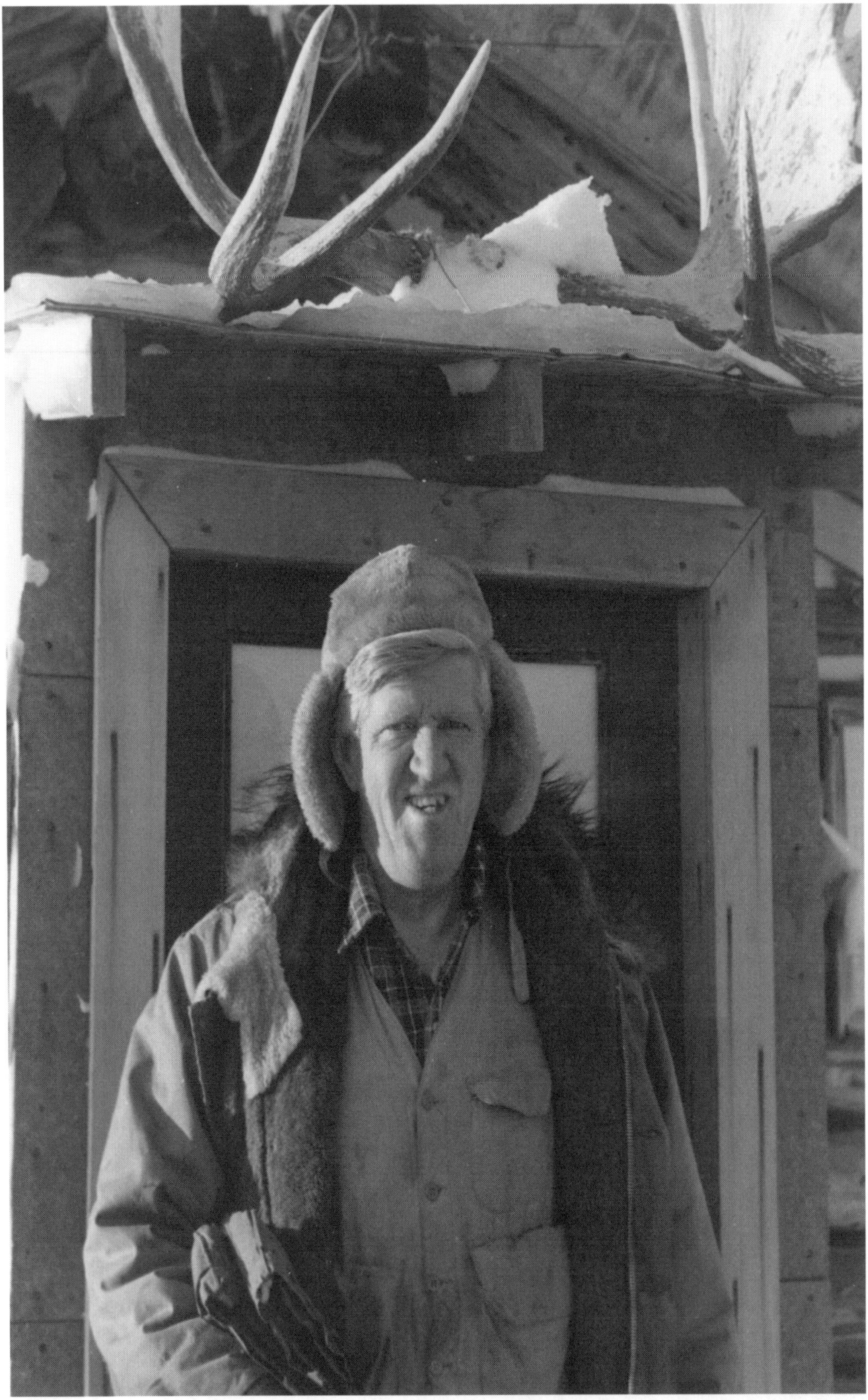

CHAPTER TWO

HOLLYWOOD IN ALASKA

M. W. "Slim" Moore (the M. stood for Morris, which Slim never used) was one of Alaska's finest and most respected registered and master hunting guides. I met him in 1950 when I arrived at Fairbanks to teach at the University of Alaska. He was big (six-foot-two), bluff, hearty, and full of solid information about Alaska's wildlife. His sense of humor constantly bubbled to the surface. He was also a philosopher and a master storyteller, with a legion of friends.

Slim arrived in Alaska from Texas in 1926 and soon immersed himself in the wilderness as a hunter, a trapper, and a packer, eventually becoming a registered guide. He was a remarkable observer of wildlife. Many professional wildlife biologists, including me, listened carefully when Slim expounded on wildlife, their problems, and how they could be better managed.

For many years Slim and his wife, Margaret, owned and operated Summit Lake Lodge on the Richardson Highway. In December 1956, I took my tape recorder to the lodge and spent a week with the Moores. During the short, cold days, Slim, Margaret and I hunted ptarmigan and tended

M.W. "Slim" Moore in 1957 at his Summit Lake Lodge in the Alaska Range. This respected hunting guide was influential in persuading authorities to set aside preserves for wildlife. He was also a great storyteller—and one of his best is the tale of his days as a wildlife wrangler for the movies.　　JIM REARDEN PHOTO

Slim's beaver traps and snares. Evenings, Slim yarned and I recorded his stories, told in a slow, humorous Texas drawl.

It was then that I recorded Slim's story of "Hollywood in Alaska." Here is the yarn Slim related to me, told in his voice.

"I want you to get us some live wolverines," the director said. He wore knickers. A golf cap drooped over one ear. A long cigarette holder, sometimes with a cigarette in it, grew from his chubby face.

"Wolverines?" I repeated foolishly, stalling for time to think. I scratched my head like I wasn't sure what a wolverine was.

"Yes. Half a dozen or so will do I guess," the little fellow allowed. "Tell your trapper friends we'll pay two hundred and fifty dollars for the first one, and two hundred dollars each for the others."

Those were my first orders on the wackiest job I've ever had. I had just signed as animal man for a Hollywood movie outfit that had come to Alaska to shoot, as they say, on location.

It was 1933. For seven years I had guided sportsmen on big game hunts, run a trapline winters, and during summers had wrangled knot-headed horses packing supplies to mines in the Alaska Range. I thought I was qualified for the animal man job. If I had known a little about lion taming, and was a trapeze artist to boot, I'd have been better suited for the job.

The fine movie *Eskimo,* written by Peter Freuchen, had appeared a couple of years earlier. *Tundra,* the low-budget picture for which I was animal man, was made on the peculiar theory that the success of *Es-*

kimo ensured success of any far-North type movie that followed. They even used a single-word title.

My guiding season was over. I had just returned from a fine season with Fred Hollander, the famed naturalist-photographer-sportsman, when this funny little Hollywood gink offered me twenty bucks a day plus expenses to work for him. It was good money then.

"We're making a gen-u-wine Alaska movie. There'll be nothing phony about it," he swore, looking me right in the eye.

I had just agreed to take the job and had shaken hands with him on it when he ordered the wolverines.

We worked in Anchorage, at the time a little railroad town surrounded by good moose, sheep, and bear country.

Carpenters started building cages and pens for all the animals we planned to acquire. While they worked, I decided to pick up a wolverine or two myself if I could. In the meantime, we spread word to backcountry trappers that we wanted live wolverines.

I took a small outfit and backpacked up the old Crow Creek Trail on the Kenai Peninsula, not far from Anchorage. Early snow had covered the high ridges and mountains, and I prowled for several days on snowshoes, hunting for wolverine sign. I finally found where one had passed and followed his wallowing trail in new snow for a few miles and found a place that looked good for a trap. I had padded a bunch of number 4 Newhouse double spring traps, and with them I made several blind sets.

Next day I packed in a fresh moose head someone had left near the old trail. This I wired a couple of feet off the ground to a tree, and set a couple of my padded traps under it, beneath the snow, with waxed paper over the pans. I expected the wolverine to find the head and start tugging at it. It wouldn't move, and the more he pulled, the angrier and more frustrated he would become, until he'd forget caution and step into a trap.

Four days later I snowshoed to the head and found an angry beady-eyed wolverine there, caught by a front foot. The bandy-legged little devil growled, then crouched to leap at me when I neared.

I backed off.

A wolverine is an unfriendly cuss at best; when you're trying to pack him out of the hills and stuff him into a pen he's damn near impossible. I didn't dare tap him on the nose to knock him cold. I might have hit too hard.

"You won't buffalo me, you little so-and-so," I told him.

I fastened another padded trap to a pole and fished until I caught one of his rear paws, then I stretched him as tightly as I could. I figured I had him then. I walked up to tape his jaws shut, but every time I neared, he yanked and struggled and growled and turned his head toward me with those big popping ivories. A wolverine can bite through bone, a pole, and even wire. I sure didn't want him chewing on me.

I finally had to mush to camp for a big tarp, which I doubled until it had about six thicknesses. I threw it over him, then lay on top of it. He couldn't bite through the canvas. But he roared. And he turned and twisted frantically under me.

I groped and found his head through the canvas and pinned it down. Then I peeled the edge of the tarp back one layer at a time so I could grab his snoot. I carefully wrapped a hand around his jaws, and with the other wrapped adhesive tape on him.

He hummed and growled, telling me what an ugly no-good two-legged buzzard I was. At the same time he snuffled noisily through his nose. I grinned and stood. He batted his nose against my leg as if he thought he was going to bite.

Next I slid my packboard under him and wrapped each paw, with its ivory claws, in adhesive tape. Next, with a stout cord, I lashed his feet to each corner of the packboard. I slipped into the shoulder straps, got into my snowshoes, and headed for camp. He weighed about twenty-five pounds, but I soon learned it was twenty-five pounds of whang-leather-toughness and coil spring power.

He found he could pump himself up and down, which he did, with every ounce of strength he had.

I went weaving down the trail like a drunk. It was all I could do to keep my feet. As he pumped, he skidded his cold nose up and down the back of my neck, growling and mumbling and snuffling. When he did that the hair on the back of my neck came up like teeth on a comb, and the shivers chased each other down and up my spine, and down again.

I wondered how well I had taped his jaws. Finally, I stopped and wrapped another half spool of tape on them.

I packed him to Girdwood, which wasn't far, and put him in a barrel. I cut one foot loose at a time until he was free, and at the last instant I slipped my knife under the tape on one side of his head. He could claw the tape off then. Then I clapped a tin tub atop the barrel.

A few days later I caught another. I hog-tied him and shoved him into a sack. I lashed the sack to the packboard so he couldn't pump, and so he couldn't get his nose on my neck.

I took my pets back to Anchorage. The big money we had offered for live wolverines was starting to bring results. Wolverine skins were worth $15 to $20. In 1933, the $200 being offered for a live wolverine was a lot of money. Soon we had eight live, growling and cussing wolverines in our pens. A big black-whiskered guy brought one from Seward. He had firearms and knives strapped to himself until you'd think he was involved in a Mexican revolution. I swear, his whiskers reached clear to his belt. With his live wolverine he had two big buckets of porcupine meat.

"This here wolverine won't eat nothin' but porky meat," he declared loudly.

But what I remember most clearly, and the thing that has puzzled me for more than twenty years, is the cage his wolverine was in. It was a beautifully built miniature log cabin, barely big enough to hold the wolverine. The animal couldn't turn around, and there was no door. We had to tear the cage apart to let it out.

How did he get the wolverine into that thing? I wish I had asked.

At first we kept the wolverines in bear cages, which were stout and lined inside with metal. But, after we had more wolverines than we had bear cages, the director, against my advice, decided wolverines weren't such fierce critters after all. He had plywood cages built for the wolverines, with three thicknesses of mink wire for doors.

These kept the wolverines fine for three or four days. But one morning as I started to open the door to the garage in which we had the wolverines caged, what sounded like a pack of loose wolverines slammed against the door crack, fighting each other and the door to get out. They had chewed through the mink wire doors of their cages. I nearly jerked the door off its hinges getting it closed.

I had a snare-pole for handling the bear cubs we had for the movie, and I decided to recapture the loose wolverines with the pole. But first I scouted around for someone to help me. The first guy I found was the cameraman.

"Say, uh, I wonder if you could come help me for a few minutes?" I asked.

"Sure, Slim. What's up?" the guy asked.

"Well, uh, some of the wolverines are loose in the garage and . . ."

He was silent for a long time, staring at me. Finally he said, nervous-like, "Gosh, Slim, I don't know anything about wolverines. Maybe you'd better get someone else."

It took all of my powers of persuasion to get him to help.

We found several empty oil drums and worked them through the door and into the garage, standing behind them for protection. The instant we cracked the door, all of them hit it again, but we were ready and braced. The noise they made was enough to curl your hair. The cameraman was pale, but he had guts and stayed with it.

When we yelled, the wolverines retreated. They growled and cussed and in general raised all kinds of hell. I was relieved to find only three of them were loose.

Once inside the garage we closed the door behind us and stood waiting behind the oil drums. A wolverine dashed toward us and came close enough for me to slip the loop over his head. I held the snare pretty tight. In fact that hot-tempered little cuss got pretty tame before I dropped him into one of the barrels and covered it.

One of the remaining two was completely wild. He charged and bounced off the barrels repeatedly, and dashed around so fast I couldn't get the snare on him. The third wolverine spent most of the time crouched under a bench, growling.

Finally the wild one dashed by and on impulse I dropped the snare and grabbed both his hind feet and picked him up. He started to double up and reach for me, and I automatically spun to keep him away.

By the time I had whirled around a couple of times, I wished I hadn't been so impulsive. It wasn't exactly like having a tiger by the tail, but it was close. I couldn't stop spinning long enough to drop him into a barrel. As the wolverine and I went around and around, I saw the cameraman's face peeking over a barrel. His eyes were like saucers. He ducked every time the wolverine swished by. I guess he was afraid I'd turn loose and dump the growling critter on him.

In about half a dozen spins I started to get dizzy. I was beginning to wonder how it would end when I staggered a bit, trying to keep my feet. As I staggered, I moved closer to a post in the garage, and the next time around I slammed the wolverine's head against it. That took most of the fight out of him, and it was easy to drop him into a barrel. I hadn't intended such rugged treatment, but it did take the "tiger" out of my hands, so to speak.

I tottered dizzily to get behind the barrels and waited until the garage quit spinning before going after the third animal. He was still under the bench and I reached in and got the snare around his neck and pulled him into the open. He braced his feet, growling, but I skidded him out anyway. I hated to lift him by the neck with the snare wire, so I asked the cameraman to lift his body while I kept the snare wire tight and controlled his head.

So help me it was accidental. I'll swear to it. The cameraman later accused me of turning the wolverine loose on purpose, but I didn't.

He grabbed the critter's tail and pulled, stretching the body tight. He intended to put one hand underneath and support most of the weight by its belly while I lifted the head with the snare; we would drop it into a barrel together.

But, as he pulled on the tail, somehow the quick little devil pulled out of the noose. I honestly don't know how he managed it. One moment I had him, the next he was out. This put the cameraman in an awkward position; he had a wolverine by the tail.

I guess he remembered how I had handled the situation a few minutes earlier. Anyway, he lifted and started to whirl. At the same time he yelled, adding his excited voice to that of the angry wolverine.

With each spin the cameraman took a couple of steps toward the post where I had clonked my wolverine. His intent was obvious.

Now, I was responsible for those animals. I took my work seriously. I didn't want all my wolverines to end up with bashed-in heads. I hadn't bammed mine against the pole on purpose, though I suspect the cameraman thought I had.

Thinking quickly, I decided the only way out was to have the cameraman release the animal, so I yelled, "Turn him loose."

He took me at my word, but his timing was bad. That wolverine catapulted directly toward me. I flung myself down, and I swear it brushed me as it flew by. I heard it bounce off a wall of the garage and ricochet off of one of the three barrels we had by the door.

I got to my feet and turned to see it staggering toward me. Automatically I held the snare-pole out, and he rammed his head into the noose as if on purpose. I jerked it tight, and without any more humane ideas of having the cameraman lift him into the barrel with me, heaved upward as if he were a big fish and dropped him into the last empty barrel.

The animals played an important role in the movie. The only human actor played the part of a doctor who was forced down while flying his small plane across arctic Alaska. He made his way south, afoot, looking for civilization. As if this weren't trouble enough, a plague had wiped out Natives in all the villages he came to. Of course, there had to be a huge tundra fire too, and that fire chased him across Alaska and practically to the state of Washington. The animals were there because they too were being driven ahead of the fire.

"A gen-u-wine Alaskan movie," the director had said. I had to laugh when I learned the so-called plot.

The actor was a 200-pound bruiser who didn't like any part of being in Alaska, and we had quite a time with him when it came to the wolverines. Getting him to go into a pen and act with them running around growling and fighting each other, and threatening him, was almost impossible. I guess he figured they were bad actors.

Every time one ran toward him with the apparent intent of sampling some raw Hollywood meat, he cringed and backed up. He was genuinely scared, and I didn't blame him.

"Magnificent acting. Did you get that?" the director would yell at the cameraman while the poor actor was dancing around defending himself. Acting was the last thought he had in mind when those feisty wolverines started for him.

Once I had the temerity to approach the director and point out, since we were filming a "gen-u-wine Alaska movie," that wolverines didn't generally run around in packs. His shrug, and explanation that we needed more action, didn't really satisfy me, but I let it go.

The wolverines got meaner and harder for me to catch every time we turned them into the pen to do some filming. I was almost as happy as the actor when the wolverine sequences were completed.

The director wanted it to appear that there were lots of animals being chased by the fire. At the time, the easiest animals to get in large numbers were porcupines. The Kenai Peninsula was loaded with them. Fox and mink ranchers fed them to their animals by the hundreds.

When we offered five dollars each for live porcupines, plus the cost of freighting them to Anchorage, we had three hundred porcupines before we could stop the flow. We had them in boxes, pens, barrels, cages, woodsheds, car trunks, and anything else we could stuff them into.

To simulate the huge tundra fire, we hired a gang in Anchorage to cut dry spruce, which we piled high. Then we threw on barrels of diesel oil and set the mass afire. Next we turned the porkies loose and started the camera.

Instead of running away from the fire, as often as not the porkies ran into it. Regardless of what we did, they wouldn't perform properly for the camera.

Someone came up with the idea of making tin chutes to slide the porkies down. Then, so the plan went, they would scuttle off past the camera, which was stationary. Smoke billowed past the camera and hid the chutes.

Of course the smoke nearly asphyxiated us. Our eyes watered so badly we couldn't see much. And have you ever tried to shove a live porcupine, head first, down a slick metal chute where it doesn't want to go?

We got the porkies to the bottom of the chutes all right by using snare poles, heavy gloves, and plenty of cussing. They dropped to the ground, but often they stupidly stood there, and the next porky to slide down the chute would drop atop them—and the one on top got a bunch of quills in its belly.

Porky feed was a problem. We spent a lot of time cutting boughs and brush for them to eat the bark from. Our outfit stayed at an old homestead belong to H. P. Allen—we called him High Power—and old High Power had about three tons of rutabagas left from the previous summer's crop. His sales pitch convinced the director that they were just the thing to feed the porkies, and he sold him the entire lot.

As it happened the porkies liked the rutabagas. The trouble was, they were high power too; the resulting diarrhea killed porkies like flies.

In desperation, we hung dead and frozen porkies from piano wire and a guy back in the brush pulled a wire to yank them in front of the camera. They bumped and bounced across the snow and ice, their feet swinging back and forth. When the film was developed, I was astonished to see they looked more natural than the live porkies. They really seemed to trot across the screen.

Next, for some obscure reason, the director decided he needed some crows, and the little fish crows from Latouche Island, near Cordova, were exactly what he wanted. He bought several hundred of them that obliging Natives trapped. The fact that crows don't exist in the area the "doctor" was supposed to be struggling through made no difference.

We photographed the crows while they were in covered fox pens. Smoke blew past, upsetting the crows, and they hollered and fluttered and acted fine.

When we were through with them, the director, who was a soft-hearted guy, told me to turn them loose. Crows were not native to Anchorage.

At the same time, we were through with the porcupines, so he ordered they too be released.

The result was bedlam. For a few days there was a porcupine or three in about every tree in town (Anchorage was pretty small in 1933). And about every other dog in town had a sore face where quills had been pulled.

One old-timer with blood in his eye looked us up. He had a shotgun under his arm. He had been awakened before daylight that morning by a rattling and crunching on his front porch. He rolled out of a warm bed, poked a flashlight and shotgun out the front door, wondering what'n hell was out there, and found a porcupine busily gnawing down a post of his porch.

The director bought him off with a fistful of cash.

The little loud-mouth fish crows darted around Anchorage for quite a while. They were confused, and often went in gangs. Some of the rowdydow boys of Anchorage got out shotguns and had some pretty good wing shooting for a while. This burned up the more staid citizens. They blamed the film crew, including me, of course.

One of the more ardent shotgun artists went too far, though. He actually knocked a high-flying crow down amidst one of our filming operations. The dead crow tumbled through the air and landed with a loud *whump* not twenty feet from the actor, who was busily hamming up the scene in which he was supposed to be staggering through some knee-high brush. His startled look toward the dead crow made the director yell, "Cut."

I was standing there admiring the guy's magnificent shot when the director yelled at me, "Say, Slim, will you go see what you can do about the wise guy with the shotgun?"

He had faded by the time I got to the spot from which he had shot. But it did give me a chance to get away where I could laugh.

And then there were the bear cubs. According to the plot, there were two cubs, orphans, that the fleeing "doctor" had adopted. We had three cubs; one was spare.

They didn't know from one day to the next how to behave. One day we petted them, and the next, for the camera, we dropped trees on them, or maybe pushed them off a cliff, or dumped them into an icy stream.

One was bigger and meaner than the others. It weighed about a hundred pounds, and I think it was a yearling, whereas the others were in their first year. We called it Queen.

One day the actor was in a pen with a big fire burning outside. Smoke drifted across, concealing the wire, and to the camera I guess it looked fine. He was supposed to rush up and grab Queen and rescue her from the fire by carrying her away.

A few hours earlier we had felled a tree on the cub, for the camera, of course, and it was kind of on the peck. The actor ran over and reached for Queen, but he hesitated when she came up on her hind feet, snorted, chomped her teeth, and peeled her lips back. He went ahead and grabbed. Queen proceeded to chomp teeth up his arm like eating corn on the cob. She must have pinched a dozen big blood blisters. At the same time, her claws worked the actor over.

The actor had few clothes on because they had supposedly been torn off by the brush, so the claws went right through to skin.

Mr. Actor promptly dropped Queen.

"Pick that bear up and get it out of there," the director instructed the actor, taking his ever-present cigarette holder from his mouth.

But the actor had had all he wanted, with bites, scratches, and blisters where his "pet" cub had worked him over. "Ta hell with this," he growled and walked off.

The director's face became livid. He threw his golf cap on the ground and leaped on it. He dashed his long cigarette holder into a snowbank and screamed, "Get back in there."

His performance easily topped that of the actor, so the actor had no choice but to back down and return. I felt sorry for the guy, and substituted one of the other cubs for Queen, and that segment of the film was completed without a bear again trying to steal the scene.

Almost everything that happened on that job had a screwball twist to it. I happened to catch a couple of falcons in a trap, so we kept them, thinking they might fit into some scene. Someone had sent us a bald eagle. One day I turned the eagle into a pen with the two falcons. The falcons, on perches, screamed bloody murder, and so help me, one of them fainted and fell from his perch to the ground, out like Schmeling.

The eagle had a bad wing, but he could fly about a hundred yards. One day as the camera started to grind, he sat on a perch watching the actor trying to catch a rabbit. The poor 200-pound guy was starving to death. As he stooped and started to sneak forward to one of the dozen or so rabbits I had turned into the pen, the eagle jumped from his perch, flopped his wings a few times, and landed on the actor's back.

He froze. "Get him off of me," he yelled. I knew if I picked the bird up his claws would tighten and really give the actor something to yell about.

"Lie down and roll over," I advised. When he did, the eagle stepped off onto the ground.

Later when the "doctor" caught a rabbit, we gave him some fried chicken, which he ate in front of the camera, hamming it up gruesomely.

Next, the director decided he had to have a lot of mink in the picture. I warned him that every trapper in Alaska would send them in if he advertised as he had for porcupines, so he made a deal with a mink rancher near Anchorage to use two hundred of his caged mink. Next, he got permission to use a big auditorium, which he had camouflaged to look like woods.

Lights were strung around the bottom of the auditorium to illuminate for the camera. At the last minute, the cameraman decided to use overhead lights only, so we unscrewed the bottom light bulbs. Those mink, fresh from cages, frantically dashed around, and half a dozen of them jammed their wet noses into these light sockets and were knocked stiff. I skinned electrocuted mink all one day.

I worked for that outfit for four months. Sometimes I laughed, and then again I was ashamed to be mixed up with a thing like that. I got so I'd slink down the street and turn my head when I met a fellow guide or trapper.

The movie is still around. I have heard that it appears on late evening TV, and it even showed up at a Fairbanks movie theater near my home a few years ago.

I am often asked what I thought of the finished movie. I usually hedge, "Well, it was a 'gen-u-wine' filmed-in-Alaska movie."

If the questioner persists, I have to answer truthfully: "I don't know. I've never seen it."

After telling me this story, Slim Moore shook his head and said that, while there was plenty to laugh at about the making of the movie, he hated the pressures put on him and on the animal "actors."

"It was a helluva way to treat animals," he said. "We didn't have time to gentle them, facilities for caring for them were makeshift, and the treatment they received when on camera wasn't very nice. I made sure they had plenty of food and water, and once their part in the movie was over, I released those that could make it back into the wild."

Slim often testified at public hearings of the Board of Fish and Game and of the later Board of Game while I was a member. His comments were pointed, usually humor-

ous, and they always reflected his concern for wildlife. During the 1960s some guides hunted brown bears with small planes, landing near when they located a bear, and leading clients to an easy but unsportsmanlike kill. Slim contemptuously referred to such guides as "crop dusters." Others had testified against aerial hunting, but the board remembered Slim's comments best. "Crop dusters" was the perfect term.

It was Slim who recommended that the world-famous McNeil River area on lower Cook Inlet be closed to hunting and set aside for the viewing of brown bears. In the early 1950s he took a client to McNeil River for a hunt and realized what a marvelous place it could be for the public to view the big bears. The Territorial Game Commission acted positively on Slim's recommendation and in 1955 closed the area to hunting. At statehood, the Board of Fish and Game retained the hunting closure.

Slim was named Alaska's Guide of the Year in 1973 by the Alaska Professional Hunters Association. In 1977 the Alaska Guide Licensing and Control Board recognized him as an honorary Master Guide for life—the only person ever so honored. In that same year Alaska's legislature congratulated him in a formal resolution for his almost half a century of ethical and active guiding. At his retirement at the age of eighty, he was the oldest active guide in Alaska.

Slim Moore died in Anchorage in April 1982 at the age of eighty-three.

This story appeared in *The Alaska Sportsman* in March 1966.

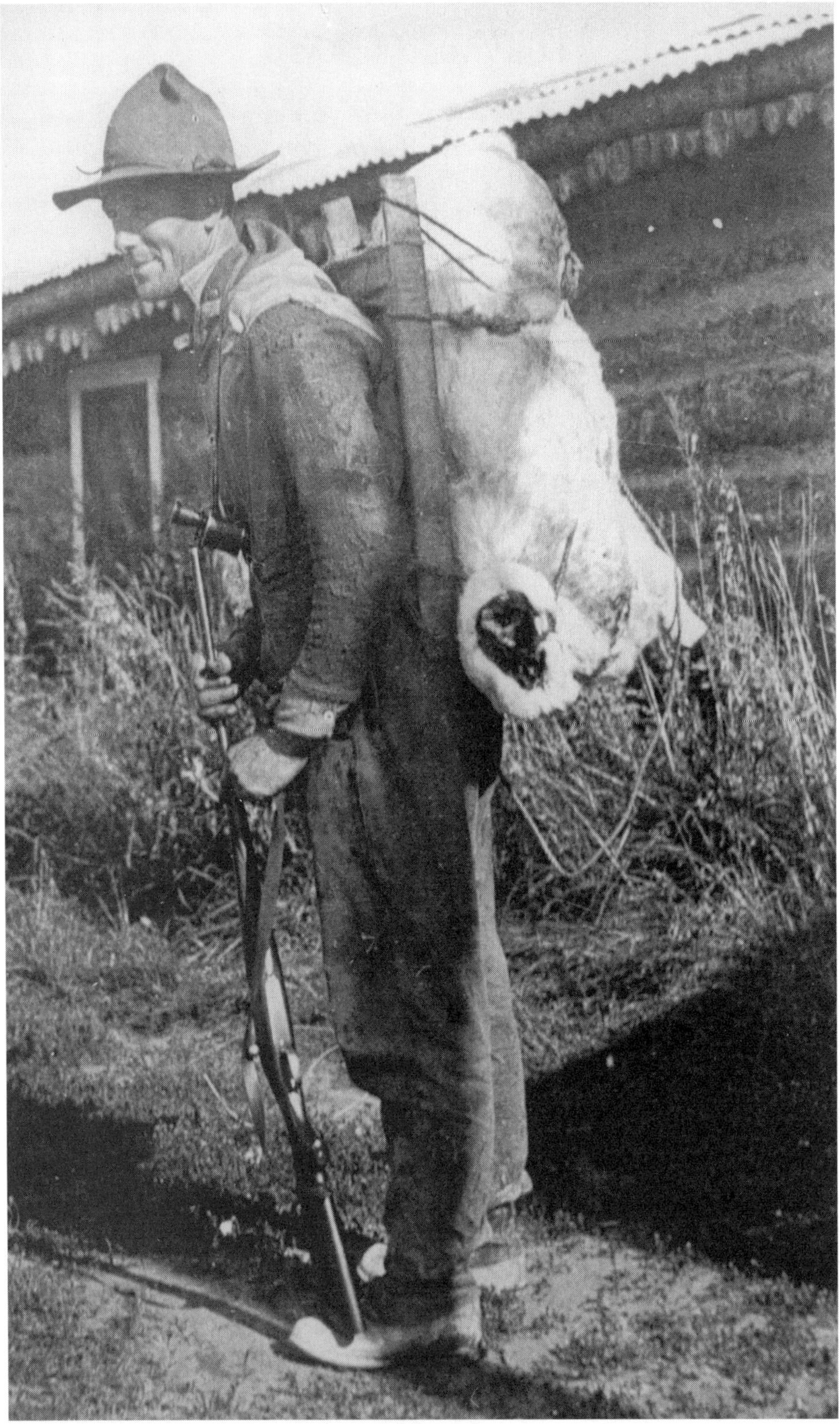

CHAPTER THREE

ADVENTURE WAS HIS LIFE

Frank Glaser was a compulsive talker who loved to tell about his many encounters with grizzly bears, his years of trapping and hunting, or how he guided the famed Murie brothers, biologists, on early Alaska expeditions. He would tell how he guided other famous men, such as the one he referred to as J. Peterpoint Morgan, meaning J. Pierpont Morgan.

He would talk endlessly about wolf hunting, dog-team trips in the Arctic, and early bush plane flights, and about an array of Indians, Eskimos, pioneer miners, hunters, and trappers. Frank carried a trim 155 pounds on his five-foot, seven-inch frame all his life. An energetic rolling gait came from years of slogging the wild places. He was past sixty when I knew him, yet he could outwalk most men half his age. This story is a true piece of history, a part of the Alaska I have known for more than half a century.

Frank Glaser in 1921, with the carcass of a Dall ram on his packboard. A hunter, trapper, and wildlife expert, Glaser knew as well as any man ever did how to live off the bounty of the Alaskan wilderness. He was a born talker who told endless tales of adventure and survival.   PHOTO COURTESY OF FRANK GLASER

The hackle-raising howl of a wolf broke the stillness of the subarctic dawn on the north slope of the great Alaska Range. The sound drifted across the snowy flats, into stunted timberline spruces, over the ice-covered Savage River, and into the log cabin where a trapper was awakening.

Again the wolf howled. Another joined in, and then another, until it became a chorus.

The trapper, Frank Glaser, left his bed, threw wood into the stove, and dressed. The outdoor thermometer read minus 40 degrees, which prompted him to pull on another pair of wool socks. He donned his parka as he headed for the door, binoculars hanging from his neck.

He grabbed his rifle from the cold entryway, strapped on snowshoes, and headed for a nearby lookout point, from which he spotted nine wolves on a flat two miles away. A wolf stood to howl, and a cloud of steam rose. A moment later, the low, lovely, wild sound reached Glaser.

Several hundred caribou were scattered across the flat beyond the wolves. The wolves were watching the caribou.

A creek meandered within rifle range of the wolves, and Frank ran down the ridge into the creek bottom. His snowshoes scraped and clattered on the hardened March snow, and he bent to remove them. Suddenly two black wolves bounded over a drift fifty yards upstream, heads up, looking. In the creek behind the trapper another wolf appeared. The wolves had heard Glaser and thought he was a caribou.

He snapped a shot at one of the wolves and saw it collapse. He centered the rifle scope on the second black, which had skidded to a stop, and saw it stagger when he fired. He spun and centered on the wolf downstream, fired, and watched it roll to a stop.

He got out of the webs and struggled up a hard snow-drift to the stream bank. His horsehide moccasins were slippery, and he had to dig in with the gun butt to pull himself up. He crawled to the top and peered over. The six surviving wolves milled three hundred yards away. At his shot they scattered. He emptied the rifle, hitting two.

He followed one of the blood trails for a mile, but lost both of the cripples and returned to skin the three he had killed. These were but three of the more than five hundred wolves killed by Glaser during his time in Alaska.

Frank Glaser was twenty-six in 1915 when he moved to Alaska from Washington state, carrying a new .30-06 box-magazine Winchester and a pair of binoculars. He came for the hunting he had heard so much about. He settled at Black Rapids Roadhouse on the Valdez Trail, where he contracted to market game meat for two bits a pound to the Alaska Road Commission, which had crews converting the Valdez Trail into what came to be called the Richardson Highway.

As a market hunter Frank hunted mostly Dall sheep, but took some caribou and moose. He used a packboard to carry the meat to the Valdez Trail, where a Road Commission wagon and team would take over.

Grizzly bears often claimed or damaged meat that he planned to return for. "I declared war on grizzlies in those years," he once told me. During his life he killed more than eighty brown and grizzly bears, many in defense of his life. Market hunters, prospectors, miners, teamsters, and others struggling to survive in the Alaska of that time commonly regarded bears as worthless, and a menace to boot.

Market hunting was halted by a new Alaska Game Commission. The Alaska Railroad now brought fresh and frozen meat directly to Interior Alaska from Seattle; game meat was no longer needed. Tiring of the constant wind at Black Rapids, in October 1924 Frank loaded his dogsled with tools, windows, and other essentials and headed for Savage River on the north side of the Alaska Range, near Mount McKinley National Park (now Denali National Park and Preserve). In a few weeks he completed a 14-by-16-foot moss-chinked, dirt-roofed log cabin, which was to be his headquarters for the next thirteen years as he became a full-time trapper

His years at Savage River were probably Frank's happiest. Fur was plentiful, and after 1926 wolves increased and were added to his catch. Each fall and winter the Kuskokwim caribou herd moved into the area and, after the rut, scattered to the flats and foothills, where Frank watched over them as if they were his cattle.

Fur prices were high, and he made several thousand dollars most years—more money than he needed. He loved rifles, and he bought almost every new model that came along. He kept a room at the Nordale Hotel in Fairbanks year-round. After trapping season he often remained at the Nordale for weeks, enjoying town.

In November 1926, he found a large, young black wolf in one of his traps, tapped it across the nose with a light club to knock it out, tied its jaws and legs, and lugged it home on his packboard. He chained it within reach of a bitch malamute, and kept two from the first batch of pups that came in March 1927, naming them Queenie and Buster. Other litters followed. Within a couple of years Frank had a team of huge, mostly wolf, sled dogs, on which he spent vast amounts of patience and time training.

Frank claimed that his wolf dogs were much better than pure malamute or husky.

"They pulled like horses, they did. I don't remember of ever having one of that breed that wasn't a good puller," he told me.

Frank frequently traveled to the village of Healy with his dog team, and the route took him across several high, bare ridges. Windblown snow often blanked visibility, occasionally with temperatures of minus 30 degrees Fahrenheit or colder.

Queenie, the 125-pound black half-wolf, was his leader. She never lost the trail, regardless of wind or snow. Sometimes mountain wind became so strong she had to crawl. When the dogs stopped in blowing snow, Frank knew their eyes were frozen shut, and he crawled up the towline to clean them. Then Queenie would go on.

He taught his team to lie down and remain in place as he harnessed them and hooked them to the towline. The eager dogs would lie with ears pricked and heads turned, watching him. They were trained to remain that way until he said, "All right."

At that command the team would leap into full run, each dog growling with every jump, and it would be all Frank could do to hang on and keep the sled upright for a couple of miles until they slowed to their usual mile-eating traveling trot.

Once, the dogs leaped away before he reached the sled, and he watched them disappear two hundred yards away around a bend, still traveling at a dead run, every dog in place. He was certain they would tangle and start fighting, and he ran to the bend, only to stop in astonishment. The team was returning at a gallop. Queenie had missed him, and had swung the team in a wide arc to return. He grabbed the sled as they went by, called "Come gee" to the big black queen wolf-dog, and grinned as she swung onto the trail, head high, ears pricked, tail wagging.

The team loved to chase caribou, and they often took Frank high into the sheep hills, or wherever the caribou went. At times, with Frank clinging to it and cussing, the powerful dogs dragged the upset sled for a mile or more through brush, across creeks, and over tundra before he could stop them. His winter clothing became torn, and he spent much time repairing sleds.

One day he tied a jerkline to a neckline that ran between two leaders he ran that day. Then he found a bunch of caribou. The dogs lit out after them with Frank grimly clinging to the flying sled. They reached a flat, and Frank stepped on the claw brake, yelling, "Whoa, whoa." He might as well have yelled at the wind.

With a last "Whoa," he wrapped the jerkline around his hand and leaped from the speeding sled.

The two leaders, running all out, with a combined weight of about 250 pounds, yanked Frank a good ten feet through the area. Snow flew as he bounced, skidded, and rolled to a dazed stop. The leaders had been somersaulted backward into the rest of the team, and they all had rolled into a huge squirming, growling, ball. The sled rammed into the pile.

He found another bunch of caribou, and the dogs lit out after them. This time Frank remained standing on the sled as he hauled back on the jerkline. Again the dogs were rolled into a confused melee, and the sled rammed into them.

It took a few more treatments, but thereafter when Frank yelled "Whoa," the dogs slowed, whether they were shagging caribou or not, eyeing their master and the sled over their shoulders. He made no more involuntary trips into the sheep hills.

In April 1937, when fur prices hit bottom, he was hired as a predator control agent by the U.S. Bureau of

Biological Survey (which became the U.S. Fish and Wild-life Service in 1939). He couldn't have asked for any-thing more to his liking.

That July, with Queenie and Buster, he met the 100,000-animal Fortymile caribou herd at the Cana-dian boundary to follow it into Alaska. His assignment was to learn its annual migration route. He described this remarkable trek to me as if it had been a simple weekend hike.

He took eighty-seven pounds of supplies, mostly dried food. He put twenty to thirty pounds each in dog packs on Queenie and Buster and carried the rest on his packboard. He took no dog food, no bedding, no tarpaulin or tent, and wore summer-weight clothing. He carried a map but no compass. He had a .30-06 rifle, fishing line, about a dozen artificial flies, and a mosquito net.

The caribou traveled west, keeping largely to the high ridges, and Frank stayed with them. At first he trav-eled at night (at this latitude it is daylight twenty-four hours a day in July). Days, he spread his mosquito net and slept under trees that would shed rain. On rainy days he didn't get much sleep because of the cold. About a third of the food he ate was grayling, which he caught at every clear stream he crossed. He boiled his, and the wolf-dogs ate theirs raw and whole.

He built log rafts to cross big streams like Charley River, and waded others.

By September, nights were too dark to travel, and he spent the darkest hours beside a fire. Then the snow started.

He shot three yearling caribou, skinned them, and worked their brains into the hides until the hides were pliant. With a buckskin needle and caribou sinew he sewed the skins, fur in, into a sleeping bag. He dried the meat over a fire. He enjoyed nights after that, sleeping warm in his caribou fur bag.

In mid-September, when snow was a foot and a half deep on the ridges, he killed a bull caribou, and over a fire bent willow limbs into snowshoe frames, whittled crosspieces, then webbed the shoes with strips of the bull's hide. Again he dried the meat. The snowshoes carried him the rest of the way on his long trek.

His assignment was carried out. He left the herd on October 15 at Circle Hot Springs, 140 straight-line miles from where he had started eleven weeks earlier. He had walked at least 450 miles across Alaska's mountains. He was travelworn, but still strong and healthy.

In 1939 Frank, then fifty, married forty-eight-year-old Nellie Gage Osborne, who had moved to Alaska in the 1920s. During the rest of Frank's years with the Fish and Wildlife Service, Nellie patiently waited while Frank made his long field trips. She also lived with him in remote Eskimo villages when he was assigned to northwestern Alaska.

When Frank went to work for the government, he didn't know how to drive a car. Sam White spent about a week teaching him. "He had quite a time keeping between the ditches on both sides of the narrow roads of the time, but he became an adequate driver," Sam remembered.

For the eighteen years Frank was a federal agent, he left his tracks in the far places of Alaska. He helped Kodiak ranchers get rid of cattle-killing brown bears; he prowled hummocky Nunivak Island in the Bering Sea to count musk ox; he flew as gunner on aerial wolf hunts; and for wolves he set his snares, traps and— when they came into use—cyanide getter guns. He even used poison during the late 1940s and early 1950s, in line with federal policy of the time. Predator control is out of fashion in Alaska today. In Glaser's time, which coincided with a period of great wolf abundance, elimination of wolves was regarded by Alaskans as the way to greater game abundance.

His wolf hunts for the government led him into many exciting adventures. In August 1939 he had a pilot fly him to the Mount Hayes area of the Alaska Range, arranging to be picked up about November 1, provided the ground was bare enough for the wheel plane to land. He wore summer-weight woolens and rubber-bottomed shoepacks but had no cold-weather gear. He lived in an old prospector's cabin.

In mid-September, he followed signs where one of his wolf traps had been dragged off along with its toggle (a log). He carried his current favorite rifle, a .220 Swift. It was a fine rifle for wolves, but not much good for bears. He was fifteen feet from a willow patch when, with a roar, a huge grizzly charged out of it. Frank shot from the hip, slowing the bear, but the tiny 48-grain bullet didn't have the needed stopping power.

The bear kept coming, and Frank shot again, leaped back, shot a third time, and leaped back once more. The bear slowed with each shot, but it kept moving. After dodging the bear several times and doing a lot of leaping and shooting, he finally dropped the animal with his eleventh shot. It fell scarcely a rifle's length away.

The grizzly was a sow whose yearling cub had wandered into Frank's wolf trap. As Glaser killed the sow, the yearling pulled free and fled.

Frank sat on the bear and had a pinch of Copenhagen snuff (he called it "Swedish dynamite") to steady his nerves. In later years he occasionally had severe gastric upsets, at which time he would denounce snuff. "It ain't fit for a man's stomach," he'd say. But he always went back to it.

He skinned the bear and tanned the hide with sulfuric acid and salt he found at the prospector's cabin. Deep snow made an airplane pickup impossible, and Frank had to walk out. In early November temperatures dropped far below zero. Frank used his skin needle to sew from the grizzly hide a pair of mittens, a fur cap, and a pair of mukluks with soles of moosehide he found at the cabin.

With packboard, axe, rifle, grub, and no bedding, he started to hike the more than one hundred miles to the Richardson Highway. On the second day he broke through the ice of a river and found himself in water up to his shoulders. Air temperature was 40 below zero. He fought his way ashore and ran to a patch of spruces as his clothing froze. He started a fire, cut a green spruce to stand on, then stripped. He stood wearing nothing but his bearskin cap, mittens, and dry moccasins from his pack. He kept the fire burning and waved wet woolen underwear, pants, and jacket through the flames to dry them.

In a few more days he reached the Richardson Highway and hitchhiked to Fairbanks. It was all in a day's work for Frank.

In 1940 the Alaska Game Commission sent Glaser to the Seward Peninsula in northwestern Alaska to control wolves that were reportedly decimating reindeer herds. The reindeer business had expanded too rapidly, and ranges were overused. In 1937 Congress made it illegal for whites to own reindeer, and the federal government was buying the animals from whites and holding them to turn over to Eskimos. Few Eskimos were interested. Hunting, not herding, is the Eskimo way.

Glaser found chaos, with reindeer starving, untended, or at best herded by disinterested Eskimos. Wolves had easy pickings. In one typical instance, Glaser searched for and finally found the Golovin reindeer herd of five thousand animals. The animals had been left to fend for themselves. Wolves had pushed the deer onto a barren mountain where there was virtually no feed. As Frank and an

Eskimo companion studied them one day, they saw eight wolves chasing reindeer in the distance. Closer, they heard the mournful howl of a wolf.

"I'll call that one," Frank told his companion.

He howled and got a reply. He waited, then howled again. As he and the Eskimo crouched out of sight, the wolf appeared on a snowbank fifty yards away. Frank shot it with his Swift. The Eskimo was impressed, and Frank's reputation grew.

Eventually, reindeer decreased to a total of 30,000 or 40,000 from a high of 641,000 in 1932, and the situation stabilized. Frank and Nellie returned to Fairbanks, where he worked as a predator control agent until his retirement in 1955.

The Glasers left Alaska after Frank's retirement and for the next fifteen years lived in Idaho, California, and Oregon. Frank tried to make a few dollars by showing his wildlife movies, but had little success.

In their old age the Glasers returned to their beloved Alaska. A friend who visited Frank at an Anchorage nursing home near the end told me the old wolfer's mind wandered, but generally he was the same old Frank. He told his friend he planned to return to his Savage River cabin and to the life he had left thirty-seven years earlier.

Perhaps Frank did go back to Savage River, for that wild and lovely region was his idea of the Happy Hunting Grounds. He died May 16, 1974, at the age of eighty-six. Nellie, with him at the nursing home to the last, died fifteen days later.

This article appeared in *Outdoor Life* in July 1975.

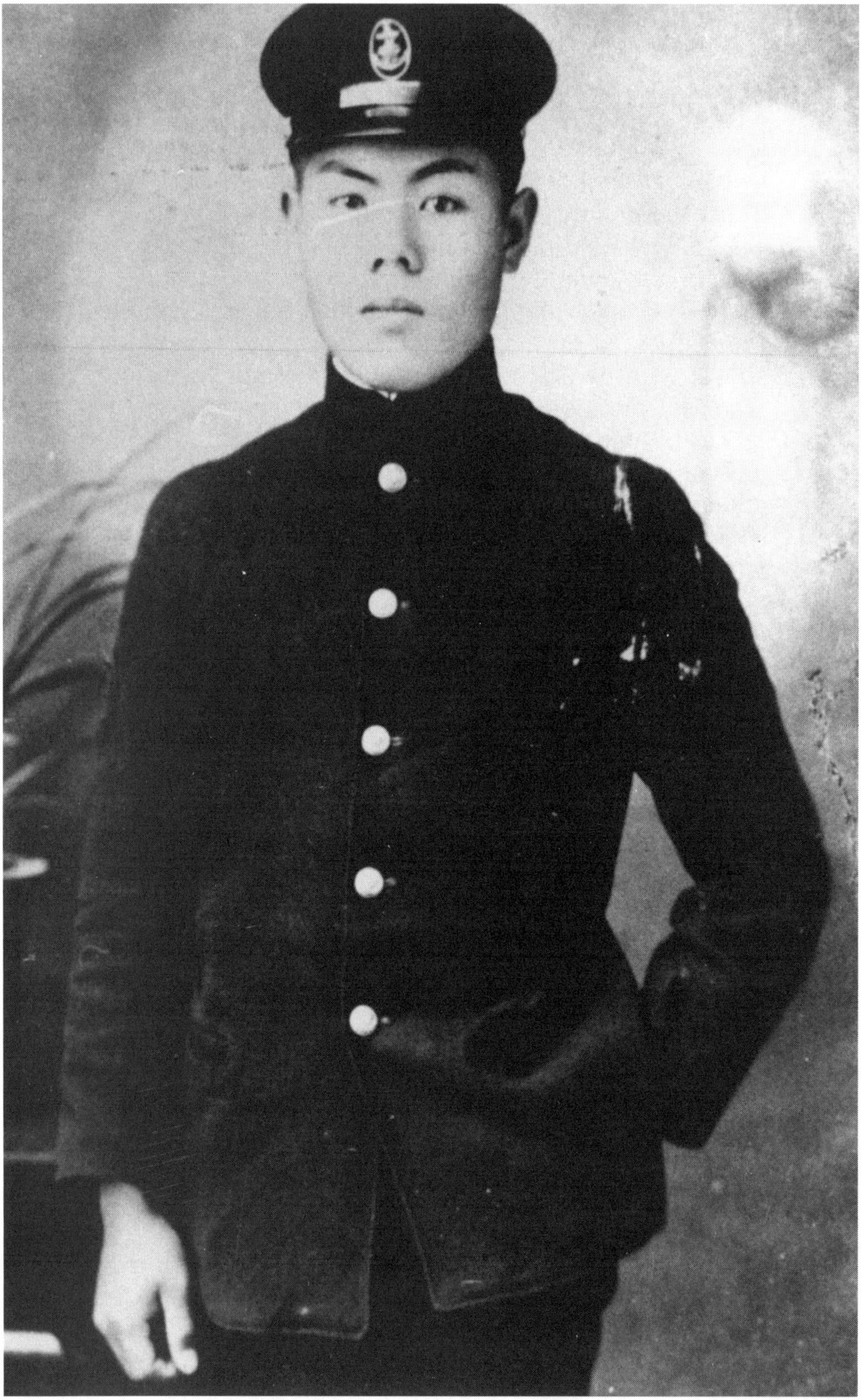

CHAPTER FOUR

KOGA'S ZERO

I first read about this Japanese Zero fighter from World War II in Brian Garfield's classic book The Thousand Mile War. *While I was at Adak Island in 1986 on an Aleutian Islands assignment for* National Geographic *magazine, I visited with retired Admiral James Russell, who further sparked my interest in this famous enemy fighter. Russell had seen the Zero at Dutch Harbor when it was newly recovered from Akutan Island, and he knew one of the test pilots who later flew it.*

In researching the subject, I became acquainted with some wonderful people—heroes—such as Bill Thies, pilot of the patrolling PBY from which the crashed Zero was discovered. In his PBY, Thies was the first to discover the invading Japanese ships at Kiska Harbor, Alaska, and with the slow, lumbering PBY he flew the first American bombing run on those ships. His insistence on taking a crew to the downed Zero, despite resistance of his commanding officer, resulted in the United States learning the secrets of the Zero.

Fighter pilot Tadayoshi Koga at the time he was reassigned to the aircraft carrier *Ryujo*. Koga, nineteen years old at the time of his death in 1942, was the first buried on Alaska's Akutan Island. His remains were later moved to Adak Island and eventually, it is believed, to Japan.

USHIO-SHOBO PUBLISHERS, COURTESY OF LT. GEN. MASATAKE OKUMIYA, JASDF, RET.

William Leonard, a Navy pilot at the time, flew the rebuilt Zero repeatedly from North Island Naval Air Station, San Diego, and provided me with an intimate description of the plane and its characteristics. Kenneth Walsh, a Marine pilot in World War II, told me exactly how the knowledge gleaned from Koga's Zero had saved his life more than once.

Two military catastrophes befell the Japanese in early summer 1942. Their defeat at Midway is well known, but few Americans are aware of the other great disaster: the acquisition by the United States of a Japanese Mitsubishi A6M2 Zero fighter. Its discovery, repair, and subsequent test flights is one of the least known stories of World War II, partly because it was top secret for many years.

On June 3, 1942, the light Japanese aircraft carriers *Ryujo* and *Junyo,* two heavy cruisers, three destroyers and a tanker, under the command of Rear Adm. Kajuki Kakuta, plowed toward our Aleutian Island navy base of Dutch Harbor at Unalaska Island. Staff Aviation Officer Masatake Okumiya, aboard the *Ryujo,* was the mastermind of the planned attack on the base.

The Japanese launched their raid near dawn. Sunlight glinted on wings as, over Dutch Harbor, Zeros rolled into screaming dives. For fifty minutes four waves of Kate level bombers serenely flew bombing runs, while Zero pilots strafed antiaircraft gun positions and other targets. Small arms fire rattled and antiaircraft guns boomed but no enemy planes were downed. Damage to Dutch was light.

At midafternoon next day, Kakuta sent another flight of Zeros, Val dive bombers, and Kate horizontal bombers to pound Dutch. Three of the Zeros were piloted by Chief Petty Officer Makoto Endo, Petty Officer Tsuguo Shikada, and Flight Petty Officer Tadayoshi Koga.

Before the Japanese dropped their bombs, soldiers at an Army outpost near Dutch saw the Zeros flown by Endo, Shikada, and Koga shoot down into the sea a Consolidated PBY-5A of Patrol Squadron VP-42. Surviving crew members climbed into a rubber raft and started for shore, but the Zero pilots strafed the raft until all in it were killed.

Damage at Dutch was heavier than from the previous raid. Seventy-eight Americans died from the two Japanese bombings; twenty-eight were wounded.

No Japanese planes fell at Dutch from the small arms and antiaircraft fire that June 4. However, Koga's Zero trailed oil as it departed Dutch. An American bullet had severed the return oil line between the oil cooler and the engine. The running engine pumped oil out of the broken line as, accompanied by Endo and Shikada, Koga flew east twenty-five miles to Akutan Island, which had been designated for emergency landings. A Japanese submarine lay nearby to pick up downed pilots.

The three Zeros circled a grassy flat. Koga lowered wheels and flaps. The wheels hit, water sprayed, and the Zero bounced, flipped, and landed upside down with a giant splash. Koga had landed in a swamp. Grass hid the water. Endo and Shikada circled, watching, but Koga remained in the plane. They returned to the *Ryujo.*

Koga and his Zero fighter, a Mitsubishi type 0 Model 21 (A6M2), lay unseen until July 10, when Lieutenant William Thies and his PBY crew spotted it as they returned to Dutch from an overnight patrol. The Zero was light gray, with rising sun on the wings and both sides of the fuselage ("meatballs," our aviators called these emblems). It had a yellow stripe encircling the after part of the fuselage. This plane has variously been called the Aleutian Zero, the Akutan Zero, or Koga's Zero.

Navy Commander Robert Larson, now retired and living in Mill Creek, Washington, was then Ensign Larson, second pilot of Thies's PBY crew. He wrote me, "We passed directly over the Zero and Thies banked and descended to have a look. The downed plane didn't look too badly damaged. We marked its position on a map and flew on to Dutch."

Thies, now a retired Navy captain living in Gig Harbor, Washington, remembers his excitement over the find. "I had considerable difficulty convincing squadron commander Paul Foley Jr. that we should be released from patrol duty to go see if the airplane could be salvaged," he told me. "We were short of crews and planes due both to losses to the Japanese and to the weather."

Thies headed the investigative party of fifteen. Koga's decomposed body, still in the plane, was buried on a nearby mound.

In 1942, Japanese technology was held in low esteem by most Americans. Larson commented, "We were rather surprised at the details of the Zero. It was well built, with simple, unique features. Inspection plates could be opened by pushing on a black dot with a finger. A latch would open and one could pull the plate out. The wing tips folded by unlatching and pushing them up by hand."

The wings were integral with the fuselage, complicating recovery, but by mid-July the Zero had been yanked from the swamp and taken to Dutch. It was cleaned and crated. The awkward crate (wings and fuselage in a single crate) was taken to North Island Naval Air Station, San Diego.

In San Diego, a twelve-foot-high stockade was erected around the Zero inside a hangar. Two Marines stood guard. Repair crews worked twenty-four hours a day, seven days a week. The Zero was ready to fly again September 20, 1942.

Navy test pilot Lieutenant Commander Eddie R. Sanders flew the tests. In May 1988, Sanders, by then a retired rear admiral, told me he made twenty-four test flights of the plane from September 20 to October 15, 1942. "The very first flight exposed weaknesses of the Zero which our pilots could exploit with proper tactics," he said.

"The Zero had superior maneuverability only at the lower speeds used in dogfighting," Sanders said, "with short turning radius and excellent aileron control at very low speeds. However, immediately apparent was the fact that the ailerons froze up at speeds above 200 knots so that rolling maneuvers at those speeds were slow and required much force on the control stick. It rolled to the left much easier than to the right. Also, its engine cut out under negative acceleration due to its float-type carburetor.

"We now had an answer for our pilots who were being outmaneuvered and unable to escape a pursuing Zero. Go into a vertical power dive, using negative acceleration if possible to open the range quickly and gain advantageous speed while the Zero's engine was stopped. At about 200 knots, roll hard right.

"This recommended tactic was radioed to the fleet after the first test flight, and soon the welcome answer came back: 'It works!'"

At the time, Sanders wrote: "The Zero, Model A6M2, is a carefully constructed and well equipped fighter except that it has no leakproof tanks and no armor whatever. Flush rivets, carefully housed steps, hand grips, landing gear, etc., provide a clean smooth exterior. Great emphasis has been given to saving weight. The original finish was a very smooth light gray, tinted blue light green.

"It is equipped with complete instruments, some of which appear to be superior to ours; two-way radio (frequency 4596 KC), radio compass (Fairchild); oxygen, droppable belly tank, provision for two bomb racks on wings; flotation bags in wings and fuselage. Landing gear, flaps and brakes are hydraulically operated. Brakes are weak because of a clumsy cable system. Tail wheel is held in position by bungee.

"Visibility is excellent with no difficulty seeing astern. Cockpit is not much more cramped than a Spitfire, except that the longest pedal position is quite short and knees stick up rather high. There are two 51.5 gallon wing tanks and a 38-gallon fuselage tank ahead of the pilot. Belly tank (droppable) holds approximately 87 gallons."

Other U.S. experts were also impressed as they studied this 23-foot-long, 5,500-pound (battle ready) airplane, for it was a lovely all-metal (except for fabric-covered control surfaces) low-wing monoplane with a clean and smooth exterior. Armament was two 7.7mm machine guns, each of which fired 680 rounds through the propeller, and two 20mm cannons, mounted in the wings, which fired 60 rounds each.

The 940 horsepower (at takeoff) Nakajima Sakae radial engine turned a three-blade constant speed propeller similar to the American Hamilton. The hydraulically powered retractable landing gear placed the wheels far apart, making it stable for takeoff, landing, and taxiing.

The plane was pitted against our fighters of the time (Bell Airacobra, Curtiss Warhawk, Lockheed Lightning, North American Mustang, Vought Corsair, and Grumman Wildcat), and the best combat maneuvers for coping with the Zero were developed for each. Many military pilots flew Koga's Zero, and it was used in mock dogfights against pilots bound for the Pacific—a preview of things to come.

Masatake Okumiya—one of Japan's leading air-sea strategists, who was present at most of the major air-sea battles in the Pacific from 1942 to 1944 including the Dutch Harbor raid—commented after the war that revelation of the Zero's secrets to Americans from that captured plane was "no less serious" than their defeat at Midway.

In 1987 I met Okumiya, all five-foot-five and ninety pounds of him, at Anchorage during the premiere of the movie *Alaska At War.* What was the greatest weakness of the Zero, I asked him. "No armor," he replied.

Admiral James S. Russell, who served in the Aleutian Campaign and was later chief of the U.S. Bureau of Aeronautics, told me, "The fact that the Zero from Akutan was recovered, repaired, and flown by our own pilots beginning in late September 1942, the tenth month of our 45-month war with Japan, is of tremendous historical significance.

"The menace of the Zero led to some far-reaching innovations in our aerial tactics. That one airplane—Koga's Zero—made possible many improvements in air tactics and in the design of new aircraft and their weapons to be used later in World War II."

Lt. Col. Kenneth A. Walsh, a retired Marine Corps officer, recipient of the Medal of Honor, and the first Corsair ace (with twenty-one Japanese aircraft, including seventeen Zeros, to his credit), told me how he first used information that came from test flights of Koga's Zero:

"On April 1, 1943, I got my first aerial victory over the Russell Islands about fifty miles northwest of [Guadalcanal's] Henderson Field. I lost altitude in doing so, and I climbed at high speed to regain altitude. As I reached something like 16,000 feet (I wanted 25,000 or 30,000 feet) I followed around the right side of a huge cumulus cloud. As I left the cloud I saw a Zero 500 or 600 feet to my left. He was doing the same thing as I was, only on the left side of the cloud. He was climbing for altitude to go home and I was climbing to get above any enemy planes I might find.

"We spotted each other at the same instant. We were both at the same level, both climbing about the same speed, and at about the same heading. I immediately turned toward him, planning a deflection shot, but before I could get on him, he rolled to the right, putting his plane right under my tail and within shooting range. He did it so fast I was flabbergasted. I had been told the Zero was extremely maneuverable, but if I hadn't seen how swiftly his plane responded I wouldn't have believed it.

"I was in real trouble, and I remembered briefings on Koga's Zero how to escape from a following Zero. I did a split S, and with its nose down and full throttle my Corsair picked up speed fast. I wanted at least 240 knots, preferably 260. Then, as prescribed, I rolled hard right. As I did this, and continued my dive, tracers from the Zero zinged past my plane's belly.

"From Koga's Zero, I knew the Zero rolled more slowly to the right than to the left. If I hadn't known which way to turn or roll, I'd have probably rolled to my left. If I had done that, that Zero would have probably turned with me, locked on, and had me.

"I used that maneuver a number of times to get away from Zeros, " Walsh said.

No one knows how many of our pilots' lives were saved by information from Koga's Zero. However, a comment by Bill Thies said it well: "If our having Koga's Zero saved even one American pilot's life, it was all worth it."

Koga's Zero came to an ignoble end in February 1945 when Commander Richard G. Crommelin was taxiing it at the San Diego Naval Air Station, preparing for a training flight. A Curtiss Helldiver overran it, chopping it into pieces from tail to cockpit. Crommelin survived.

The wreckage was discarded. Saved were the manifold pressure gauge, airspeed indicator, the folding panel of the port wing-tip, two manufacturer identification plates, and a wing inspection plate. Most are in the Navy Museum at Washington Navy Yard in Washington, D.C. The manufacturer identification plates are in the Alaska Aviation Heritage Museum at Anchorage.

This article, adapted from my 1995 book *Koga's Zero: The Fighter That Changed World War II,* appeared in *Aviation History* magazine in November 2000.

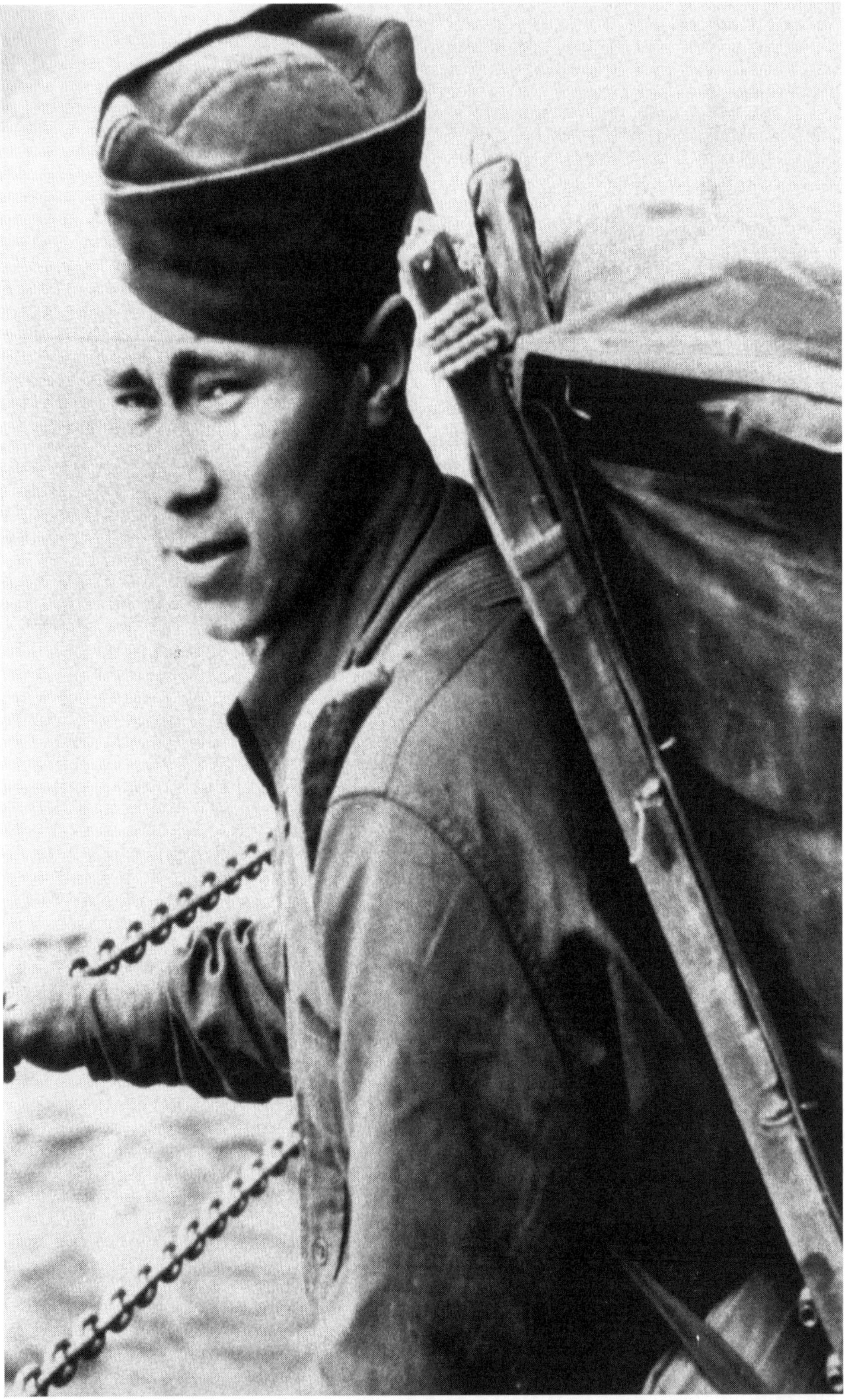

CHAPTER FIVE

CASTNER'S CUTTHROATS

World War II had ended two years before I arrived in Alaska in 1947, and it was still a fresh memory for everyone. I heard Alaskans talk about Castner's Cutthroats. It seemed as if every Alaskan knew former members of that wartime outfit—officially designated as the Alaska Combat Intelligence Platoon, and also known as the Alaska Scouts. They were held almost in awe.

Attu and Kiska Islands in the Aleutians were the only parts of North America in which Americans fought the enemy on the ground and in the air during World War II. Castner's Cutthroats played an important role in defeating the Japanese on this American soil.

Over the years I met more than a dozen of the former members of the outfit, and I came to know well eight of these. Commencing in 1950, when I became acquainted with Ivar Skarland, head of the Department of Anthropology at the University of Alaska and a one-time Alaska Scout, I started making notes on their wartime experiences. Over nearly forty years I jotted notes about the Alaska

Alaska Scout Simeon Pletnikoff (Aleut Pete), aboard the transport *Bell* taking him to Attu Island for the invasion to displace the Japanese. His Trapper Nelson packboard and sack was standard issue to men of the unit known as Castner's Cutthroats, which used a mix of military and civilian clothing and equipment.

NATIONAL ARCHIVES

Scouts as told to me by Skarland, Wayne (Red) Adney, Truman (Slim) Emberg, Wilbur Church, Ernest Shupert, George Bishop, Ed Walker, and Bob Garr. This is their story.

Col. Lawrence V. Castner, intelligence officer of the Alaska Defense Command, conceived of the Alaska Combat Intelligence Platoon, and he personally handpicked for the outfit only expert outdoorsmen, mostly Alaskans. Included were big game guides, sportsmen, trappers, prospectors, miners, and commercial fishermen, as well as Indians, Eskimos, and Aleuts accustomed to living from the land. They had hunted everything from whales to hump-shouldered coastal brown bears.

Their nicknames give a clue to their character: Bad Whiskey Red, Quicksilver, Bucko, Trader Joe, The Quill, Indian Joe, and Aleut Pete were a few. Their wilderness experience made them better scouts than the Army could have created with years of training. Castner taught them how to gather military intelligence.

Castner chose sixty-nine draftees and regular Army soldiers for this elite force. At age thirty-five, George Bishop was the oldest; the others called him Pop. He had trapped, guided big game hunters, and traded in furs. Unmarried, he was drafted into the army in February 1942 and sent to Fort Richardson, near Anchorage.

"I had lived in the woods all my life. I knew nothing else," he told me. "The Army asked me how I made my living. I told them I was a trapper."

An intelligence officer asked Bishop if he could drive a dog team, handle a riverboat, use an axe.

"That's all I've done for years," answered the perplexed Bishop. The officer sent him to Castner.

With other Alaska Scouts, Bishop learned mapmaking, hand-to-hand combat, and other military skills. No one needed to show Bishop how to handle a rifle, however. Six scope-sighted Springfield rifles were issued to the platoon. Scouts who scored highest on targets at 300, 400, and 500 yards were issued these rifles.

"I got lucky and got the highest score," Bishop remembered. He wasn't lucky; he was a marvelous shot. I know, for I hunted with him in the 1950s and 1960s.

Alaska Scouts did not operate as a single unit, except once, at Adak Island. Generally, Castner sent them out in small detachments. They used civilian Trapper Nelson packboards, belt knives, tin (canvas) pants and jackets, civilian shoepacks, and other non-GI equipment. Some carried their personal .30-06 hunting rifles.

On June 3 and 4, 1942, Japanese carrier planes bombed Dutch Harbor, an American base in the Aleutian Islands. Seventy eight Americans died. An Alaska Scout, Sergeant Donald Spaulding, who was camped in the mountains above Dutch, radioed a bomb-by-bomb account of the raid to Castner at Fort Richardson.

Those exploding bombs marked the beginning of the fifteen-month-long Aleutian Campaign. Next, the Japanese landed on and fortified Attu and Kiska Islands in the western Aleutians.

Soon, detachments of four or five Alaska Scouts started slipping ashore from submarines, fishing boats, and amphibious Navy planes on lonely, remote Aleutian Islands, scouting for Japanese invaders. They also sought sites for airstrips and beaches suitable for amphibious landings, and mapped previously uncharted islands.

The Aleutian Islands stretch from mainland Alaska 1,000-miles across the North Pacific toward Japan. Attu is the westernmost; Kiska lies 175 miles closer to Alaska. To drive the Japanese from the first North American soil captured by enemy forces in modern times, the United States leapfrogged island to island toward Attu and Kiska.

First, General Simon Bolivar Buckner, commanding the Alaska Defense Command, wanted an aircraft runway on Adak Island, 450 miles west of Dutch Harbor. Buckner flew to Adak in a Navy PBY seaplane, accompanied by several Alaska Scouts. Sergeant Ed "Hiram" Walker was one of them.

Adak, treeless like all of the Aleutians, rises abruptly from the sea in a jumble of sharp peaks, with narrow valleys. In summer, flapping seabirds, eagles, and ravens swarm about the island. Seals, sea otters, and sea lions squirm on the beaches. No human lived there. But American pilots had reported seeing Japanese patrols on Adak.

Walker described for me his trip to Adak with Buckner. For most of a day the general fruitlessly searched for a level runway site. As he impatiently strode about, Alaska Scouts kept to high ground, guarding the general against possible lurking Japanese. Finally, a Scout pointed to a coastal lagoon. "Drain that, general, and it'll make your runway," he suggested.

Buckner seized on the idea, and the drained lagoon became the Adak runway.

But first, the United States had to fortify Adak. On the night of August 27, 1942, the submarine *Tuna* quietly surfaced a mile from Adak. Led by Castner, twenty-three Alaska Scouts paddled five rubber rafts ashore. Next night the submarine *Triton* eased her bow onto a sandy Adak beach, and another twenty-three Alaska Scouts silently slipped ashore.

Former Alaska Scout Bob Garr, at Adak with Castner, told me, "Three of us hiked forty-five miles around Mount Moffett as fast as we could. Our orders were to kill any Japanese we found, before they could send a radio message.

"I got back to the beach at three o'clock in the morning and reported my sector clear, then I flopped on the tundra and was instantly asleep. I awoke two hours later, soaked from rain. The bay was full of ships. Castner had heard from all the scouts, and had given the fleet the all-clear."

Ed Walker described for me how, on Adak, after the landing, the Scouts camped at a trapper's shack. Scouts dove twenty feet down in the icy water to catch half a dozen ten-pound king crab. Others caught Dungeness crab and dug clams. One Scout killed a mess of Dolly Varden with a grenade. Driftwood fires smoked, and the tired men cooked, ate, snoozed, and relaxed.

A newly landed soldier wandered near. "My God! What outfit is that?" he asked an insignia-free Castner.

For a moment Castner, a West Point graduate, must have seen his Scouts through the eyes of the curious soldier. Most wore a mix of Army and rough civilian woodsmen's garb. A couple wore fringed buckskin jackets. All wore belt knives. Some had beards. Spit-and-polish military they weren't.

"Why, they're Castner's . . . uh, cutthroats," he replied, with a grin.

The name stuck. The press especially liked the colorful title, although *Time* magazine called them "Tundra Troopers." *Yank* called them "The Alaska Scouts," reporting that none of the Scouts liked the cutthroat title. But *Collier's* called them Castner's Cutthroats, and so did Alaska's newspapers and *The Alaska Sportsman* magazine.

Within weeks Adak became a U.S. stronghold from which fighter planes and bombers flew to attack Japanese-held Kiska and Attu. Next was Amchitka, 190 miles from Adak and within sight of Kiska. Twice during the winter of 1942-43, Scouts flew there in Navy PBY amphibians, with P-38 twin-tail fighters buzzing protectively overhead. Under the noses of the Japanese, they searched for a site for an aircraft runway.

Engineer Colonel Benjamin Talley accompanied the Scouts on their second trip to Amchitka. Talley told me that once while he and the Scouts were on the island, a Japanese patrol plane flew over. "It was so low I could see the pilot's eyes," he said.

He and the Scouts escaped discovery.

Amidst a howling Aleutian storm, on January 13, 1943, American infantry and engineers landed on Amchitka. A destroyer sank, and men drowned. Alaska Scouts, including Pop Bishop, were the first ashore. One Scout, whose name I have been unable to learn, rescued twelve infantrymen when their boat capsized in the surf.

"Most of the food was lost during the landing, and we had to live partly off the land," Bishop told me. "For a time every soldier on Amchitka lived on one or two cans of C rations per day.

"A day or two after we landed, I spotted emperor geese on the tundra. I crawled to within forty yards and shot one. The others stood, heads up, staring. They had never been hunted. I shot two more before they flew," he remembered.

"We Scouts killed hundreds of these six-pound geese. They fed a lot of soldiers. Later, I killed a sea lion, and we ate it too. We caught cod, greenling, and an occasional halibut. I shot many Amchitka ptarmigan with my .22 handgun."

As engineers built the airstrip, six Alaska Scouts, including Bishop and Lieutenant Earl Acuff, built an observation post of driftwood covered with grass and sod on the northern tip of Amchitka. From it, with binoculars, they occasionally spotted Japanese planes high over Kiska, fifty miles away.

The astounded Japanese could hardly believe that Americans had landed on Amchitka. They were certain the constant winter storms made a landing impossible. With pontoon-equipped Zero fighters, they bombed and strafed the Americans on Amchitka, trying to stop airfield construction. Some Americans were killed. After they built the observation post on the north end of the island, Alaska Scouts radioed warnings when Zeros approached.

Engineers completed the runway in days. A squadron of Curtiss P-40 Warhawk fighters arrived. When next Alaska Scouts radioed that Zeros were approaching from Kiska, a flight of P-40 fighters snarled into the air and climbed high. When the Zeros arrived, the P-40 pilots dived and shot down two of the enemy planes. Japanese air raids to Amchitka almost ceased.

From Amchitka, American bombers dropped tons of bombs on the dug-in Japanese on Kiska and Attu.

With Amchitka, Adak, and Dutch Harbor as support bases, it was time to meet the Japanese invaders on the ground. On May 11, 1943, in the first-ever amphibious island landing by U.S. infantry, Americans stormed four beaches of rugged forty-mile-long Attu. Alaska Scouts were guides, map readers, messengers, snipers, and advisers.

Pop Bishop was assigned to guide the 240-man 7th Scout Battalion, a longtime regular Army outfit, which sailed to Attu from Dutch Harbor aboard a destroyer and two gigantic submarines, *Nautilus* and *Narwhal.*

"At Attu, we climbed snow-covered 3,000-foot mountains that rise straight from the sea. I led. We got into position above and behind the Japanese camp. Other forces attacked from the beach. The Japanese were caught between us. We had food for one day, and no bedding. I carried three hundred rounds of ammo, four grenades, dry socks—about seventy-five pounds," he remembered.

Bishop and the men of the 7th Scouts were in the mountains for three nights. Their clothing was inadequate for the fog, rain, snow, and wind. Slick-soled leather blucher boots issued for the campaign gave no protection from the deep snow, and on steep slopes the soldiers could scarcely stand. Alaska Scouts, wearing shoepacks (rubber-bottom, leather-top boots), changed socks frequently and had no foot trouble.

Chilled, wet, and hungry, the soldiers lay shivering in trenches they dug in the snow between rock ledges. There they were reasonably safe from Japanese bullets and shell fragments. They lobbed mortar shells into the Japanese camp and at Japanese who climbed into the mountains.

Said Bishop, "Alone, I slipped down a draw and dug a peekhole through a snowdrift and watched. The Japanese were confused, and they didn't have enough men to fight on the several fronts from which attacks came.

"On the fourth day we had to pull out. We couldn't stay longer without grub. Some of the men were sick. Many had frostbitten or swollen feet. My shoepacks kept my feet dry. I kept socks drying next to my skin, and changed frequently.

"Before we left, I went again to my snowdrift peekhole and found no change with the Japanese. I was ready to return when the habits of a lifetime in the woods probably saved my life; I looked around before moving. There, between me and my outfit, were three Japanese soldiers walking toward me. I had to shoot my way out.

"The nearest was about fifty yards. I killed him with a shot to the chest. The second, at about seventy yards, stopped when I shot his companion, and, rifle ready, tried to locate me. My next shot hit his shoulder, and he staggered. I fired two more shots before he went down. I jammed a fresh clip into the Springfield. Before I could fire again, the third Japanese ran into a creek-bottom washout.

"He was pinned. But so was I. If I had moved it would have given him a clear shot at me. It was too far to throw a grenade, so I rolled one. It bounced over the washout before it exploded. I rolled the next grenade very gently— a deadly game of golf. The grenade dropped into the hole where the Japanese lay, killing him. I then returned to my outfit leaving three dead Japanese soldiers behind."

Two weeks into the battle, Bishop and two other Alaska Scouts came upon a camp of forty American soldiers. The men had not had a full meal in three days because of defective oil stoves. Their food consisted mostly of bacon and flour.

"Why don't you burn driftwood?" Bishop asked. "You could cook over open fires."

One of the soldiers laughed. "The driftwood is wet. It won't burn. We even threw oil on it."

"I'll show you how to burn driftwood," Bishop said. He trotted to the nearby beach where lay a jackstraw pile of bleached driftwood logs. He swung his axe and cut away wet outer layers of a log, exposing dry wood.

"I'll be damned!" exploded the officer in charge. "I didn't think there was dry wood within a thousand miles."

With his sheath knife Bishop made shavings. He split kindling wood and quickly had several fires. The hungry men soon ate sizzling bacon and hotcakes.

Early in the battle for Attu, Bishop carried a message to the powder-stained commander of an artillery unit. Moments before he arrived, a sniper had killed one of the artillerymen.

"Are you one of Castner's Scouts?" the upset officer asked.

Bishop nodded. "Do you want to go up and get that damned sniper?" the officer asked.

Thirteen years after the event, in 1956, Bishop told me, "Hell no, I didn't want to climb that mountain after a sniper. However, someone had to go.

"I went up a steep draw. At a snowdrift I tossed my rifle ahead and crawled after it. A Japanese machine-gun cut loose at me. Snow flew and bullets hammered near. I shoved my rifle forward and dived after it. The snow had formed a dam, with meltwater above it. I slid headfirst into a foot of ice water. It was a shock, but it was welcome—I was still alive.

"One bullet had cut through my coat, shirt, and underwear, but it didn't draw blood. I climbed higher and for hours lay among low willows, watching. Occasionally, the sniper slowly raised his head, peeking. He had been lucky to hit anyone, for the range to the artillery outfit where he had killed the man was eight or nine hundred yards. I was within three hundred yards of him.

"I kept my scope-mounted Springfield on the spot. When enough of his head showed, I put a bullet into it. A mortar wiped out the crew of the machine-gun that had shot at me."

Bishop emerged from the three-week Battle of Attu without a scratch. But proportionately, the Battle of Attu was the second bloodiest in the Pacific. For every hundred Japanese who died, seventy-one Americans died or were wounded. In the Pacific, only the Battle of Iwo Jima had a higher ratio.

On Attu, 1,700 Americans were hit by Japanese gunfire; 549 died.

Afterward, Americans buried 2,351 Japanese. Twenty eight Japanese were taken prisoner.

Bad Whiskey Red (Willis Cruden), one of Castner's Scouts, was killed in action at Attu; Raymond Conrad and Edward Bagby received Silver Stars for heroism and gallantry in action there. Clyde Peters was seriously wounded.

In August 1943, American and Canadian troops landed on Kiska. As usual, Alaska Scouts, including Pop Bishop, were the first ashore. They were pleasantly surprised. Weeks earlier, amidst concealing fog, the five thousand Japanese on the island had fled.

That ended the Aleutian Campaign. During the remainder of the war, Alaska Scouts mapped and explored far places of unknown Alaska. They field-tested military equipment and functioned as search and rescue teams.

For leading the Alaska Combat Intelligence Platoon, Colonel Lawrence V. Castner, who died in 1948, received the Distinguished Service Medal. The platoon—Castner's Cutthroats—received the Presidential Unit Citation for its leadership and performance in action during the Aleutian Campaign.

Traditionally during wartime, America's outdoorsmen have become her military scouts. Survival knowledge, path-finding ability, sharpshooting skills, and toughness have characterized such men. Members of Castner's band exemplified this great tradition.

This article was printed in *Alaska* magazine in December 1991. It won a silver award in the historical feature category at the following year's Regional Publishers Association competition. (My book *Castner's Cutthroats: Saga of the Alaska Scouts,* reprinted in paperback in 2001, is a partly fictionalized account of the Alaska Combat Intelligence Platoon.)

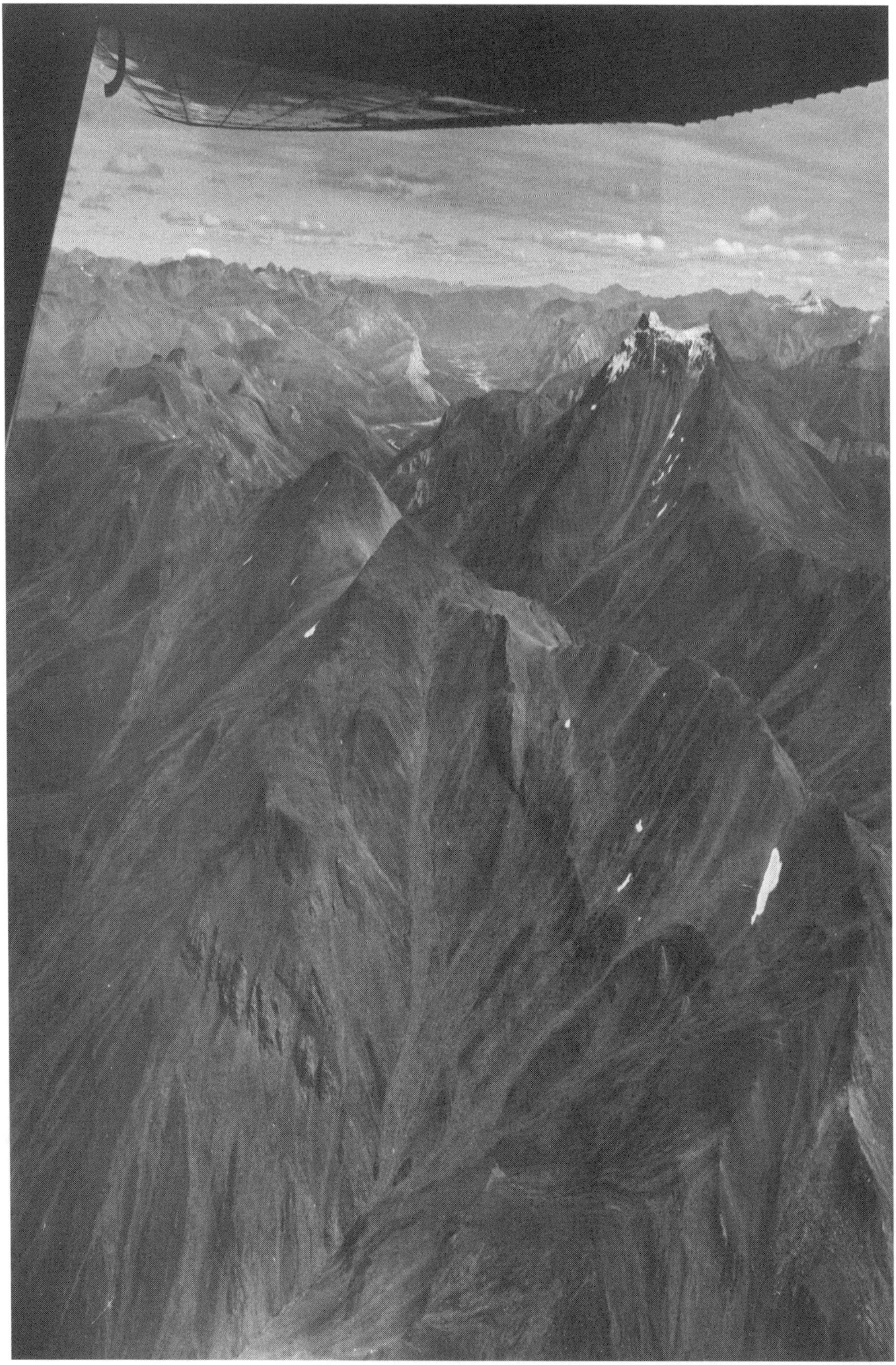

CHAPTER SIX

LOST IN THE TALKEETNAS

The story of Pat O'Donnell is a classic of Alaska survival. A recording of O'Donnell telling of his experience was broadcast over Fairbanks radio station KFAR soon after his ordeal. His emotional recounting made such an impact that KFAR manager Al Bramstedt Sr. broadcast it again during hunting season the following year. He also broadcast it the next year, and the next, eventually broadcasting it each hunting season for nearly a decade as a warning to hunters about to go afield.

I was living at Fairbanks when I heard it for the first time in 1955. I contacted O'Donnell at his Anchorage home and received permission to write the story, based on the recording broadcast by KFAR. Here is the story, told in his voice.

On Labor Day 1949 with my wife and two friends—pilot Francis "Dizzy" Brownfield and Earl Bogle—I went

The unforgiving Talkeetna Mountians northeast of Anchorage. Left alone in this wild land, Pat O'Donnell was forced into an epic trek for survival. He climbed over ridge after ridge and crossed a series of rivers in his struggle to reach saftey.

JIM REARDEN PHOTO

85

on an Alaskan hunt I'll remember to my dying day. Not because of the game I killed, but because to get home I walked more than two hundred miles, alone, through the rugged Talkeetna Mountains.

It was to be a caribou and bear hunt. From our camp, Dizzy was to fly us daily in his Piper cruiser J-5B airplane to the Little Nelchina River in order to hunt. This river is about twenty air miles north of Sheep Mountain, a landmark on the Glenn Highway, 128 miles northeast of Anchorage.

We saw caribou the first day, but didn't manage to kill anything. The next morning Dizzy flew Earl about twelve miles upriver and landed him on a gravel bar so he could hunt his way back to camp. Flying back after leaving Earl, Dizzy sighted a herd of caribou.

"Come on, Pat," he said when he landed at our camp a few miles from the Glenn Highway. "I'll take you up to where the caribou are. Hunt toward camp and you'll walk right into them."

My wife remained in camp and I got into the plane and we took off. Diz thought he knew a shortcut, so he flew north. We went through several big valleys, and somehow he got twisted around.

"Pat, I'm lost," he told me.

"Lost?" I was surprised.

"Yeah, and look at this fog coming in. I think we'd better set her down and wait it out."

He landed on a short gravel bar next to the river, just barely managing to stop before reaching the water.

"Good landing, Diz," I complimented him.

"Yep. Any landing you walk away from is a good one," he kidded, with a grin. I didn't realize then how far I was going to have walk back from that one.

He tried to contact Sheep Mountain by radio, but he didn't get through. We sat around smoking cigarettes, waiting for the fog to lift. Diz was low on cigarettes, and I had maybe a dozen, so we divided them evenly. About then I saw a caribou standing on the bank across the river.

"Shall I shoot it, Diz?" I asked.

"Sure, let's go get it," he replied.

I sneaked the door of the plane open so that the caribou couldn't hear it, got the gun, and crawled under the plane. I had borrowed a .30-40 Winchester, and hadn't sighted it in or taken any practice shots with it.

I aimed at the caribou and saw the ground at his feet jump when I shot. By the time I got ready to shoot again the caribou had moved off.

I jumped into the water, excited, wanting to dash up there and get him. I came out of that cold water fast, and Diz grabbed the gun.

We fooled around like that for a long time until finally the caribou wandered over the top of a nearby ridge. Then we decided to take off and return to camp, as the fog had lifted.

After turning the plane around, we got in, and Diz revved her up and started off. The runway was short, bumpy, and wet, and the next thing I knew my face was full of water. We had hit a big puddle and the plane had twisted around and been shaken up.

We checked the plane over and found a hole ripped in the fabric on the underside, loading the fuselage with water. We tilted it out. One of the wing tips had scratched the ground just enough to break the inside of it a bit, but it hadn't broken the fabric.

I looked at the short airstrip with all the rough spots and made up my mind.

"Diz, you'd better take off alone. You can fly on up the river, and I'll walk. If you find a longer bar, you can land, and I'll meet you there."

"You take the rifle then," he said, "because I'm low on gas. I might fly out and refuel and come back to get you."

He took off, just barely making it. Then he circled, waggling his wings at me as he went by, and up the river he flew. That was the last time I ever saw him.

I began wading up the river, cutting from bank to bank, walking steadily. I watched each gravel bar as I passed to see if a plane could land on it, and after about three hours spotted one that looked pretty fair. I pulled a pile of driftwood aside and cleared away weeds and dirt that had been washed up. Then I sat down to have a cigarette and to relax.

Just then a small plane came over at several thousand feet. I was sitting under some bushes. It hadn't dawned on me that I was lost and that Dizzy would never come back.

I got up and walked on the bar to look at the plane. It kept going. I started a fire with my cigarette lighter, and began to worry. Four hours had gone by.

"I wonder if Diz could have cracked up going up the river?" I asked myself.

To my left was a high mountain, so I crossed the river and climbed it. From the top I could see about ten miles, I imagine. While there I saw a real good-looking gravel bar, but I couldn't see an airplane anywhere.

So down off the mountain I went and made my way to this good gravel bar. By then I was getting dazed and chilly. It was late in the day and dark was coming on. I picked up a lot of driftwood and got another fire going. Then I smoked my last cigarette and went to sleep.

In the morning, after a mighty uncomfortable night of feeding the fire and dozing beside it, I was undecided whether to move or stay there. After a while I half made up my mind.

"I think I'll go west," I told myself. I knew I'd have to hit the Alaska Railroad if I did. So I climbed to the top of the mountain to the west.

"No, you'd better stay here," I said.

So down I went to where I had my fire. I sat and waited, wondering, and then began to get nervous, so up the mountain I went again. I did that several times, and each time went a bit farther. Finally I looked on the other side of the mountain and saw a whole herd of caribou. They were close, so I banged away at them three times. They just looked at me and walked off.

"Boy, Pat, you're really a good shot. The first thing you know you won't have a bullet left," I told myself.

I had eight cartridges: five in the rifle, and three in a box. I folded the box and put it in my pocket to use for starting fires, and put the three cartridges in my trouser pocket.

Soon the caribou began moving back. A big bull in particular got my interest. He was coming toward me.

"I'm going to play Indian on you," I thought.

The brush was pretty high, so I lay down and peeked at him. He kept coming. The wind was blowing in my direction, so I started easing toward him. Soon I was within thirty feet.

I reared up and leveled the rifle at him. He raised his head and looked at me. "Bang!" I fired. He just stood there. I thought I had missed again, and not wanting to waste any more ammunition, threw the rifle down, drew my sheath knife and charged. He collapsed just before I reached him. It was my first caribou.

I stood looking at the dead animal, realizing what I had done.

"I'm way up here, now I've got to pack you all the way down this mountain," I addressed the carcass.

"Yeah, but Diz ain't down there."

"I'll just cut your hindquarters off and take them down the mountain."

I finally reached the bottom, then waded and fell through the river to the camp I had set up. My fire was still warm, so I threw wood on it and it blazed up again.

I sliced off some meat and began cooking it. I was hungry, not having eaten all day, but it was tasteless, and it didn't seem right that I should eat freshly killed meat that hadn't cooled.

I hung the quarters in a tree and went to sleep. I spent another very uncomfortable night trying to stay warm near the fire and dozing off. Morning finally came. I ate more meat, and continued to wait and watch for Diz. About noon I began to get excited again and wanted to move west.

"No," I finally told myself, "I think you'd better go up the river for a ways because Diz could have landed somewhere up there, or maybe he even cracked up, and you might see him."

So, carrying one of the hindquarters on my shoulder, I went up the river. It started to rain toward evening, getting cold and miserable. My feet hurt, and I stopped often to rest. One of my clearest memories is sitting in the rain eating blueberries that day.

I saw a gorge ahead, across a bend of the river, so I cut straight across. I found a nice gravel bar there with a lot of good wood on it. Just as I hit the bar an airplane came over. I fired a shot in desperation, hoping they would hear it, but of course they didn't.

It was dreary, windy, and wet. I gathered wood, started a fire after some difficulties, cooked more meat, and went to sleep. Next day I made several fires and fed them through the day and night. No more planes flew over.

The following day was clear and bright. I cut the meat off the caribou leg and cooked it, wrapping eighteen pieces the size of a hamburger in my handkerchief, figuring I'd eat one of them three times a day, giving me enough for six days. And I cooked and ate more meat right then. It didn't taste very good without salt.

By then I had decided I would have to get out on my own. I knew it would be rough. I wore light underwear, GI fatigue trousers and jacket, one pair of wool socks, leather Chippewa boots and my wife's red mackinaw. No hat. I had my rifle, cigarette lighter, a sheath knife, and a switchblade pocketknife. In that outfit, with no blanket, I got mighty cold on those September nights in the high Talkeetna mountains.

I headed upriver, unable to cross because even in the riffles the water was too deep. When I did find a place and tried to cross, the water picked me up and turned me over and over. The old Winchester was scraping on the rocks and I was afraid it would break. Just then, while rolling over and over, I heard an airplane. I couldn't get out of the water quickly enough, and it was gone when I fired a futile shot into the air.

There I was, wringing wet, cold, mad—and desperate. If I could have gotten my hands on that plane I'd have ripped the wings off.

I came to a lot of marshy land, sinking to my ankles with every step. I heard ducks and wished for a shotgun. I came to a big lake, and as I looked around, saw human footprints. I yelled; the footprints looked pretty fresh. There was a tin can on a stick in the ground, just beginning to rust on the inside. It hadn't been too long since a plane and people had been there.

About twenty-five yards away was another stick in the ground with a piece of canvas hanging on it. I decided that the lake had been used for duck hunting and these markers had been a guide into it.

I climbed a high mountain in front of me, thinking maybe I'd see a floatplane from the top. There was nothing. I thought I was on top of the mountains, but as I continued trudging west I always saw a higher one ahead. On top of this one, it was nice and level and I walked fast.

I would steer a course to one mountain, then to another. Once I heard airplanes high above. I took my undershirt off and waved, but they flew right over. I ran into caribou and moose. Each time I'd look at them and talk with myself.

"Should I shoot another one?"

Then I would remember that I still had meat from the caribou I had killed.

"No. You can travel faster without a load."

So I kept going. The mountains began to decrease in size, and in the distance I could see trees and water. I hadn't been drinking water up there; I ate blueberries.

When I reached the water I found it milky—glacier water. And it was moving fast, with big boulders rolling in it. I had to get across, but I was afraid to attempt it for fear that I might be thrown again, and I'd break a leg. And if I broke a leg I was finished. So I sat on the bank and thought.

I remembered that three fires means SOS, and I could still hear an occasional airplane going over. So I built three big fires and put a lot of green Christmas trees on them for smoke. I did that for two days.

In my wanderings after wood I found an old wagon and a lantern, both rotten. They gave me courage.

"Someone else was here, even with a wagon. They had to bring it in here, and they must have gotten out, so I can get out."

I couldn't get it into my head to go down this river. I wanted to cross it, so I followed toward its source and found a place where I waded through about to my shoulders. I held my lighter in one hand and my gun in the other. I had to keep that lighter dry.

The water was still, and there was sand in front of me when I came out. I stepped into that and sank clear to my hips.

"Quicksand, Pat, you're done!"

"Aw, no, you ain't," I said. I fell forward on my face and pulled myself out, but I got the cigarette lighter in the sand. When I reached solid ground again it didn't work.

That made me disgusted. I sat down, took my pocketknife, and cleaned all the particles of sand away from the lighter's wheel and finally got it so it would turn. Then I started walking again.

I got to the top of another mountain where there were a lot of streams, so I lay down to get a drink at one. While drinking I saw something glitter, and reached down and picked it up. It was a gold nugget.

"Why, Pat, you lucky dog. Here you gotta be lost and find this. No pan to pan it, and even if you panned it, where would you put it?" I was talking to myself freely by this time.

"Well, I ain't going to pan it, but I'll take this back as a memory." I put the gold in my back pocket and continued walking.

I hit snow on the next mountain, and circled, following the edge of a deep gorge. I thought I saw a house or something down at the bottom of it, but I didn't want to go see for fear that I'd find I was mistaken. I had been fooled too many times by logs that resembled crashed airplanes. I walked back and forth on the rim twice, undecided.

"Aw, forget that," I said finally. "I've still got a little meat, and maybe just over the next hill I'll see a highway or something." So I took off again and dropped down into a nice wide valley. Things looked familiar to me in that valley. I still don't understand why; I'm sure I had never seen it before.

My lighter didn't work that night, and I had to sleep without a fire. I was miserable and chilled to the bone by daylight. In the morning I headed for a stream

I had seen across the valley. My feet were badly bruised and blistered, and they hurt with every step.

It was rocky and tough traveling up the stream, and as I climbed I saw a group of mountain sheep. When I reached the top the sun was setting, and it was beginning to get cold. I couldn't find a place to get out of the weather there, so finally I backtracked to some rocks I had seen and used my army field jacket, with two sticks across the rocks, as a shelter for the night.

I soon became cold, and I could reach right out and cut the fog. I had strange dreams as I drowsed: helicopters were hovering just above me, offering to take me to safety. I awoke cold and shivering and had to walk around in the dark to get warm. I wrung the water out of my jacket—it was raining again—and covered myself up again. Then I tried to get some more rest. That went on all that long, cold night.

Next morning when I reached the top of the next hill I found snow, but that disappeared as the sun rose. I was on a black, rock-strewn mountain. Next I came to a deep gorge, in the bottom of which were three big pools of water. There was no way down but over big black crags. Down I went, stepping from rock to rock. My boots were worn on the heels and showing the nails, so they often slipped.

I found a stick with a natural crook on one end, and used that to test rocks before I stepped on them. The next mountain was level on top, and after quite a distance I came to another deep gorge. It looked too steep for me to go down. I searched around here and there, but every place I looked was steep.

"Pat, do you think you can make that? You know, that looks mighty steep. I think that if you got halfway and you couldn't go down, you ain't comin' back. Do you want to take a chance?" asked my cautious self.

"Yeah, let's go," answered my reckless side.

It was a desperate climb. I edged down slowly, hitting a sheer drop of about eight feet. Nearby were some black rocks with water falling on them, and on one side they jutted out enough so that I could get my hands on them. I got one toe in a crack so I could reach down with my stick to hit a black rock beneath me.

I edged, sat, slid and crawled backward down the steep drop. The loose rocks there scared me; if I slipped on one and fell, I might have broken a leg or worse. I think it was here that I lost my sheath knife. When I reached bottom I found swift water loaded with boulders. It hurt my feet to walk on the boulders.

Following the bank I found that the water plunged into a deep gorge, so I had to backtrack. I came to another river with a wide bed filled with glacier water. It was impassable. Again I had to backtrack. Finally I got around the streams by jumping from boulder to boulder and got out of that gorge. Then I started down the wide-bedded river—it was about half-a-mile across, I guess—traveling along the bank where the walking was good. I came around a bend and there, incredibly, was a cabin.

I walked up to the cabin and yelled. No answer. The door was nailed shut, but a hammer hung nearby. Over the door a sign read, "Welcome."

"Boy, I'm welcome," I said. "I'm coming in, too." I took the hammer, pulled the nails, and walked in. The cabin belonged to Oscar Vogel. I later learned he was a long-time trapper and guide in the Talkeetna country.

There was a bedroll hanging from the rafters, a bed on one side of the cabin, and a stove in the middle of the floor with some stove pipe. Next to the door were four sticks driven into the ground, each with a tin can on it, where the stove belonged.

After I had the stove set up I looked around and found a can of rough-cut tobacco and an old corncob pipe. While smoking away I looked for coffee, and found it. I went after water and soon had a coffeepot on. Then I heard some noise outside. I thought it was the man who owned the cabin coming back.

In my excitement I pulled the door open and started out. Two big grizzly bears looked me right in the eye. Another step and I could have slapped 'em right in the face. I ran back into the cabin, slammed the door, grabbed my gun and jumped up on the bunk, shaking. I was ready to shoot if they touched the door.

They didn't, and I finally walked over to it, pressed and pulled at it at the same time and peeked out, but they weren't in sight. I went out and peeked around each side of the cabin, but didn't see any bears. So I went back and finished making coffee.

I cooked some beans I found and ate them. Beans never tasted so good. I stayed there the rest of the day, that night, the next day and night. I had never appreciated a simple thing like sleeping warm before.

The following morning my feet felt pretty good. I filled a jar I had found with cooked beans, then borrowed a piece of Mr. Vogel's canvas and a woolen blanket. I also took matches. I left my leather shoes, which were nearly worn out, and wore a pair of good rubber-bottomed shoepacks Mr. Vogel had left.

I started downstream again, my hopes up. Before I had traveled a hundred yards my feet were wet—the shoepacks leaked where the leather and rubber joined—but they were still better than my leather boots.

Late in the day I looked up, and lo and behold there was another of Mr. Vogel's cabins—a big one. It seemed to be his base cabin, because in it he had a list of groceries with "Talkeetna River" written on it. I was on the headwaters of the Talkeetna River, I later learned.

I took some candles and matches when I left that cabin the next morning, and that evening I found a third cabin that belonged to Mr. Vogel, right on the riverbank. I got pitched several times crossing the river to get to it. I realized I was getting weak then, for I often had difficulty with my footing.

Mr. Vogel mustn't have liked that cabin, because he had written on the door, "Vogel's no-good cabin." It looked plenty good to me. He didn't have much food there, but I still had a jar of cooked beans and a can of milk. I also smoked more of Mr. Vogel's tobacco.

I took a pair of Mr. Vogel's woolen socks with me the next morning when I left; mine were worn out. I went on down the river. For four more days I traveled, crossing high mountains and wading stream after stream. My feet felt like hamburger.

Near the end of those four days it started raining again. I was out of food and had nothing but matches and candles left. I found a pool of water along the river with a six-inch fish swimming in it, which I caught with my hands. I figured I would make a fire and roast him. I was pretty hungry after eating nothing but berries for a day. They didn't agree with me.

I couldn't find any dry wood, but in my searching I found some beer cans and bean cans that had washed up on the shore. I knew that someone had to be around somewhere close.

I looked up one of the streams I had just crossed and saw a tent. I had to cross several streams to get there, and when I arrived I found a log cabin, a log cache, and the tent. I went into the cabin, which was unlocked, and found butter and eggs on the table. There was also bacon, pancake flour, beans, coffee, sugar, and potatoes. Soon I sat down and had a real feast. That cabin belonged to Glenn Hudson, and I later learned that the fresh food had been left by a Fourth of July party.

I cut some wood to leave at the cabin and decided to go on next morning. But it rained all night. Gosh, I enjoyed sleeping inside, listening to the rain on the roof! I left the cabin and stepped into the river to wade across, and it threw me. I didn't care.

"I'll go right back to that cabin, build a nice fire, take my clothes off and dry them, and stay there another day," I told myself.

So back to the cabin I went. While there I heard lots of planes, and that night in the distance I saw a beacon. I knew then that I was close. The beacon looked to be five or ten miles away.

I soaked an old blanket in kerosene and had three fires ready to go. As I heard planes, I'd light them. But it rained for the next four days that I remained there. I was fogged in, and they couldn't see the fires.

Every day I tried to cross the streams in front of the cabin, but I would get tossed on my ear and have to go back. I was afraid the current would pull me into deep water and drown me. I finally got disgusted. I wrote a note to my wife on a paper towel, leaving it in the cabin, knowing it would be found, and decided to go on, come what may. It was the twenty-fourth day I had been lost.

I went upstream and let the water throw me until I got to the other side, then I tumbled to my feet. Then I repeated it three times in other branches of the river. The pancakes I had made and carried in my shirt became mush.

The next stream was deep, and I had to clear a place on the bank so I could run and jump to grab a tree that beavers had felled from the other side. When I grabbed the branches, my rifle slipped over my shoulder. I couldn't raise my arm, and my pack slipped down. I was hanging to this tree over deep water, one leg and one arm hanging on for dear life. Finally I squirmed up and got the blanket out of the water. It was wool, and must have weighed twenty pounds; it felt as if it were trying to pull the river up with it.

I continued downstream. I must have walked for about four hours when I happened to look up and see an airplane that had just taken off, flying low above the trees. I got so excited I couldn't see straight. I dropped my pack and fired a shot, but by that time the plane was gone.

Five minutes later I heard a dog barking. Then I started hollering and whistling. Every hundred feet or so I would yell. Finally I even heard chickens clucking. I kept yelling. Finally a man's voice answered. We yelled back and forth and finally I parted the brush just as the other guy did the same, and we looked at each other across a stream.

"You've got the sweetest face of any man I've ever seen," I told him.

"What's the matter?" he asked.

"Man, I've been lost up there in those mountains. I thought I'd never see another human face again!"

"Well, you'll have to cross the stream and get all wet before I can help you," he said.

"Huh, I'll drink all the water in it if I have to get across!" I told him.

"Give me that duffel," he said as I came dripping out of the water.

"You don't have to carry that. Where am I?"

"On the railroad, about a mile from Talkeetna," he answered.

Officers of the Air Force 10th Air Rescue Squadron told me that I had traveled approximately one hundred air miles. In doing so I walked at least two hundred miles. To this day I cannot retrace my steps, and no one has been able to determine just where I was until I arrived at the first of Oscar Vogel's trapline cabins.

After Diz and I disappeared, my wife and Earl Bogle had walked to the Glenn Highway and Sheep Mountain Lodge, where they reported us missing. Diz's airplane was discovered by a 10th Air Rescue team after three days of searching.

Traces of Diz's route after he left his plane were discovered, but he was never found. Perhaps the world will learn his fate one day, but until then, it will simply be another of the many haunting mysteries of the Far North.

I came close to being part of that mystery.

When Pat O'Donnell arrived at Anchorage after his long desperate trek through the Talkeetnas, still exhausted, he was interviewed at Anchorage radio station KENI, and the interview was recorded and broadcast. It was the recording that later was heard annually on KFAR in Fairbanks. The Anchorage interviewer asked O'Donnell to tell his story, and with memories still vivid, he recounted it without a single break. At the end, emotionally overwrought, his voice breaking, O'Donnell urged that the search for his friend Dizzy Brownfield be continued.

Brownfield's fate is still unknown. His airplane was found on a hill thirty or thirty-five miles northeast of where he had left Pat O'Donnell, and only three miles from the Indian village of Tyone. The plane was out of gas and had one flat tire. One leg of the landing gear was broken and twisted, and the tail wheel was torn off. Otherwise it was essentially undamaged and upright.

Later a message was found in a cabin eighty miles away, indicating Brownfield had traveled afoot at least that far after his forced landing. He left no indication of the direction he planned to take upon leaving the cabin. Five blaze marks that he might have made were found on trees leading upstream from the cabin.

If Brownfield had climbed to the top of the hill where he landed his plane, he could have seen the cabins of Tyone on the shore of Tyone Lake. It is possible the hilltop was covered with low clouds at the time, and Brownfield headed downhill and hiked away from the village. And why Brownfield flew north when he left O'Donnell will forever be a mystery. To reach Sheep Mountain Lodge on the Glenn Highway to get fuel, he needed to fly south.

Another irony of the story is that O'Donnell could have walked to the Glenn Highway over an easy and short route had he gone south. It is only twenty to twenty-five air miles from the Little Nelchina River to the Glenn Highway. Compared with the steep, high, and rugged Talkeetna Mountains that O'Donnell penetrated, the ridges between the Little Nelchina and the Glenn Highway are easy traveling for a man afoot.

Pat O'Donnell, a carpenter, continued to live in Anchorage until his death in the late 1990s.

This story appeared in *The Alaska Sportsman* in August 1956 and again in its successor, *Alaska* magazine, in October 1986.

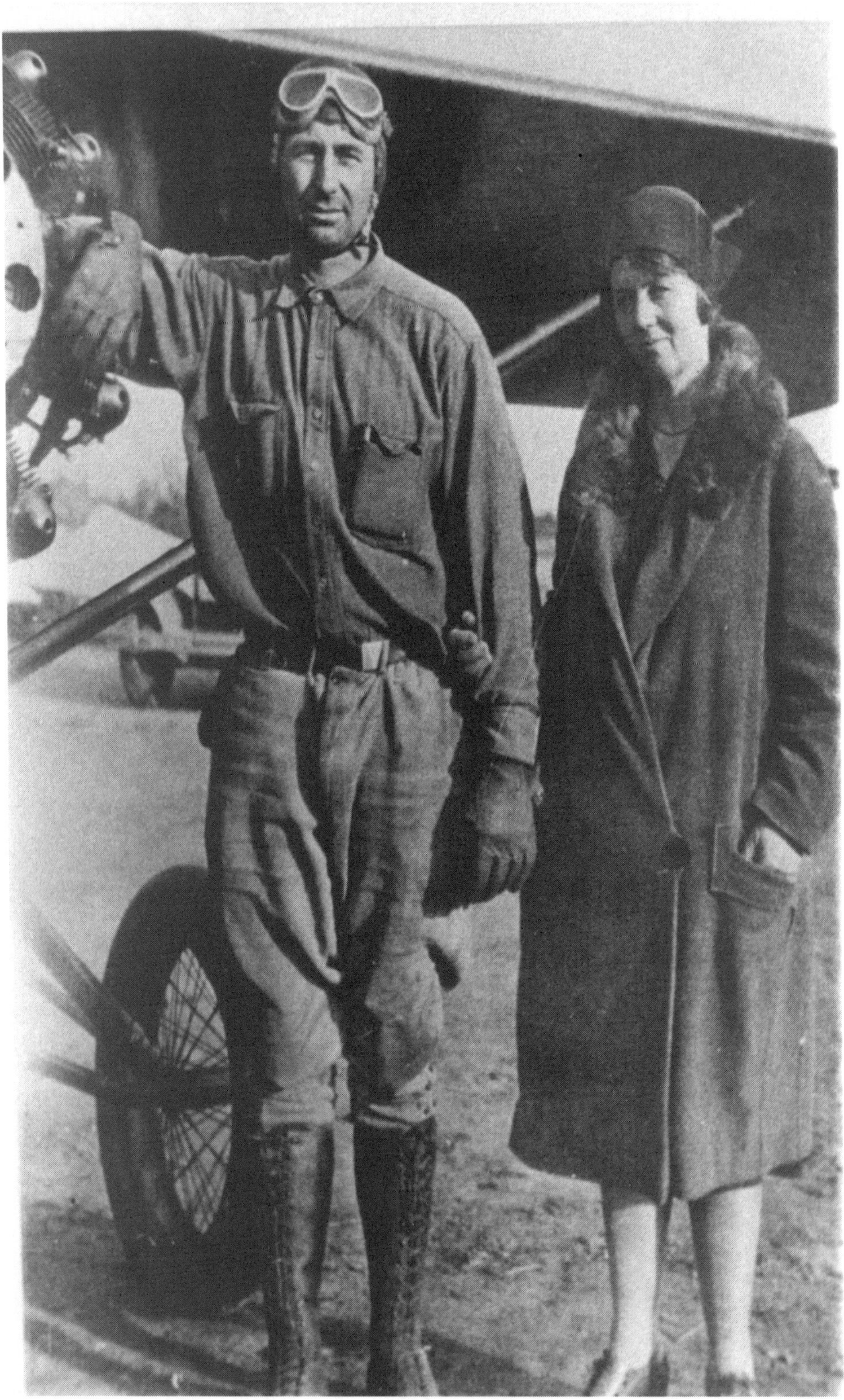

CHAPTER SEVEN

LEGENDARY BUSH PILOTS

Winter 1927. Alaska game warden Sam White, patrolling north of Fairbanks, drove his dog team over the crest of a ridge. The sled stopped. Sam heaved on it, snapped the towline, yelled. Nothing happened. Fouled towline, he thought. He climbed over the top—to find his fifteen dogs stretched out in the sun, half of them asleep.

"That helped me make up my mind. There had to be a better way. I bought an airplane so I could fly my patrols," he told me in 1950. "After years of dealing with freethinking dogs, I really appreciated it when I finally got airborne."

Sam was the world's first flying game warden. He was also a respected early-day Alaska bush pilot. A former Maine guide, a World War I Ranger, and a trapper, he was a master woodsman. Long-time Alaska bush residents recall Sam with respect and affection.

Pilot Sam and his wife, Mary, in the late 1920s. White became the world's first flying game warden, patrolling for the U.S. Biological Survey in Alaska in his own airplanes. He often had to pay for his own gas and airplane expenses.

For $3,500 Sam White bought a two-place, open-cockpit Swallow biplane. It cruised about 100 mph and had a three-hour, twenty-minute range. Pioneer pilot Noel Wien and his brother Ralph taught Sam to fly it in 1928-29. At the time there were eight airplanes in Alaska. Sam flew it for hundreds of hours on wildlife patrol, often buying gasoline with his own money.

Sam's boss, Frank DuFresne, later a well-known outdoors writer, disapprovingly told him, "Our most successful wardens travel on snowshoes."

Sam ignored him. In his Swallow in mere hours he patrolled wilderness regions that had once taken him weeks to cover. From aloft he could see traps that were set illegally too close to a beaver house. He could tell when a trapper illegally fed moose, caribou, or Dall sheep meat to sled dogs. He took his first airplane-caught poacher to court in 1930.

For nearly ten years Sam flew his own plane on patrols. It took the Alaska Game Commission until 1938 to get around to buying two Fairchild 24 airplanes for wildlife work. By 1944, when airplanes were commonly used for wildlife work in Alaska and elsewhere, DuFresne bragged that the Alaska Game Commission had pioneered the use of airplanes in game management.

Sam was the first in Alaska, and perhaps the first anywhere, to use an airplane to count big game from the air. His first aerial count of moose and caribou was in January 1929.

Sam resigned his warden job in 1941 when ordered to ignore wildlife hunting violations by Army brass. War was coming, and the military in Alaska brought prosperity. Politics (as usual) put quick bucks over the welfare of wildlife. Sam refused to accept that.

He went to work as a commercial pilot at double his warden salary, and he flew in Alaska as a bush pilot for the rest of his active life. In forty years, Sam logged more than 11,500 hours in the air. In addition to his Swallow, he flew Bellancas, Stinsons, American Pilgrims, a Curtiss Robin, a Fairchild 71, a Travel Air 6000B—all early bush planes. He made eleven forced landings and had only two accidents, both minor. Sam died in 1976.

Sam was a great storyteller. Here's one I like: In 1953, with his L-5G Stinson, he flew charter for Coast and Geodetic Survey crews in the Kuskokwim country. One day he landed on a lake where he had left a crew at a spike camp. The crew asked Sam to fly some pike they had caught back to the main camp.

Sam demurred. An earlier load of poorly packaged pike caught by this crew had left his plane smelly for days. The gang at main camp had complained about having to eat fish.

Nevertheless, when Sam was ready to leave, he found two cartons of pike—about eighty pounds worth—perched on his right pontoon. The slimy fish were a day or two old, and the cartons holding them were falling apart.

Sam told me, "I climbed into the front office [pilot's seat] and left the cartons on the float. I figured they'd wash into the lake on takeoff."

They didn't. The fish remained on the float as Sam roared into the air. As he flew over a ridge he spotted a black bear sow with three cubs. Mama bear heard the low-flying plane and stood up to look. Sam dipped the right wing and kicked the rudder. The pike plummeted to the ground and hit within a few feet of the bears.

"It was an explosion of fish. Those pike flew everywhere," Sam grinned.

The bears hightailed it in four directions. Soon, the sow turned back to round up her family. She must have picked up the strong smell of fish.

Sam turned and flew over the bears at greater altitude. Three bears were gobbling fish, and the fourth was running to get his share.

Sam White and other pilots of the 1920s and 1930s broke trail. They learned to land on river bars and smooth ridge tops. They had no weather forecasts, no radios. Maps of Alaska had many blank areas. They navigated by mountain ranges, rivers, sled dog trails. They often walked for days to return to civilization when balky engines quit, stranding them in the wilderness. They were gutsy pioneers.

Bush pilot Don Sheldon, who flew from Talkeetna, a skip and a jump from Mount McKinley (Denali), made a name for himself as one of Alaska's great bush pilots. In addition to flying hunters and fishermen, miners, prospectors, trappers, and sightseers, he flew climbers high onto the slopes of McKinley, landing on steep glaciers, the kind of flying that requires guts and great skill.

Sheldon's 1955 rescue of an eight-man Army patrol from almost sure death was one of the most remarkable feats of flying ever. The Army men were sent with a fifty-foot boat to chart navigable stretches of the Susitna River. This required penetrating Devils Canyon, one of the wildest stretches of rocks and rapids anywhere. It was damn foolishness on the Army's part.

While flying two fishermen to a lake in his float-equipped Aeronca Sedan, Sheldon flew over Devils Canyon to check on the Army crew, a courtesy on his part. He saw parts of a smashed boat and floating debris. He left the fishermen at the lake and flew search along the rim of the six-hundred-foot-deep canyon. Chunks of boat, floating gas drums, and other debris were scattered along the river for miles.

He spotted seven Army men huddled on a ledge at the base of the sheer canyon wall. The men were wet, their clothing and life jackets torn. They were almost sure to be swept to death as their strength gave out. No boat could handle the rapids. There wasn't much time.

The canyon is fifty yards wide, full of house-size boulders. The river boils through it at thirty miles an hour. It was too rough and swift to land where the men were. Sheldon flew upriver, found a tiny smooth patch of water, and landed—no small feat in the swift current. He kept the Aeronca aligned with the current using engine power, and allowed the plane to drift backward downstream. Waves rolled higher than the wingtips. Water beat at the wing struts. Spray covered the windows. It was a wild, dangerous, gut-wrenching roller-coaster ride. The engine sputtered as spray sucked into the carburetor. A dead engine would have meant death to Sheldon.

When he arrived where the men were clinging to the ledge, he stopped the plane's backward travel with full throttle. It required all of Sheldon's skill—and lots of luck—for him to taxi close enough in that furious water so a man could get to his plane without damaging a wing on rocks or the canyon wall. If any man making the leap were to miss the plane, he would be swept downstream instantly with no hope of help.

Sheldon jockeyed close, and one of the men leaped, caught a pontoon, and climbed on. With the man inside, Sheldon allowed the plane to drift backward for a mile and a half through plunging white water.

With smooth water in sight, he turned the plane and flew off.

Sheldon landed in the gorge three more times, hauling out two more men on each trip.

Afterward, far downriver, he found and rescued the eighth and last soaked, skinned, bruised, and chilled member of the patrol.

A citation from the Army to Sheldon for the rescue said, in part, "His intrepid feat adds luster to the memory of those stalwart pilots whose rare courage and indomitable spirit have conquered the vastness of the Alaskan Territory, and merits the deepest respect and admiration."

Don Sheldon is gone, taken by cancer in 1975.

Bush pilots must sometimes use ingenuity to remain aloft. Frank Barr once flew his big Pilgrim back to Fairbanks with a shovel attached where the tail wheel had been. He had broken the wheel off in landing, and a villager had helped Frank tie the shovel in its place to act as a skid.

When I knew Barr at Fairbanks fifty years ago, he advertised, "If you want to get there in the worst way, fly with Barr." He was a frontiersman all the way, including his sense of humor.

Frank Barr hated to leave a damaged airplane in the wilderness, and he became famous for rebuilding his wrecked planes and flying them out.

In the winter of 1933-34, wind flipped and wrecked his parked Moth airplane in the wilderness of the Yukon Territory. Working in 50-degree-below-zero temperatures, Barr repaired it in six weeks. He flew the plane out with a broken wing strut splinted with an axe handle and moosehide babiche, a shortened propeller he had recut with his belt knife, and metal from a gas can nailed across the leading edge of one wing. While rebuilding the biplane, he had lived on snowshoe hares he snared, and ptarmigan he shot with a .22.

In August 1938, while Barr was flying over the Fortymile country of interior Alaska, his beloved American Pilgrim's engine blew a cylinder and he was forced down. The tail section was wrecked when he landed on a rough ridge top. He had to leave the plane there for the winter.

While his Pilgrim waited on the lonely ridge, Barr, living at Fairbanks, learned to weld. With his new skill he built a new Pilgrim tail section. It was a hungry winter, for the Pilgrim was his sole source of income. He referred to it as "the winter of the rabbit," for he and his wife, Mary Kate, lived mostly on snowshoe hares he shot.

In the spring, he returned to the Pilgrim. With a small welding outfit, he glued on the new tail section. After three weeks of welding, recovering the fabric, and building a runway with a shovel and axe, he flew her out.

Frank died of cancer in 1983.

Flying isn't always straightforward, with normal takeoffs, landings. Another bush pilot I knew, just before the breakup of ice one spring, landed his Aeronca Sedan on the river ice at a Bering Sea coast village. He came to an abrupt stop and his plane almost went up on its nose as the wheels sank into loose, honeycombed, corn ice.

He delivered his mail and freight. When he was ready to leave, villagers pushed on the plane as he gunned the engine. The Sedan wouldn't move.

In the village he found some abandoned corrugated iron roofing. He nailed two-by-four cribs on two pieces of the metal, turned up the front ends like a toboggan, then lifted the plane's wheels into the makeshift skis.

He figured the skis made of iron roofing would support the plane until he was airborne. Then, theoretically, they would drop off.

The iron slid reluctantly, but with villagers pushing and the engine wide open, the Aeronca started to move. Finally, it was going so fast the pushers couldn't keep up. As lift developed, the iron slid more easily, and the plane gained more and more speed.

When she was ready to lift off, he did it a bit too fancy: he horsed back on the controls. The tail, which had been up, went down. The airplane flew as the nose came up, but the instant she took to the air, one of the makeshift skis whipped back and hung up on the horizontal tail feathers. The other bounced on the tail once, and dropped off as planned.

So, suddenly, our hero was flying ten feet above the river ice with a slab of galvanized roofing folded across his tail. He was headed toward the riverbank, and the horrified villagers were sure he was going to pile her up. He cleared the bank by about a foot. He didn't dare climb; it seemed likely he would come down suddenly.

He flew upriver, cutting bends, using full rudder and plenty of side stick to stay in the air. The roofing remained glued to his tail.

He came to the only stretch of solid ice on the river for ten miles, and made a perfect landing. He didn't even shut the engine off; he climbed out, took the iron off his tail, tossed it aside, and nonchalantly took off, headed for home.

Flying stories are legion in Alaska, and some are even true. I don't claim credit for the following. I leave it to the reader to decide on its veracity. I've heard it attributed to two different longtime pilots.

Frank Barr, flying his big American Pilgrim, picked up one passenger and a load of twenty-five live bald eagles at a small British Columbia village. The eagles, trapped by local Indians, were wrapped in fish net. They were going to a research station in Juneau.

Frank started through the Coast Mountains toward Juneau. He ran into snow and clouds, and the plane began to ice up. The passenger became uneasy when

Frank increased rpm's of the big radial engine to keep the airplane flying. Ice continued to build. The Pilgrim began to wallow. The passenger was now scared.

Barr's hand came through the small opening from the cockpit, waving a piece of paper. The passenger climbed through the load of eagles and grabbed the note. It read: "Cut some eagles loose and get them flying."

The passenger removed netting from a dozen of the birds and coaxed them into flying. As the eagles took to the air, the laboring Pilgrim seemed to fly more easily.

The plane flew fine for a time, but ice continued to build. Soon the Pilgrim was again laboring. It wallowed through the clouds, sluggishly responding to the controls. Barr's hand again came through the opening. This time he just waved.

The passenger got the message and swiftly cut the rest of the eagles loose. Some didn't want to fly, but he prodded them into the air. Soon the cabin of the old Pilgrim was a mass of flapping eagles. Again the Pilgrim flew more easily. Eagle wings battered the passenger, who had to retreat into the toilet compartment in the rear.

Finally Barr fought the Pilgrim through the last mountain pass, and, as the plane neared the coast and warmer air, ice melted from the wings. The plane was out of danger.

Barr claimed he had a tough time bringing the Pilgrim down at Juneau. The flying eagles, he said, made her so light that she flew kind of like a dirigible. But Frank pointed the nose down and gave her a little power and managed to land safely.

Inside, the plane was splattered with eagle whitewash, but Barr and the passenger didn't mind: they were alive.

They climbed out of the plane and were trying to decide how to recapture the eagles when the research institute truck arrived with a load of cages. The driver attached a hose to the truck exhaust and ran it into

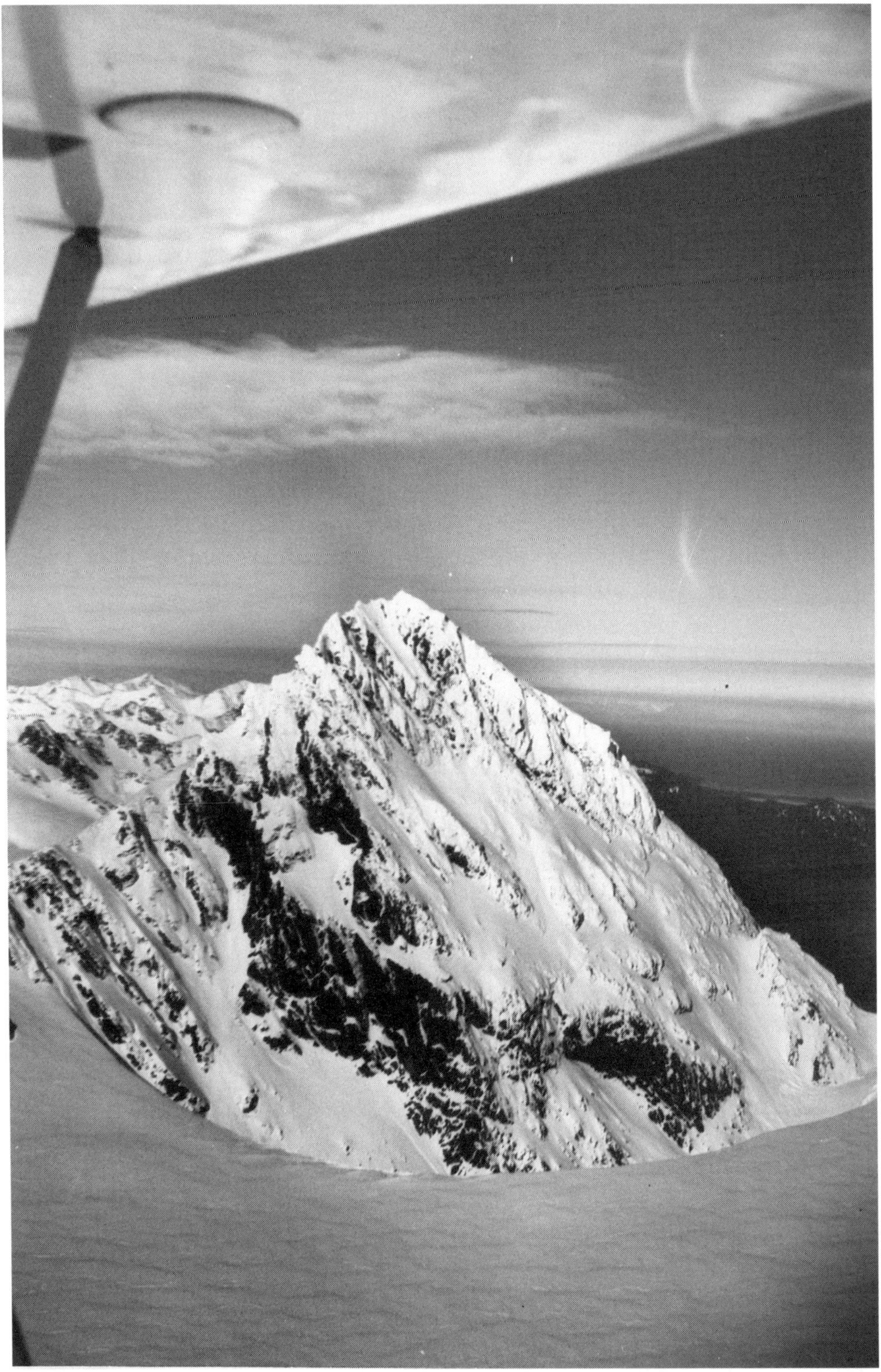

the Pilgrim's cabin. Soon all the birds were asleep. It was no problem to put them into the cages.

Every Alaskan has tales to tell about the famous pilots of the Territory and the state. The lure of flying is inescapable. After more than thirty years of chartering planes for hunting and fishing trips, at the age of fifty-nine I bought a Piper Pacer airplane and learned to fly. The reason is simple. Alaska has but a few thousand miles of road. Most of the state is accessible only by airplane. The best hunting and fishing can be reached only by plane. I no longer had to wait for scheduled flights to visit distant places.

I've written numerous aviation articles and several aviation books. Having a pilot's license made the writing much easier; I understand aviation terms, and some of the problems of flying.

Then in 1989 I bought an Avid Flyer kit—a welded fuselage and a gazillion parts—and over about a thousand hours built in my basement this two-place, side-by-side airplane. It was inspected by the FAA, and I flew it for a time. But I felt my years as a safe pilot had run out, so I voluntarily grounded myself.

I miss being able to fly.

This article was done on assignment for *Outdoor Life* magazine in 1992. They paid for it, but it was never published. The manuscript was returned years later.

Spectacular Alaska scenery from the air. Pilots get a front row seat for viewing the mountains and other natural wonders of Alaska. This is an unnamed peak in the Kenai Mountains that front the Gulf of Alaska.   JIM REARDEN PHOTO

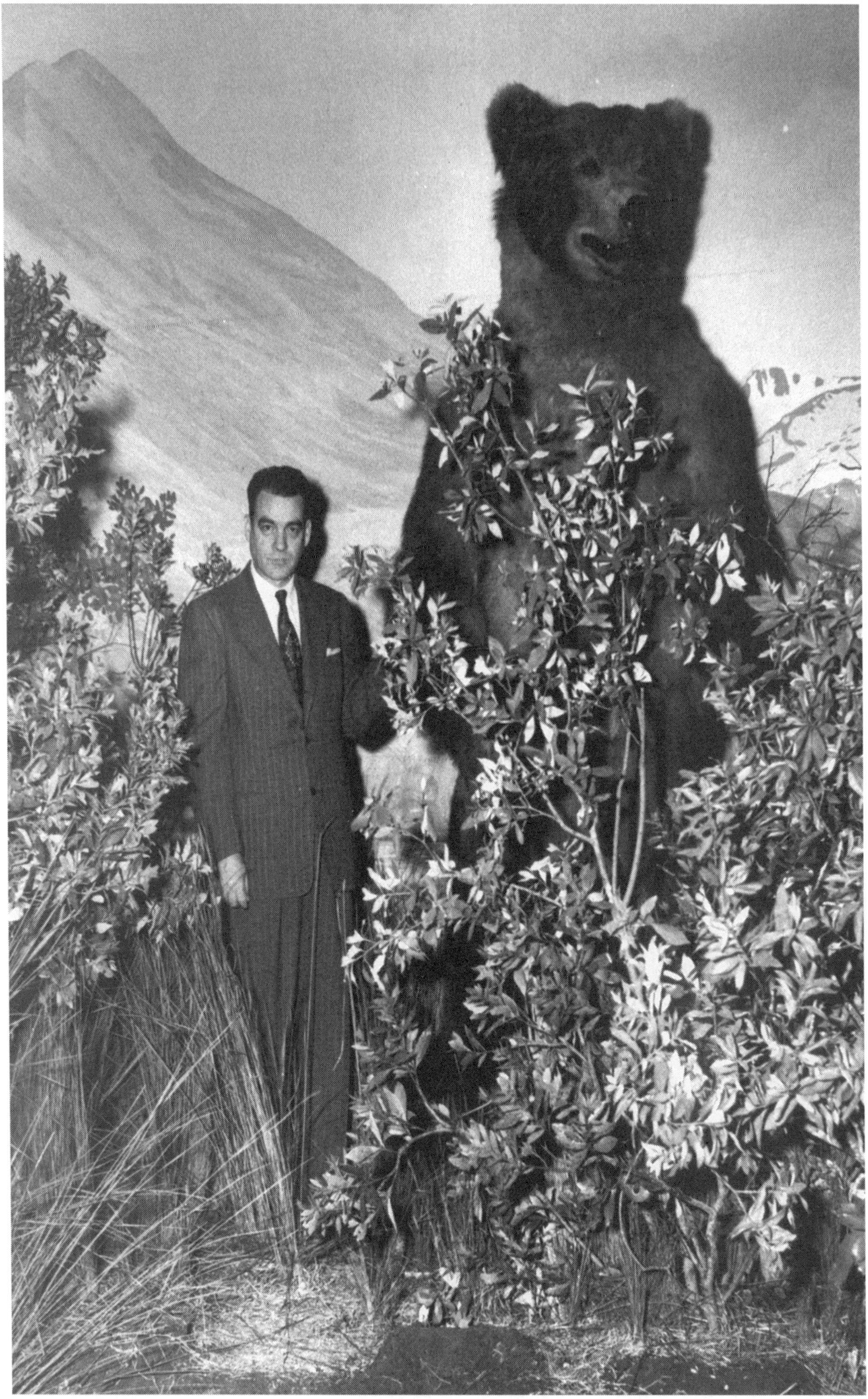

ALASKA'S BEARS: HOW BIG ARE THEY?

While hunting, Mike and Jim saw an Alaskan brown bear. Mike suggested, "You hurry to that narrow place in the valley. I'll sneak up on him. If he smells or sees me and runs, he'll go right by you."

The plan worked; when Mike attempted a stalk, the bear spooked and ran. However, no shot was fired by the waiting Jim.

When the two rejoined, Mike asked, "Did he go by you?"

"Yep," said Jim.

"Close?"

"Yep."

"Why didn't you shoot?"

"Well, he stood this high," said Jim, holding a hand over his head."

"Why, that's nothing. A lot of bears stand higher than that."

"He was still on all fours," said Jim, his eyes huge.

Roy Lindsley with the mounted world's record brown bear he shot, in a photo taken at the Los Angeles County Museum in 1958. The bear mount stands eight feet, eight inches tall. Heavier bears have been weighed, but the skull of Lindsley's bear is still the largest ever measured.   LOS ANGELES COUNTY

Alaska's great coastal brown bears do grow big, and many a hunter facing a burly hump-shouldered brownie with a head the size of a beer keg and paws like snowshoes has looked at his puny rifle and decided not to shoot. Alaska abounds with both bears and bear tales, and commonly the storied bears grow bigger with the telling.

What are some honest weights of Alaska's big bears? Is the height at the shoulders of some bears standing on all fours taller than a man, as apocryphal hunter Jim claimed?

Thirty years ago it would have been difficult to answer these questions, for few of Alaska's bears had been weighed or measured. Even today there is uncertainty as to how heavy a coastal brown bear may become, despite an abundance of known weights of tranquilized bears.

We're really talking here about grizzly bears, of which there is only one highly variable species. Commonly the huge coastal animals are called brown bears, and are generally considered to be the world's largest land carnivore. (Polar bears, a marine mammal, probably grow larger than brown bears). And brown bears found in Alaska's Interior are generally referred to as grizzlies, although both forms are the same species. Wildlife biologists commonly refer to these bears as brown/grizzly bears. The greater abundance of food of coastal Alaska, including salmon, is probably the reason the coastal bears have evolved to a larger size than their Interior relatives.

About 65 percent of the grizzly bears of North America live in Alaska. Today, Alaska's brown/grizzly bears are probably as numerous as they have been at any time over the past century. Hunting seasons are generous (a nonresident hunter seeking a brown/grizzly bear must be accompanied by a registered guide), and currently 1,100 to 1,200 brown/grizzlies are annually killed in Alaska by sportsmen.

Relatively few of the really big wild brownies have been weighed. One of the earliest recorded weights I consider to be accurate is that of a boar shot in the Uyak Bay drainage of Kodiak Island during the spring of 1936 by New York sportsman Frederick Hollander. Frank Glaser, one of his guides, carried a portable beam scale as Hollander bucked alders, steep mountain slopes, and late spring snow on his search for a big bear. He finally killed the monster in a tangle of alders on a steep hillside, and weighed it, piecemeal, on the spot.

Hollander reported the big boar was in poor condition with little body fat, with empty stomach and intestines. This outstanding bruin tipped the scales at 1,016 pounds, including eight pounds estimated for lost blood.

The hide alone, which squared 9 feet, 9 inches (average of greatest width and greatest length), weighed 105 pounds.

Based on known spring and fall weights of adult brown bears live-captured by game biologists, by late fall Hollander's bear might have weighed as much as 1,300 pounds.

Another Kodiak bear with a known accurate weight is the famous world-record brown bear killed by Roy Lindsley on May 23, 1952. Lindsley—tall, slim, and a fine woodsman—was an Alaska commercial fisherman, trapper, and bounty hunter during his first years in the Territory. When he killed the big bear he was fishery management supervisor for the U.S. Fish and Wildlife Service on Kodiak Island.

At that time, the Los Angeles County Museum had a permit to take a giant boar brown bear. Melville Lincoln, the museum's senior habitat curator, taxidermist Herman Beck, and artist Robert Sewell asked Lindsley and Russell Hoffman, manager of the Kodiak National Wildlife Refuge, to accompany them to hunt the bear.

Lindsley and Hoffman took the party to Karluk Lake. Lindsley didn't own a rifle at the time, so he borrowed a .405 Winchester. After one day of hunting, during which the collectors turned down several small bears, Russ Hoffman was recalled to Kodiak on urgent business. Roy asked him to leave his .30-06, preferring it to the borrowed .405 smokepole.

Late on the second day Roy and taxidermist Herman Beck spotted a large brownie in a good spot for a stalk. The two fought uphill through thick brush and broke into a grassy swale, where they stopped to rest. They couldn't see the bear.

They went on, and suddenly from nearby alders came piglike grunts and the sound of a bear popping brush as it ran. Roy stood ready to shoot, but the bear remained out of sight.

For ten minutes the two waited, hoping the animal would appear. It didn't.

Roy looked around, hoping to spot another. On cue, he saw a bear seventy-five yards away, walking directly toward him. Through binoculars all he could see was head and shoulders—both big.

Herman also peered through the glasses. "I can't tell how big it is, but I can tell it's getting awful close!" he whispered.

Roy wasn't sure of the size of the bear. He didn't want to shoot a small boar, and he didn't want to shoot a sow. Maybe he could get a better look.

He leaped up, waved his arms, and shouted, "Hi you, hey there!" He expected the bear to stand on hind legs to look, or at least to turn broadside. Either way he could estimate its size.

The bear evidently didn't understand what Roy expected of him, because he simply kept walking. At about twenty-five yards he went out of sight into thick alders.

Roy decided to take the animal. He sat, raised his knees to rest his arms on, and aimed Russ Hoffman's .30-06 about where he expected the bear to appear. In moments the animal's front half materialized out of the alders. There the critter stopped and with its piglike eyes stared at the two men. Roy aimed between its eyes, then realized he might ruin a scientifically valuable skull. He dropped his aiming point to just below the jaw.

Herman was nervous. "Shoot, shoot," he whispered.

The gun barked and the 180-grain bullet hit the bear's jawbone, breaking it loose from the skull. The slug then ranged through the neck and emerged between the shoulders. The bear fell and rolled downhill, crashing through the brush. He remained still for a short time, then slowly struggled to a sitting position, head hanging low. Roy put three more shots into the animal's spine, and he sprawled flat and lay still.

Wary, Roy and Herman sat for about five minutes, watching the prone bear.

Later, with a steel tape, Roy measured the distance from which he had shot the bear at thirty-two feet.

The giant animal was well furred, with a small rubbed spot on the back of his head. One canine tooth was broken, and his face was scratched as if from a fight. Next day with a 100-pound capacity scale the four collectors weighed every ounce of meat and bone. They added 30 pounds for blood and lost body fluid for a total of 1,033 pounds, not including the hide.

The 157-pound hide was 11 feet, 2-1/4 inches wide and 9 feet, 8-1/2 inches long, thus squaring 10 feet, 5-3/8 inches. It was too heavy for the field scales and had to be weighed later at camp.

Total weight of the bear was 1,190 pounds—huge for a spring bear without an ounce of fat.

"Fall fat, he would have weighed several hundred pounds more," Roy told me.

Using the 30 percent rule-of-thumb figure that some biologists consider for comparing spring and fall weights of the big bears, Lindsley's monster might have weighed near 1,550 pounds when he went into hibernation five months earlier.

The skull of the bear killed by Lindsley scored 30-12/16 (added length and width) after it had dried for a year. Half a century after it was collected, it is still the world record Alaska brown bear.

Today that bear, mounted, stands eight feet, eight inches tall, dominating his Los Angeles County Museum family of a sow and two yearling cubs.

Two other weights I am aware of are worth listing. The late Alf Madsen, a longtime Kodiak Island bear guide, once told me he had weighed a Kodiak boar brownie that tipped the scales at 1,320 pounds. And longtime Kodiak bear guides Bill Pinnell and Morris Tollefson once listed in a brochure that a bear killed by one of their hunters was weighed by the Kodiak National Wildlife Refuge manager (name not given) at 1,407 pounds.

The number two brown bear of record (skull measurement 30-11/16) was killed on October 15, 1961, near Madsen's camp at Uganik Bay, Kodiak Island, by Seattle hunter Erling Hansen. Madsen estimated its weight at 1,250 pounds.

The number three bear (skull 30-9/16; now owned by the Los Angeles County Museum) was also killed on Kodiak Island, in 1938, by longtime Alaskan Fred Henton.

The Boone and Crockett Club committee that settled on using skull length plus width, without the lower jaw, for judging bear size—the biggest skull being considered the largest bear—made a good choice. Alaska's state game biologists have measured many thousands of brown/grizzly skulls. Each brown/grizzly taken by a hunter must be sealed by a state official, and the skull must accompany the hide. Male brown/grizzly skulls continue to grow as the bear becomes older. Leland Glenn, an Alaska biologist, determined the skulls of these animals reach 98 percent of their length by the time the animal is ten years old and 98 percent of their width when they are twelve years old.

Generally speaking then, the Boone and Crockett system is reasonably accurate, although some small bears have large skulls, and some large bears have small skulls.

Boone and Crockett has drawn an arbitrary line about seventy-five miles inland along Alaska's coast as far north as the 62nd parallel. Bears found west and south of this line are termed Alaska brown bears, and those found east and north of the line are grizzly bears. If this line hadn't been established, all brown/grizzly records would belong to the great coastal brownie.

What have Alaska's game scientists learned about the size of coastal brownies? "It hasn't been a priority with us to weigh the biggest bears," said Roger Smith, one-time Alaska Department of Fish and Game biologist at Kodiak. "Many times these animals are so large that, even tranquilized, they are almost unmanageable," he told me.

Karl Schneider, longtime game research coordinator for the Department of Fish and Game in Anchorage, put it more succinctly: "Measured weights of brown/grizzly bears too large to lift with a helicopter are not in our samples."

Commonly, in research studies bears are located from a helicopter. After a short chase a tranquilizer dart is put into the animal. It is frightened and often heads for the nearest cover. Often the bear collapses amidst dense alders, perhaps on a steep hillside. A relaxed and unconscious bear that weighs 1,000 pounds or more—the weight of a small horse—is difficult for two men to move, or even roll over. Add the hurry factor (when is this sucker going to recover consciousness?) and you begin to see the difficulties.

The big old boars—the animals that weigh the most—are not as abundant as they once were. The reason is simple: Hunting regulations are tailored to allow a large number of hunters to bag reasonably big bears, with an occasionally really big and old bear. This has reduced the average age (and average size) of Alaska's brown/grizzlies. This in turn has probably created a more productive population. Further, big old boars are usually more wary; they didn't become big bears by being stupid and hanging around people.

Is the weight of a bear a good indication of size? Or, putting it another way, is the heaviest bear likely to be the largest bear? Yes, and no. The weight of a bear fluctuates annually probably more than that of any other big game animal. A good example is a grizzly sow that was live-captured in the Alaska Range three times over a period of three years by darting from a helicopter. She was sixteen years old and full grown when first captured on June 9, 1982. Her weight was 311 pounds (weighed by hoisting on a scale with a helicopter).

Almost a year later, on May 17, 1983, she was again captured and weighed—at 280 pounds. Two years later, on July 22, 1985, she was nailed again with a tranquilizer dart. This time she weighed 480 pounds. That's a 200-pound variance—an increase of 71 percent over her first weighing.

Another example is a bear that was live-trapped at Hood Bay, Admiralty Island, in Southeastern Alaska. First caught September 13, 1973, this big sow was almost thirteen years old and weighed 500 pounds (actual weight). One year later, less a day, she weighed 315 pounds. She had lost 37 percent of her weight in a year.

Today, thanks to helicopters, darting guns, and demobilizing drugs—and sportsmen's dollars spent on research—we know a good deal about average weights and sizes of Alaska's brown/grizzly bears.

The largest set of coastal brownie measurements were collected by Fish and Game biologist Leland Glenn from the great brown bears of the Alaska Peninsula, which probably grow fully as large as Kodiak Island bears. He captured 344 different bears a total of 502 times. The largest boar weighed 975 pounds and stood 57.4 inches at the shoulders. Another big boar weighed 840 to 860 pounds and was an even 60 inches, or five feet, at the shoulders.

His largest sow, 15.5 years old, weighed 610 pounds and was 51.8 inches at the shoulders. Another unusually large sow measured 54.6 inches at the shoulders and weighed an estimated 480 pounds. Glenn's work was mostly in the spring, and therefore the bears he weighed were probably substantially lighter than they would have been in the fall.

There are stories of almost incredibly huge brownies. One of the most believable is an account from the late George C. Folta, one-time U.S. District judge for Alaska's first judicial division, whose passion was bear hunting. He killed 142 of Alaska's bears over a period of about four decades. In 1913, he told a reporter, he saw a brown bear hide that was 13 feet, 6 inches long at the Alaska Commercial dock at the town of Kodiak. Even if that hide was long and skinny from being stretched, it must have been worn by one huge bear.

Judge Folta told the same reporter that in 1914 he measured at more than 13 feet long (using a rifle barrel of known length) the hide from a bear he killed near

Zachar River, Kodiak Island. He lost that hide when he tried to raft it down Zachar River and the raft overturned. Another hide from a bear he killed on the same hunt was, he said, 10 feet, 9 inches long.

There is little doubt that unusually big coastal brownies can weigh as much as 1,500 pounds. Perhaps even 1,600-pound brownies are possible, although Roger Smith, former Kodiak Island state game biologist, said he finds it unlikely.

When I think of oversize brown bears, I remember what Roy Lindsley shouted when he wanted a better view of the great bear he shot.

"Hi you, hey there!"

What a novel approach to hunting the world's record brown bear.

In my half-century-plus in Alaska, the attitude toward brown/grizzly bears has changed almost 180 degrees. In 1947, commercial salmon fishermen along the coast commonly carried a rifle aboard their boats and, though it was illegal, any bear seen on the beach was considered a legitimate target, at least by some.

The great value of these animals is now recognized by most Alaskans. Bears on the beach are no longer considered a target to be shot at for fun.

One of the most popular wildlife attractions in the state is the McNeil River bear sanctuary on the west side of lower Cook Inlet. McNeil River was part of the commercial fisheries area that I was management biologist for from 1960 to 1969. I flew there many times each summer, counting salmon in rivers and along the saltwater shoreline. In those years there was no restriction on the number of people who could visit the bears.

Today, hundreds of applicants from around the world annually spend $25 each (nonrefundable) to toss their names into a drawing to see who can go to McNeil River when bears are feeding on salmon. Ten permit holders at a time are allowed to visit. Hundreds of thousands of photos have been taken of McNeil River bears and jillions of feet of videotape exposed. Nine out of ten photos of Alaska brown bears that reach print in magazines are taken at McNeil River. The bears there are habituated to humans, and not infrequently, bears and humans are within dozens of feet of one another.

This article was published in the 1990 *Outdoor Life Hunting Annual.*

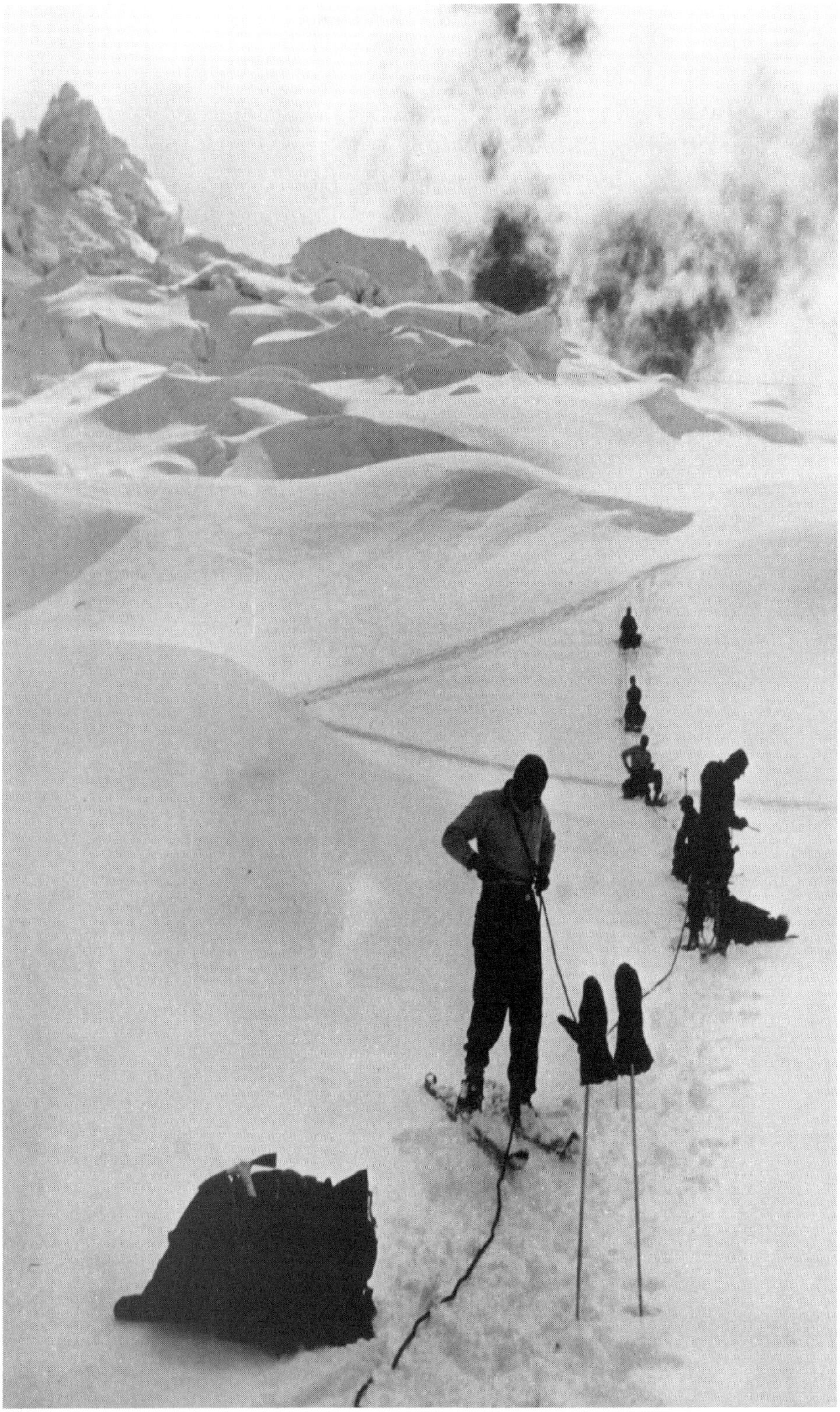

CHAPTER NINE

RESCUE ON MOUNT McKINLEY

Only a handful of climbers had successfully reached the summit of Mount McKinley by 1954, the time of this story. The dramatic news of an injured climber awaiting rescue high on North America's highest peak attracted national interest, and details of the rescue were followed day-by-day by major news media across the country.

When Dr. John McCall, an exhausted rescuer, arrived back at his home in College, Alaska, near Fairbanks, he isolated himself from reporters in order to rest. Several days later, I asked in a note to John if he would tell me the story of the rescue. John and I had been faculty members together at the University of Alaska, and we had become friends. John agreed to the tape-recorded interview that is the basis for this story, told here in his voice.

On May 26, 1954, with a companion, Fred Milan, I started to climb Muldrow Glacier, which flows off Mount

The Muldrow Glacier, on the northern flank of Mount McKinley, during the operation to rescue injured climber George Argus. With some of rescuers on skis, others on snowshoes, and all roped together, the trek seemed to take forever.
JOHN MCCALL PHOTO

McKinley, on a rescue mission—an assignment that all mountain climbers dread. George Argus, a friend, lay injured and helpless from a fall, alone in a tent at the 11,000-foot level of the extremely rough and dangerous Muldrow. We had to reach him quickly, for he was low on food and fuel.

Before they fell, Argus and three companions, all former students at the University of Alaska, had successfully climbed McKinley. Elton Thayer, leader of the group, was a ranger at Mount McKinley National Park (now Denali National Park and Preserve); Morton Wood was a tourist camp operator; Leslie Viereck and Argus were both Army privates, stationed in Alaska.

Others before them had successfully made the ascent of McKinley. But their climb was unique in that they climbed the South Buttress, a heretofore unconquered approach to the top. The ascent was difficult; at two places they had to hack steps in ice, one wall requiring 1,038 of them. After topping the South Buttress, the relatively easy climb to the summit was anticlimactic.

Leaving their names in a can at the peak, they started to descend the north side of McKinley, following the conventional route used by most of the half-dozen previous parties that had climbed the mountain. As they moved past the site of their High Camp and down knife-edged Karstens Ridge, conditions were hazardous, and they traveled on belay only—that is, one man would move at a time on the rope while the other three braced themselves on the chance he might slip.

Elton Thayer slipped and fell. The others couldn't hold him, and they fell and rolled down the steep slope for about 1,000 feet. Fifty yards from a sheer granite precipice, Viereck dropped into a crevasse, stopping the others short. Wood was the only one able to struggle to his feet. He found Elton Thayer dead, his back broken; George Argus unconscious with a dislocated or broken hip; Leslie Viereck suffering from shock and cracked ribs where the rope had yanked him as he stopped their headlong descent.

Viereck, although shaky and in pain, helped erect a tent almost on the spot. There Wood nursed the two injured men for a week. During that time Wood and Viereck buried Thayer nearby. They then bundled Argus, still on his air mattress, in the tent and sleeping bags, and dragged him to a somewhat safer spot at the 11,000-foot level of huge, heavily crevassed Muldrow Glacier.

Wood and Viereck put Argus in their three-man tent, left most of their food and fuel within his reach, and raced down the dangerous glacier for help, hoping a rescue party could reach the injured climber before he ran out of supplies or before a heavy snowfall buried him in his tent.

In April, when Elton Thayer had come to me and asked if I would be one of a four-member standby climbing group for his party, as required by McKinley Park regulations, it was easy to say yes. A mere formality, I thought. He asked me, along with two others of the group, because we had all climbed on McKinley at one time or another. I had reached the top with two other men in 1948. Elton left us a detailed account of the proposed climb.

The climbers were ten days overdue when Ginny Wood, wife of Morton Wood, and I chartered a Civil Air Patrol DC3 to fly over and search the route the climbers had planned to follow. The flight was canceled because of mechanical difficulties. About midnight of the evening of the planned flight, I received word of the accident from the 74th Air Rescue Squadron at Ladd Air Force Base, Fairbanks, five miles from the University of Alaska, where I teach geology. The news was sketchy: Two of the climbers were back, exhausted; one man had been killed;

another was left alone and injured on the mountain. Someone had to go after the injured man.

I was the only one available of the original standby party of four. The others had scattered on summer projects. Fortunately the previous day I had bumped into Fred Milan, another University of Alaska alumnus, who had volunteered to go if I needed him.

Arrangements were made through the 74th Air Rescue Squadron for a CAP plane and pilot to take Fred and me to a rendezvous point at McKinley Park Station airstrip. The Army Arctic Indoctrination School at Big Delta, one hundred miles east of Fairbanks, agreed to send some experienced climbers for the rescue attempt. Coincidentally, George Argus, the injured man on the mountain, was stationed at this school.

We decided to use skis, although they had been more or less unofficially banned on Mount McKinley. Theodore Koven and Allen Carpé, who were killed on the mountain in 1932, used them, and it is believed skis were partly to blame for their deaths. I personally think skis are far superior to snowshoes on a glacier; I hoped, too, we could get to the injured man on a quick dash, and of course skis are much faster than webs.

It was about 4:00 a.m. when pilot Dick McIntyre landed Fred and me at McKinley Park Station. The 74th Air Rescue Squadron helicopter from Ladd Air Force Base had arrived, and Viereck and Wood were waiting for us.

Viereck and Wood described where they had left George. I visualized it immediately, recalling it from my 1948 climb. They had left George in a warm sleeping bag, in the tent, with food for six days and four day's gasoline for his primus stove. He had been alone going on three days.

The plane arrived from Big Delta with six climbers. They were Peter Gabriel, of Engadine, Switzerland, a civilian climbing instructor; Lieutenant Colonel Edmund L. Mueller, commandant of the Army Arctic Indoctrination School; Captain Ray Zoberski of Leadville, Colorado; and three sergeants: Donald L. Nightingale of South Gate, California, George H. Wolcott of Ludlow, Vermont, and Charles D. Inskeep of Norfork, Arkansas. After introductions I outlined my ideas on how to proceed.

I wanted to get into the helicopter immediately with Fred and fly to McGonagall Pass, 6,000 feet up on Muldrow Glacier. There we would try to pick up the trail left by Viereck and Wood as they had descended, and with luck we might reach George in eighteen hours. The rest of the climbers would act as a support team, and to help bring George down. All agreed the plan sounded plausible.

I was shaking from the cold and nervous tension. Wood, bless him, handed me his heavy parka, which I put on and used on the entire trip.

Under other circumstances I would have enjoyed the helicopter flight. Caribou ran from the low-flying helicopter, and in the early morning calm the park was beautiful. The rotors of the helicopter were soon almost beating against a cloud ceiling that hung over the glacier, and that bothered the pilot, Captain Ralph D. Searle, of Tooele, Utah—as it did Fred and me. It was then I saw a gap to the north I thought was McGonagall Pass, our goal. I have never been more wrong, but I pointed to it and shouted above the roar of the engine, "Captain, if you can get us there we've got it made."

Unfortunately, the clouds closed down, and he decided to attempt a landing about a mile short of the gap. Loose snow, whipped by the helicopter, obscured our view as it neared the glacier surface. After several attempts to land, we dropped our packs from low altitude and flew about two miles lower to a snowless rocky moraine, where Searle landed.

He flew off in the whirlybird, leaving Fred and me about three miles short of what we thought was McGonagall Pass, with our packs and ski boots two miles up the glacier. It took three to four hours to walk that distance. Going was rough, and we were tired, having gone without sleep the previous night. Our skis, carried over our shoulders, made an awkward load. My spirits dropped, as did the clouds around us, and I kept thinking about Elton Thayer and George Argus and the terrible fall that made our rescue attempt necessary. I respect Muldrow Glacier, too, and I wasn't looking forward to climbing it.

Snow began to fall as we roped together after reaching the packs and started off on skis. We knew then the rest of the party couldn't get onto the glacier that day. Visibility was zero in heavy snow, and even the helicopter couldn't fly in that. We soon realized, too, the nearby pass wasn't McGonagall, but Oastler Pass, somewhat similar in appearance, but 1,500 feet lower.

We encountered bad crevasses and because of falling snow, couldn't see well; every foot of travel had to be probed. It was scary. At four o'clock that afternoon we were still fighting deep and wide crevasses. It was snowing hard, a cold wind blew up the glacier, and we were both tired and discouraged.

We came to a five-foot-wide crevasse that wasn't bridged. We saw holes in the snow all along it. I was ahead on the 120-foot rope, and I reached out with my ski pole to tap the bridge in front of me, testing. It gave a loud crack, and the whole thing, for a distance of about twenty yards, disappeared. We listened to the echoes and the sound of ice and snow bouncing from side to side in the big hole.

I moved to the left and tried again. Crunch, another twenty-yard section of bridge disappeared, leaving a yawning hole.

We moved farther and found a small bridge that appeared to be supported by ice. I started to ease my way to it, but just before I got there I put my foot into a little offshoot crack and dropped to my hips. The bridge, except for a thin strip of ice, broke loose and went thundering out of sight. In that poor visibility, and with tired minds and bodies, that little ice bridge looked to us like a three-eighths-inch rope bridging a veritable Grand Canyon.

I pulled myself out and walked back to Fred. "Would we be a couple of swine if we camped here?" I asked. He agreed it was wise, so we immediately put up our little tent. After eating, we crawled into sleeping bags.

It snowed all night, and we slept fitfully. As I fell asleep I remember dimly thinking that now George had only three days food left and gasoline for one day.

Next morning, the weather was clearing, and our hopes began to rise. Soon we heard the floppity-floppity of the helicopter. As the pilot hovered, the terrific blast from the whirling blades created a regular blizzard and almost blew our tent down. The chopper circled and approached camp again. Colonel Mueller crawled out, swung down the step, and hung like a trapeze artist. He must have been twenty feet up when he turned loose and plummeted into the snow. He did a nice tumble and came up smiling. Then Peter Gabriel, the civilian climbing instructor, made a nice drop and also came up smiling.

Colonel Mueller is tall, rugged, collected in his thinking, very dependable. He was a strong traveler. Peter Gabriel, oldest man in the party, was an extremely accomplished climber. It was good to have them.

Colonel Mueller and Peter, on snowshoes, shouldered their packs and went ahead, crossing a small ice bridge Fred and I had found the previous night. Fred and I gathered our camp gear and followed.

Peter led, probing, circling, and working around and through a most damnable maze of crevasses. His judgment of what would hold us and what wouldn't was wonderful, and from watching him, my badly shaken confidence began to be restored. Soon we could see McGonagall Pass not far above. The helicopter flew over and disappeared up the glacier, ferrying other members of the party ahead of us. They were to wait for us.

About two-thirds through that terribly crevassed area Peter started to show signs of exhaustion. It was hot and extremely hard going. He led for a long way, breaking trail and carrying a heavy pack. Later I learned he has a serious heart murmur. He started getting a little jumpy, as would anyone traveling under those conditions. It was something like standing in an open field and giving a blindfolded man a machine-gun and letting him try to hit you: eventually he might succeed. The bridges on crevasses usually hold, but occasionally one lets go.

I relieved Peter of the lead, and Fred and I on one rope went ahead while Colonel Mueller and Peter followed on the other. The snow was perfect for our skis, and we slid along smoothly, while the colonel and Peter plodded along on their snowshoes. We broke out of the crevassed area and reached McGonagall Pass.

We made good time that afternoon, guiding ourselves through thick falling snow by keeping the north wall of the glacier in view. There were no crevasses. Late in the day, at Gunsight Pass, we reached the four men who had been flown ahead of us. Now we were all together at what we called Base Camp and could function as a team.

Two of the men, Captain Ray Zoberski and Sergeant Donald Nightingale, were to go to the head of the glacier with Colonel Mueller, Fred, and me. Sergeants George Wolcott and Charles Inskeep were to be the support party, carrying supplies from Base Camp as needed.

Things now looked good. George still should have food for two days, even though he might be out of gasoline. We had eight men, plenty of food, radio contact with Air Force planes, and we were at about 7,000 feet on the glacier.

Another foot of snow fell that night. Periodically we had to knock it from the tents to keep them from collapsing. I wondered how George would make out with the snow on his tent.

Next morning, Peter couldn't go on. He had overdone it the previous day when he had led us through the heavily crevassed region below McGonagall Pass. Fred and I roped up and left camp first that morning, skiing across a big flat stretch of deep snow. The second rope, consisting of Mueller, Zoberski, and Nightingale, soon followed, and caught us after about an hour.

They took the lead and broke trail. Fred and I, following their broad snowshoe trail, didn't even get our ski boots wet. It was then that we encountered the first area of seracs—pinnacles of ice among crevasses. We ran into a whole series of crevasses, running all directions.

We alternated the lead, working slowly through that very rough area. We were all tired, and getting "glacier lassitude"—a feeling of weakness and thirst, and of being harassed. The altitude was beginning to get to us.

At six o'clock, when we were at about 8,500 feet, we set up what we called Support Camp, on a more-or-less level, crevasse-free site that was clearly visible from the air. We realized it would take us another day, perhaps two, to reach George. This was Friday night; George now had one day of food left.

Next morning, the Big Delta people led off early. As we started into a second serac area, Colonel Mueller suddenly dropped up to his arms in a crevasse. Captain Zoberski and Sergeant Nightingale held him with their rope as I moved in to give a hand. First, though, I snapped his picture, which brought a growl—"Damn photographers," I think he said, but he grinned afterward.

After more delays, I resumed the lead, and I suddenly became very impatient. I desperately wanted to reach George that day, and every time we slowed to belay across a crevasse, or to detour, I had to grit my teeth. We broke into the clear at a long gradual climb and we began to see, vaguely, Viereck and Wood's trail. The snowfall had apparently occurred mostly at lower levels.

We followed exactly where they had traveled, knowing it was fairly safe. Then we got well into the last bad stretch of the second serac area, where deep snow again obliterated the trail. When we had traversed this area, we saw obstructions in every direction above us, so we stopped and had lunch. As we ate, for a time the heat became almost unbearable; next it would turn icy cold as a cloud covered the sun.

Most of us had tape or cream on our faces to keep from being sunburned. We wore dark glasses, without which a person on a snowy glacier would soon become helpless. Despite precautions, by the end of the trip, my face was peeling and my lips were badly cracked, and ends of my fingers had split open. All of us were parched.

We came to one crevasse with a bridge about six feet wide, but only eighteen inches thick. It didn't look good. I could see Viereck and Wood's faint tracks on it, so I took a deep breath and crossed very carefully. Then

I recrossed in order to pick up our packs, which we had left while searching for a way through. When I got back across, I went into the shakes. Nightingale, who is as solid as a rock and apparently worries about nothing, looked at me and kidded, "You're too damned high-strung. You educated people are all like that!"

I was to get my revenge. I didn't see it, but Zoberski told me later that Nightingale fell into a terribly deep and wide crevasse the next day, and his nerves acted up just as mine had. He sat on the edge, shaking and looking down. It was a crevasse that one could easily drop a house into. I wish I had been there to ask him where he'd gotten his education.

I was afraid to think about what we might find when we arrived at our destination. Would it be an empty tent? A frozen body? A gibbering idiot? The strain of being injured and alone for so long would break the nerves of many, and it would be no discredit to them. I wondered about George.

Seemingly we couldn't travel ten minutes without crossing a crevasse. When finally we broke into the clear, a cold wind hit us, and the ski boots that Fred and I wore started to freeze, binding our ankles.

Our hearts were set on going the remainder of the distance that night, but we were very tired. About then Colonel Mueller again stepped into a big crevasse, and again he was saved by his rope. That was just too much. We realized we still had some distance to go, and that our judgment was suffering because of mental and physical fatigue. Visibility was poor, too. We decided to camp until three o'clock next morning. We had climbed for fourteen hours straight.

As soon as we stopped, Colonel Mueller radioed the L-20 DeHavilland Beaver aircraft that was flying in support, requesting sleeping bags. All of us had brought just half of our double sleeping bags, and each night we had progressively been colder as we had climbed higher up the glacier. Exactly one hour and fifteen minutes later, the bags rained down on us. More food was also dropped. We put up tents and designated the site as High Camp.

About three o'clock Sunday morning, the plane flew over to check on us. That got Fred and me off to an early start. We all felt the altitude. A person gets a kind of morning sickness when abruptly climbing into high elevation. We left our tents and sleeping bags at High Camp and traveled light. Fred and I took the radio; the remainder of the party was to follow on their slower snowshoes.

By eight o'clock Sunday morning, May 30, Fred and I were nearing George's tent. Clouds were starting to boil over Karstens Ridge ahead, and it looked as if it were going to sock in again.

The Beaver came over and dropped us an ahkio, a stretcherlike sled. We stood it on end, draped its bright yellow parachute over it, and kept going; the others could pick it up as they came along behind. We wanted to get to George.

Farther along, I suddenly dropped through a deep crevasse, catching myself by my elbows for a moment, then terrifyingly dropping farther as the sides crumbled. I landed, teetering, on a ledge about seven feet down. The crevasse was about three feet wide, and as far as I could see ahead, there wasn't another ledge. I wriggled out of my pack and shoved it to the top. Fred started to pull on the rope, but I yelled, "Hold it." I shoved my ski poles up, then my ice axe, and one ski. I turned the second ski crossways on top, grabbed it, and chinned myself out.

By the time I got out of the crevasse and recovered my nerve enough to travel, the clouds had come in again, and it was snowing. We climbed over a little rise and saw a small black triangle on the snow ahead.

"It's the tent, it's the tent," we both shouted.

The suspense was terrible. We moved closer and I yelled, "Hey, George." A "hey" came back, but it could have been an echo.

Then we moved still closer, and I yelled, "Hey, George, are you all right?" And then we heard, "Of course I am." The chills ran up and down my spine. That was one of the biggest thrills of my life.

We radioed to the plane the news that George was still alive, then slogged on through deep snow to the tent. When we got there George had his bearded, matted face sticking out, looking up at us with a kind of a funny grin.

"Who is it?" he wanted to know.

"It's McCall and Milan," we told him.

"Oh, my God, you guys," he said. "Gee, it's nice to have someone I know come up here."

We collapsed in front of the tent, shaking his hand and rubbing his head. We all got tears in our eyes.

"George," I kidded, "there's a bunch of MPs behind us. They're after you because you're AWOL."

That broke the spell, and we all laughed, it was so ridiculous.

To our amazement we found he had food and gas for another four days. His food, though, looked old and moldy to us, almost with hair growing on it. "C'mon, fellows, what'll you have?" he kept asking. We finally convinced him that we weren't hungry, and had plenty of C-rations. He ate a can of C-ration pears with evident pleasure, and after that wolfed down a can of spaghetti and meatballs.

He couldn't sit up because of his injured hip. One of his eyeballs was badly bruised, and his glasses had been lost, so he couldn't see well. A couple of his teeth had been broken and twisted. But he was cheerful.

He had thought seriously of trying to get himself out by devising crutches of some sort, but he couldn't begin to see where he was, and even if he could see, he realized it would have been suicidal. He had passed part of the time reading a book of Mark Twain stories, and by drawing everything in sight.

We chatted for about three hours, waiting for the Big Delta people to arrive with the ahkio. I fell asleep for a few minutes in the warm tent, with George talking a mile a minute all the while.

He had been warm except for his feet, and one sunny day, snow had melted, wetting the foot of his sleeping bag. He managed to change socks, with a great deal of painful effort, and he remained awake all one night wriggling his toes to keep them from freezing. He got off with only a few spots of frostbite.

When the Big Delta people arrived, pulling the ahkio, George said, "This is just like old home week." He knew them all, of course, because he too was based at Big Delta.

We slid the ahkio inside the tent and lifted him, air mattress and all, onto it. I put rock specimens he had collected and his film in my rucksack, someone else rolled up his tent, and we started back down, following the trail we had made coming up. George was lashed in, and fairly comfortable. The weather started to lift, and we made good time.

It was on the way down that we really began to work as a team. The Big Delta people were experts at rigging and handling the sled. We reached High Camp in two hours. It had taken us five hours to climb that distance.

We spent the night there. Nightingale slept in the tent with George. I think George talked to him even after he was asleep. George didn't care. He just wanted to talk. He spent a restless night, and next morning volunteered to take morphine, which Colonel Mueller administered.

We were under way at nine o'clock, the entire party roped together, with the sled also roped in. The ahkio crossed the bridges nicely. Snowshoes were poor for such work, the skis better. Inskeep and Wolcott met us at noon. That put four men behind the sled and three in front, giving Zoberski and Nightingale some relief.

Every parachute that was dropped to us during the rescue was accompanied by cloth streamers in a color than can best be described as shocking pink. We were in a festive mood at Support Camp, so we bedecked ourselves and George with pink streamers. It was a colorful, cheerful procession that moved down Muldrow Glacier that day.

Peter had hot food ready, and was in fine shape himself when we reached Base Camp at six o'clock. We didn't waste time there, and Peter hooked onto the back of the procession as we left. It was quite a sight: nine beribboned men, including George, all roped together.

It was nine o'clock when we got to McGonagall Pass, and within fifteen minutes the helicopter flapped in. Dr. Donald E. Eiber from the Army Arctic Indoctrination School was in the helicopter to look George over. We lashed George into the basket of the helicopter, and away he went. The rest of us were shuttled off, two at a time, after the helicopter returned from taking George to safety. He was flown to Ladd Air Force Base at Fairbanks, and then to a military hospital at Anchorage, where it was found that his hip was severely dislocated.

Dr. Eiber and I were the last to leave the Muldrow. While waiting, we stood the ahkio on end and piled a rock cairn about it. It was midnight when the helicopter carrying us took off in the dim night light of the

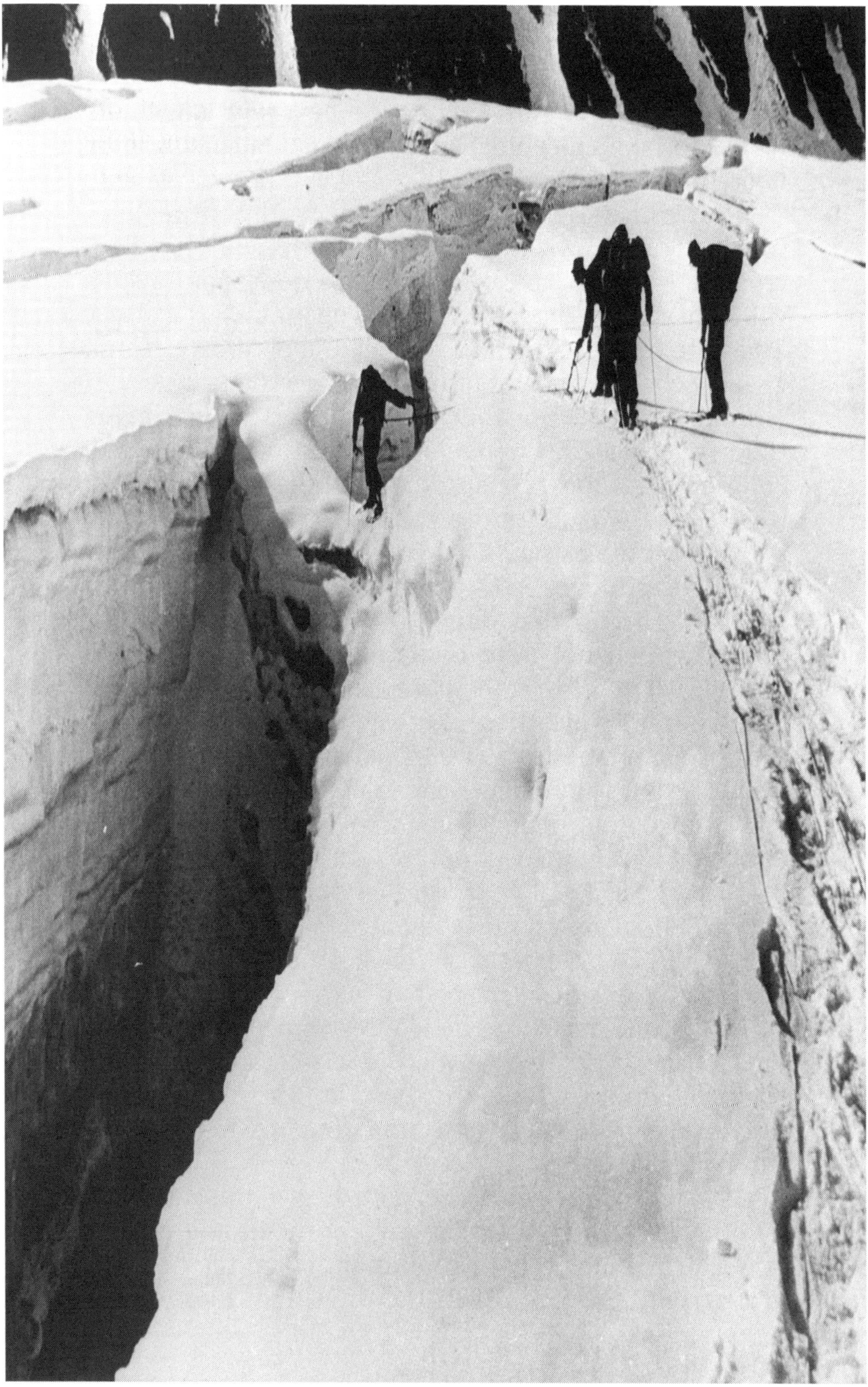

low subarctic sun. I turned and looked back at the ahkio. It was an appropriate monument, standing alone on the glacier against the twilight sky, its canvas gently flapping in the breeze.

Shortly after our interview, John McCall was hospitalized with polio and died of the disease, leaving a wife and four young children. His loss was a terrible blow to his family and to all who knew him.

Elton Thayer, who was killed in the fall on the mountain and whose body still lies buried high on Muldrow Glacier, was an undergraduate studying wildlife management under me at the University of Alaska. He was an outstanding young man, with top grades, just starting a promising career with the National Park Service.

Leslie Viereck, also on the climb, was a graduate student also studying wildlife management at the University of Alaska when I was on the faculty. He went on to a distinguished career as a plant ecologist with the U.S. Forest Service in Alaska.

Morton Wood and his wife continued to operate a summer tourist camp at Wonder Lake, north of Mount McKinley.

I have been unable to learn the whereabouts or status of George Argus, but that's not surprising; almost half a century has passed since his rescue.

This story appeared in *Saga* magazine in March 1955.

One of the many Muldrow Glacier crevasses, a major hazard to the rescue party. Often fresh snow concealed them, and one misstep could be fatal. The rescuers crossed each crevasse on belay: roped together, and one at a time.

JOHN MCCALL PHOTO

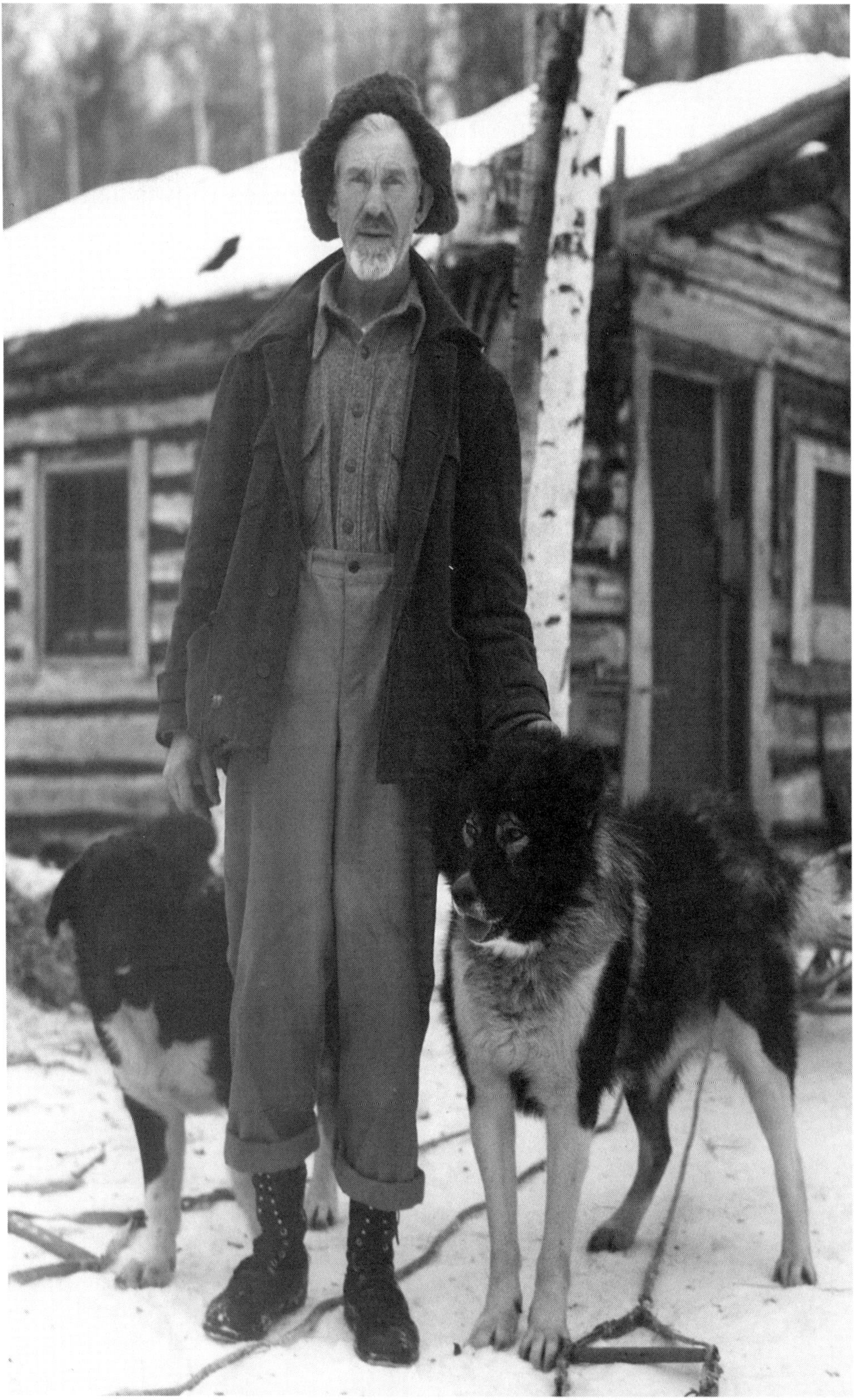

CHAPTER TEN

FIFTY-SEVEN YEARS ALONE

In October 1955, I spent three weeks with Swedish-born Hjalmar (Slim) Carlson, a trapper who lived on the shore of interior Alaska's Lake Minchumina. A local legend, he was famed for his woodsmanship, his trapping skill, and the fact he had lived alone in the wilderness for decades. In those three weeks I became acquainted with a friendly loner who was full of wonderful stories, a man who was as one with the wilderness, and a tough outdoorsman with sharply honed survival skills.

There are probably few red-blooded young men or boys—and nowadays, women—who haven't dreamed of living off the land in a wilderness as Slim did. He lived alone under the northern lights, drove a dog team, trapped valuable fur animals, occasionally fought off bears, lived in log cabins he built, and hunted and fished for his food.

Sounds exciting—romantic even. Is it? The weeks I spent with Slim gave me some answers.

Slim Carlson, in the mid-1950s, in front of his cabin with two of his dogs. Famous for his outdoors skills, Slim constructed the log cabin, built his own dogsled, made his furniture, made clothing from moose and caribou skins, performed emergency surgery on himself, and survived many close calls.

JIM REARDEN PHOTO

145

Slim Carlson was among the last of the old breed of Alaskan trappers. Most of today's trappers in Alaska use snow machines; only a handful are full-timers. Slim lived and trapped as had trappers since the Territory was settled in the first years of the last century.

I'd met Slim twice while he was in Fairbanks, and he'd invited me to visit. He was seventy years old at the time, and he had lived alone for thirty-seven years within a hundred miles of perpetually snowcapped Denali (Mount McKinley), North America's loftiest peak. "That feller, he's Slim's partner," he said one day, pointing with twinkling eyes at the mountain that dominates the region. Actually, all of the wilderness was Slim's partner.

Before I left my Fairbanks home I told a sourdough friend of my planned visit. He laughed, "You mean that dumb Swede, White Moose Carlson?"

Slim earned the nickname after he came across a rare white moose and decided it should be saved for science. He shot and skinned the animal and tried to give the hide to the University of Alaska museum. He was arrested for shooting a cow moose, and for shooting a moose out of season.

The judge asked Slim, "Did you need the meat?" Slim's guilt or innocence hinged on his answer; a law in Alaska allows anyone in the wilderness in need of food to kill game regardless of season or sex.

"No. I wanted to save the moose for science," Slim answered.

The judge fined him $250. If Slim had said he needed the meat he'd have gotten off.

To reach Slim's home, I boarded a bush plane and flew 130 miles from Fairbanks to the gravel airstrip at Lake Minchumina. There I borrowed a boat and outboard from CAA station manager Dick Collins to cross the lake to Slim's cabin.

Rounding a point, I saw Slim in a small boat untangling fish from a gill net. As I cut the motor and drifted near, he straightened his six-foot-one frame and pushed back his worn beaver cap, revealing a luxurious shock of silver-gray hair. He greeted me in a thick Swedish accent. His blue eyes and his friendly, weathered, old-young face with white goatee, reddish mustache, and large ears gave him a pixieish, wise look.

"Fishing's a cold, one-man yob," he said, when I offered to help. The bottom of his boat was covered with fish, ice, snow, and frozen slime.

Bare-handed despite the 18-degree temperature and raw wind, he used a handle with a nail in it to untangle the nylon net from the whitefish, an occasional scaleless ling, or sucker. Once he cut a six-pound pike in half to get it loose.

With the net empty and reset, we landed on the beach near his cabin and Slim added the fish to his pile of about four hundred frozen ones. He needed two thousand to take him through trapping season; they were fuel for his sled dogs.

His tied dogs set up a melancholy howl as we entered Slim's 11-by-14-foot cabin. The moss-chinked logs were flattened on both sides. A wood-burning kitchen range with a connected homemade barrel stove furnished cooking space and heat. The gable roof, built of poles, was covered with sod and moss.

Two windows let in light. A gasoline lantern hung from one of the two purlins, and a multiple-band radio perched on empty wood boxes in a corner.

Four rifles hung from the wall above a steel cot that was covered by a caribou hide, hair side up, and a sleeping bag. Magazines were piled on a shelf; mukluks (fur boots), work clothing, parkas, and a dog harness hung on the walls. A girly calendar, dates crossed off, hung over the oilcloth-covered table. Two wooden boxes served as chairs.

Overhead were several dozen fur-stretching boards and a rolled-up caribou hide. By the door were a wash basin, towel, mirror, comb, two five-gallon gasoline tins serving as water buckets, files, gun oil and solvent, straps, insect repellent, and hand tools.

Everything had its place—and everything was spotless. As we entered, Slim hung his wet canvas gloves on a nail over the stove and turned on the radio.

For nearly thirty years Slim's entertainment consisted of a phonograph, books, and magazines. In 1948 he bought his first radio, and when I visited him radio was his biggest interest. He often listened to foreign stations, comparing their versions of news with the American twist.

He prepared a moose stew and baked cantaloupe-size yeast rolls. With them he served coleslaw and turnips and a huge pot of very black coffee. He used a hundred pounds of coffee a year. The meal was so good I didn't mind the moose hairs in my portion.

As Slim washed dishes he told me that, except for occasionally building a cabin for someone or hauling a little freight with his dog team, he hadn't worked for wages since 1919. He had never gone hungry, though he'd had some tough years.

Born in 1886, Slim left Sweden for America when he was eighteen. He worked in logging camps in the Pacific Northwest before arriving in Alaska in 1914. He worked as a laborer building the Seward-to-Fairbanks Alaska Railroad until 1919, when he quit and wandered into the Denali mountain region.

At first he prospected for gold, and with virtually no income could afford only flour, sugar, salt, and coffee. He lived mostly off the land, killing Dall sheep, caribou, moose, and black bear for food. Ptarmigan, spruce grouse, and snowshoe hare offered variety. He whipsawed lumber for furniture, cabin floors, doors. He made sleeping bags from caribou and sheep skins. He tanned moose and caribou skins, from which he made clothing and moccasins.

During one of the first winters he froze one of his big toes; when it turned black he cut it off. Doctors cost money, and besides, the nearest one was a hundred miles away.

On October 27, when it was 10 below with six inches of snow, Slim and I went to haul home the meat he'd killed in September. Slim loaded his .30-06 to take along. "We might meet a brown bear," he said. "When you don't look for him, that's when you meet him."

He pulled his dogsled into place and positioned harnesses. The dogs yammered and leaped. Slim turned all ten loose. They ran in all directions, growling, playing, lifting legs, scratching snow, and tumbling with one another while he stood calling them in turn. Eventually each animal obeyed. "Such a dog you fellers is," he said affectionately in his quaint old-country way as he petted and harnessed each. Slim loved his dogs and was gentle with them.

I rode in the basket while Slim stood on the runners as the dogs sped through woods and across frozen ponds and clearings. We crossed a fox track. "Look at the marks left in the snow by his tail," I commented.

"Fox always drag his tail. So does wolf. That's their blanket," Slim mused. At another fox track with curious drag marks on each side: "That fox was carrying a rabbit."

At his meat cache Slim pointed to a nearby wolf's bed and its tracks, then to the chewed nose of the bull moose. Moose nose was Slim's favorite delicacy—he boiled it—and the fact that wolves had beaten him to it disgusted him. We loaded the meat, putting the heaviest toward the rear of the sled. Before leaving, Slim set a few wolf traps. He used bare hands and spit brown tobacco juice copiously about.

"Should you leave your scent on the traps like that?" I finally asked. Wolves are wary and difficult to trap.

"The wolf knows I'm here," he pointed out as he sprinkled moose hair and loose snow over the set traps. Other trappers later told me Slim caught his share of wolves.

Wolves were special to Slim. We heard their distant, musical howls on several evenings. "Listen," he hissed, "they sing to me!"

During his career he kept several wolves captive— animals he had trapped. He told me about one he grew fond of. "He didn't even show his teeth to me in the trap," he said. "I pushed a stick into his mouth and tied it. I tied his legs and hauled him home in the sled."

Slim put a collar on the wolf and chained him to a doghouse. "I kept him about two months. For the first ten days he never ate anything. Finally he ate a piece of meat as big as my fist, and after that he ate all the time. I wanted to breed him to two of my malamute bitches that came into heat, but he wouldn't even look at them.

"I had a big red dog that sometimes got loose. He wanted to fight the wolf. That wolf wouldn't fight. He lay on his back and wouldn't even bite.

"I couldn't kill him, not even for the bounty and his hide. It would have been like killing one of my dogs. I turned him loose. He ran about a hundred yards and sat and howled. He came close to the cabin three times after that. I talked to him and he yust sat there. Then he was gone. I never saw him again."

If any one object symbolized Slim Carlson's way of life it was his axe. He carried it with him almost always, and in his huge hands it was almost an extension of his arms. He used it for cutting ice, chopping wood, blazing trails, butchering game, and hacking frozen fish. He was proud of his axmanship and was mortified in the early 1950s when the handle of the keen-edged tool caught in loose clothing while he was splitting kindling and he cut off his left thumb.

He tried sewing the thumb back on, holding it in his mouth as he stitched. No go. He stopped the bleeding with a cauterant and a wad of cotton.

He often proudly displayed the alcohol-preserved thumb to sometimes-horrified visitors. Once when he had difficulty untangling fish from his net, he remarked to me, "I 'tink I go get my udder t'umb."

Two days after Slim and I tended his nets from his boat we walked across clear, snapping ice to them. Ominous cracking made Slim dance a bit. "I got into trouble once this ways," he said with a laugh.

He explained that while returning from freighting supplies to a line cabin, he broke through a rotten ice bridge over a river. Clinging to the sled he yelled frantically to the dogs. "If they stop, I sink," he said. The dogs swam, climbed the far bank, and yanked their master out of the drink.

During my visit the lake ice thickened and re-sounded continuously, the distinctive sounds echoing for miles through the water, ice, and air. "This ole lake talks sometimes. Sound like thunder—nice music," he mused. He could tell when the temperature changed by varying sounds of the forming ice.

Slim trapped mostly marten, but he also caught wolves, wolverine, mink, otter, fox, and beaver. From spring into November he prepared for the mid-November through January trapping season.

In March and April with his dog team he hauled supplies to his fifteen line cabins scattered six to fifteen miles apart. The 7-by-9-foot log structures were simple, tight overnight shelters that took Slim about a week each to build. Each had a bunk, table, stove (half of a 55-gallon oil drum), shelves, a wax-cloth window, cooking utensils, and firewood. Even when it was 30 or 40 below zero they became warm fifteen minutes after he lit a fire.

Slim ran three to five traplines from each line cabin, and he had as many as nine hundred traps set at one time on two hundred miles of trapline. The dogs knew every set; when they stopped, he realized they were at one of his traps, even though he couldn't remember setting that particular one. When he was free of other chores he cleared the lines of brush to make for easier winter travel with the dog team.

He preferred at least 20-below for trapping. He wore a heavy fur-lined parka, and when running the dogs, bearskin mittens and down-filled pants. Footgear was horsehide moccasins, or fur or canvas mukluks.

In early winter before deep cold, Slim used metal on his dogsled runners. Later, in deep cold, he removed the metal; wood slides easier in deep cold. In winter he shaved or trimmed his mustache and beard so they wouldn't collect ice.

For marten he used a cubby set—a shelter, commonly formed with branches leaned against the base of a spruce tree. The trap was set in the doorway, beneath an odoriferous lure—a fish-based scent soaked into burlap strips. Slim disliked finding a live marten in a trap, for he hated to kill anything. "I'm getting more softhearted every year," he admitted. In deep cold, trapped animals die quickly.

Often he was on the trail from before daylight (9 or 10 a. m.) until 9 or 10 p.m. When he arrived at a cabin he fed the dogs fish—and sometimes frozen marten carcasses—and then thawed his day's catch. After supper he skinned the marten and rolled and froze the skins. He fleshed, stretched, and dried them at the base cabin at the end of the season.

Slim caught 250 marten in his best year, and 175 in 1954, the season before my visit. With the mid-1950s price for marten around $10, this didn't give Slim many dollars for flour, sugar, ammunition, clothing, and other trading post items he needed. In the mid-1950s he needed an annual income of $2,500 to break even.

If any of his traplines failed to produce, Slim rested it for a year or more. He also alternated traplines from season to season. "I leave plenty seeds," he explained.

He used the same cubbies each winter, leaving traps hanging in them all year. Thus they appeared natural, and marten entered without hesitation when he baited up. Every few years he hauled traps to his cabin to clean them with a solution he made from alder bark.

Prolonged days of 40 and 50 below zero sometimes cut the frequency with which he could cover his traplines during the brief season. Shrews or ravens can damage fur of trapped animals, and jays frequently spring traps. Bears often broke into his line cabins during summer or early fall.

"Trapping's a gamble," Slim said. "Lots of fellers trap for fun. I see no fun to it."

Slim sometimes became so cold on the trapline that he threatened to quit. Each time, as soon as he reached a warm cabin and got a belly full of grub, he decided to stick it out.

During winter '54 while he was running a trapline, the temperature dropped to 58 below. On another occasion when it was 60 below he became so cold that he drove his dogs right into a line cabin. He was too cold to remove harnesses until he warmed himself with a fire. At such temperatures fog hovered over the dogs on the trail so he could hardly see the leader.

"But," he said, "I yust have to get out and work my traps. If I didn't I go hungry next year."

Some of his closest calls occurred in deep winter. In January 1949, in one of his line cabins, Slim piled kindling near the stove, fed the fire, and lit a candle for light. Two sled dog pups scratched on the door to be let in. One knocked over the lighted candle, momentarily unnoticed, onto birch bark and split kindling.

Within seconds the bark, the kindling, and soon the dry cabin exploded in flames. Slim barely had time to grab his rifle as he leaped out the door. The two pups were trapped on the far side of the fire.

"I yumped out yust in my long underwear," he told me. He wore no socks; his feet were in rubber bottoms cut from shoepacks. It was 12 below. "I called the pups again and again, but they didn't listen to me."

With an axe he tried to cut a hole in the cabin, but it was frozen. Hopeless.

"The worst part was hearing the pups shriek," Slim said. The mother, standing beside Slim, howled forlornly as her pups died.

Slim remained at the fire for two hours; it kept him from freezing. In that time he had to decide what to do. "If it had been 30 or 40 below I'd have shot myself," he told me. It would have been a faster and more merciful death than freezing.

"I thought maybe I should kill some of my dogs and make clothes out of their hides, but I decided I'd rather freeze. I liked my dogs too much."

When there was no heat left from the fire, Slim harnessed the dogs and drove eight miles to his nearest cabin. The dogs moved slowly in the deep snow and unbroken trail. His shoepack bottoms filled with snow. The last mile was in an exposed area, with a brisk breeze.

At the cabin, despite a roaring fire Slim couldn't get warm and he lay shivering under a sleeping bag. It was nearly noon the next day before he felt warm. He had frozen his left heel. His fingers and fingernails turned black. His face was frozen, but only skin deep. He feared he had frozen his private parts, but he had protected them all he could on the trail and got off with minor frostbite.

He once forgot that a trap holding a lynx had an unusually long chain. He moved in to tap the animal on the nose. Before he could swing the stick the lynx leaped atop Slim's head, raking his face and chest with its hind claws. The big cat had jumped the length of the chain and couldn't get balanced, so Slim got off with two nasty scratches.

One fall he returned to a cache in a tree, where he had left meat of a moose and a black bear. With him were several loose sled dogs. He carried his .30/06 Winchester.

The dogs, trotting ahead, stopped, hackles up, near the cache. Slim's pale blue eyes squinted through the forest shadows. His cache was empty. Beneath it was a mound of leaves, moss, and sod. He realized a bear had yanked his meat down and buried it.

Something big and yellow under a spruce tree turned into a charging grizzly bear. The dogs yelped and scattered. Slim unlimbered his rifle. The kick of the gun rocked his arms. He had no time to raise it to his shoulder.

He yanked the bolt and snapped a second shot. The grizzly accidentally bumped into Slim as it chased the scattering dogs, staggering him. His next frantic trigger tug produced only a click; the rifle was empty. He felt in his pocket and found a shell, but his big fist stuck and it took forever for it to pull free.

The bear bounded toward Slim. At the last moment the elusive shell came free, Slim popped it into the barrel, slammed the action shut, pointed, and pulled the trigger. It was his last cartridge, and, Slim said, "It yust had to do the yob." It did; the bear turned and left, staggering.

Later, with more ammunition, Slim trailed the bear and found it dead. His first two shots had caused little damage; the third had been fatal.

Slim trapped beaver through the ice during March and seldom had difficulty catching the limit of fifteen. He never took more than two from the same lodge if he could help it because, "I have to trap every year." Beaver ponds attract other furbearers, and he wanted every colony to remain active.

Each April, after his furs were fleshed, stretched, and dried, he arranged for someone to care for his dogs while he flew to Fairbanks to sell his catch. He paid bills and bought his outfit for the coming year. He often chartered a plane to fly his supplies to Minchumina. Once home he hauled the supplies to his line cabins, getting ready for the next trapping season.

In May he went back to fishing for the dogs, in mild weather drying the fish the dogs couldn't eat fresh. He also readied his vegetable garden. Through the short warm summer he continued to fish and to repair his cabins and equipment. He often had to build another dogsled. He cared for his garden, cut grass away from his cabin to eliminate mosquitoes and fire hazard, and cut firewood. After ticking off all these chores, Slim remarked: "Sometimes when I'm tired I sit and look at the lake."

In September he killed his winter's meat—usually a moose, sometimes caribou or black bear. In the fall of 1955 and in 1954 Slim fired his .30-06 only four times to get his meat. Hunting and shooting game was no fun to Slim. "Yust hard work, that's all," he said.

In early fall Slim picked tubs full of mostly wild cranberries (lingonberries) and blueberries. The wild cranberries kept without care; the blueberries he preserved with a thick syrup.

One winter in his early years, before he started trapping, Slim was "hibernating" in his tiny remote cabin when he developed such a craving for fruit that he shoveled through three feet of snow for frozen cranberries. "They were sour, but I never tasted anything so good," he remembered. He had lived for two months on nothing but meat.

When I visited Slim he was eligible for an old-age pension, but he didn't want to be "like dose udder fellers and sit around waiting to die on government money."

I asked him if he ever got bushy or talked to himself.

"It takes brains to get bushy, and I didn't have that." He admits to talking to himself but said he had nothing to worry about until he started answering.

Slim Carlson loved the beauty and quiet of the Alaska wilderness. To some, the life he led would have been unutterably lonely, discouraging, difficult, and disagreeable. It wasn't a simple life; it required careful planning, as well as much hard physical labor. He didn't consider his life romantic. However it was clear that Slim gained much satisfaction in wresting a living from the wilderness.

After being with Slim for three weeks I knew why he had earned the nickname White Moose Carlson. He knew he could have told a white lie and explained to the judge that he needed the moose meat and gotten off. But proud Slim Carlson refused to lie to save himself. Some may have labeled him "dumb Swede," but Slim Carlson wasn't stupid; he was one of the most intelligent, level-headed, and at peace men I've ever known.

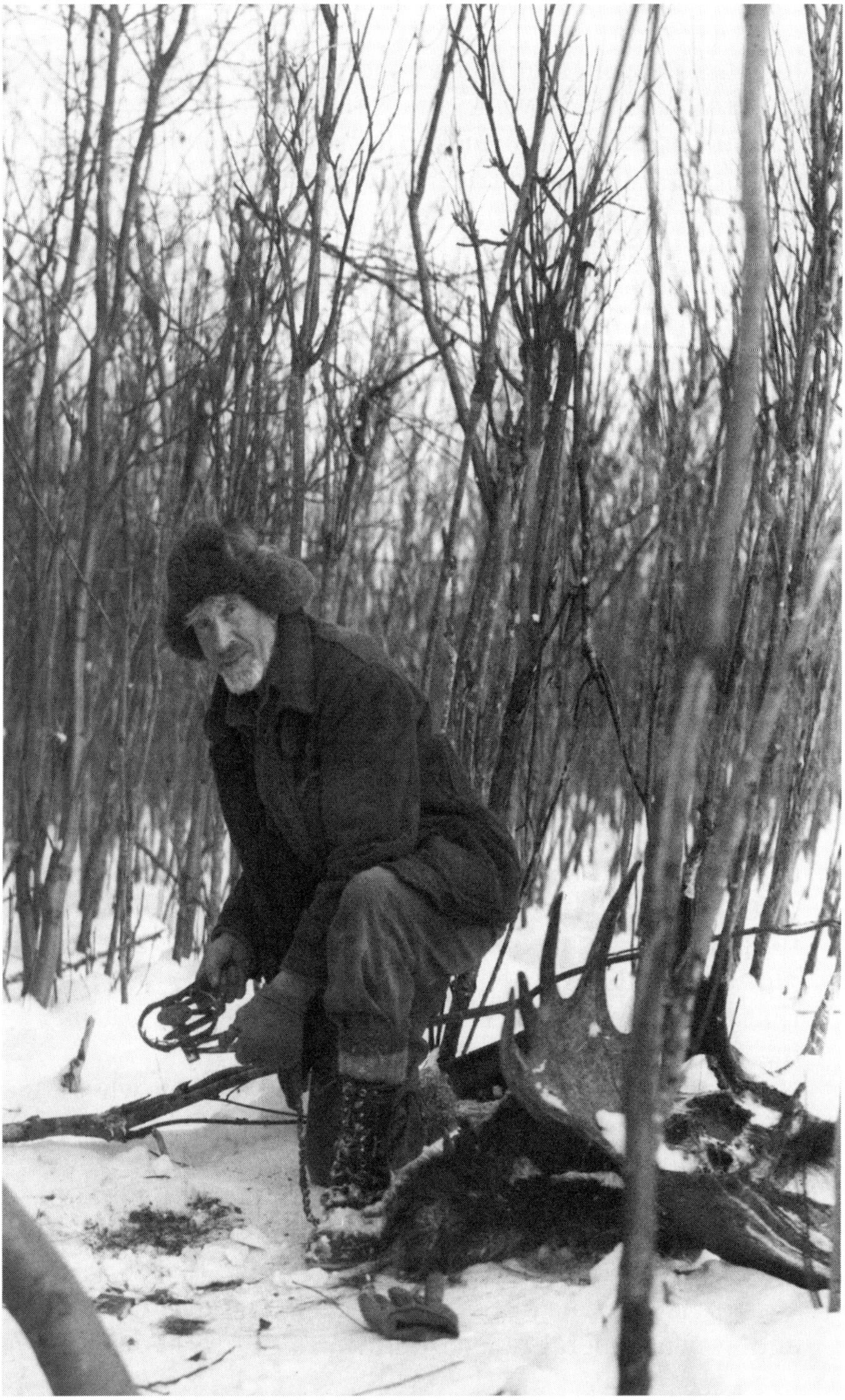

On my return home, three weeks after I skimmed across Lake Minchumina in a skiff, Slim took me over the identical route with his dog team. Now it was covered with six inches of ice.

During the years after my 1955 visit, I kept track of Slim through mutual friends. In 1970, when he was eighty-four, he walked with his dogs fifty miles across country from Lake Minchumina to his Slippery Creek cabin where, the previous spring, he had left his dogsled and other winter gear. He then trapped through that and several more winters.

His health failed in 1974 and he was forced to move to Fairbanks. He died at the Fairbanks Pioneers home in 1975 at the age of eighty-nine. The Dick Collins family, his nearest neighbors, scattered his ashes at Lonely Lake, near his Slippery Creek cabin.

Miki and Julie Collins, Dick's daughters, inherited Slim's trapline. Following Slim's tradition, they still trap it today using dog teams, unusual in our snowmobile culture. Fur is still abundant there, for Slim had cared well for the land he loved.

The original of this article was titled "Thirty Seven Years Alone in Alaska" and appeared in *Outdoor Life* in June 1956. I updated it in 2001 for this collection.

Slim Carlson, setting a wolf trap near remnants of the moose he killed for his winter meat. Asked if he wasn't concerned that wolves would sense the odor from his bare hand and stay away, he snorted, "The wolf knows I'm here."

JIM REARDEN PHOTO

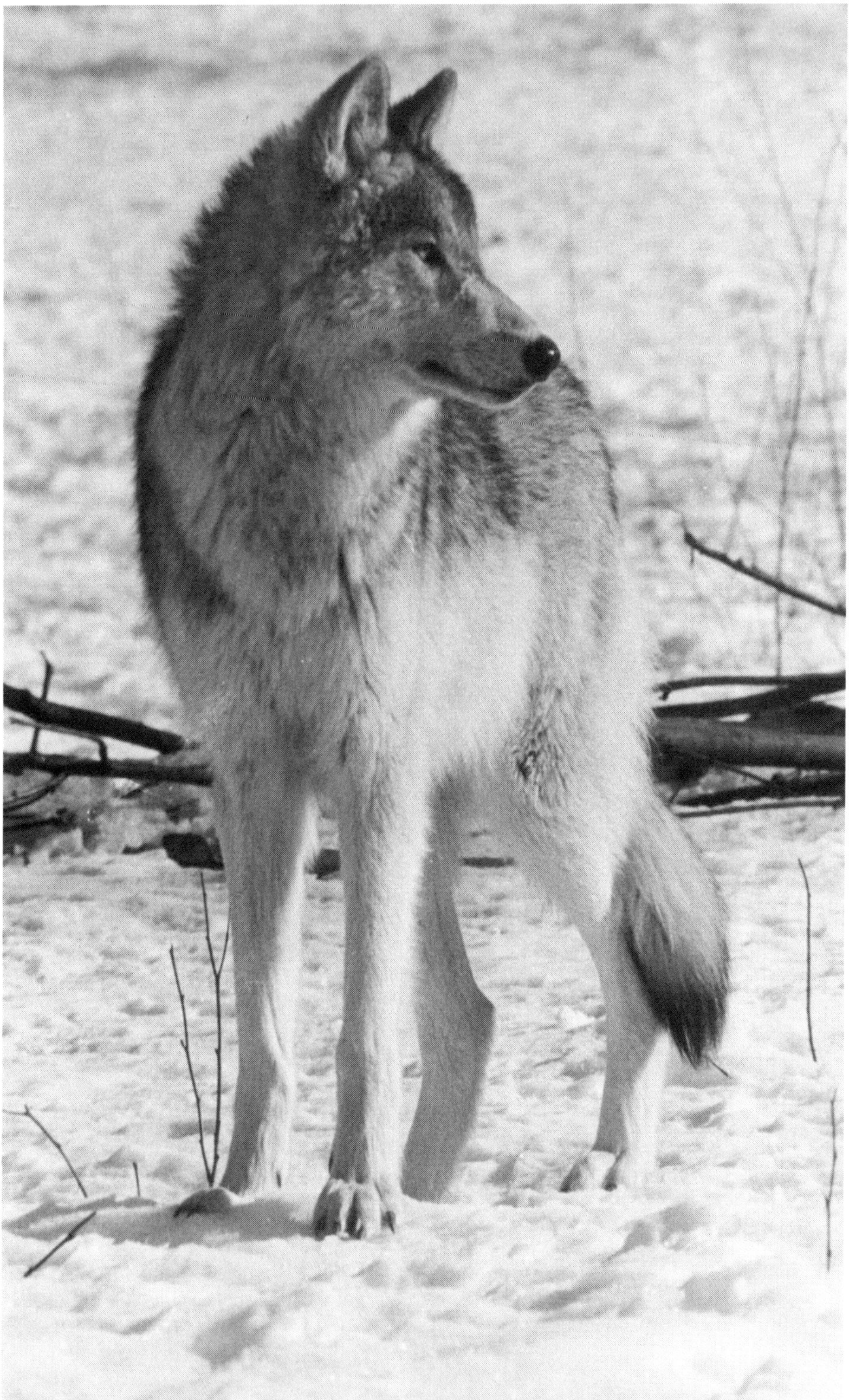

CHAPTER ELEVEN

SAVAGE RIVER WOLVES

Frank Glaser's years of living on the Savage River near Mount McKinley National Park (now Denali National Park) gave him a remarkable inside look at the daily lives of Alaska wolves. His experience as a hunter and trapper—and in developing a team of sled dogs that were part wolf, part malamute—earned him his reputation as a wolf expert.

He had a marvelous memory for names, dates, and places, and humor punctuated his yarns. He was an audible text on the history, geography, climate, personalities, and wildlife of Alaska.

I tape-recorded some of Glaser's stories about his life, including this eyewitness account of wolf behavior along the Savage, told here in his voice.

I never saw a wolf track or heard a wolf howl during the winter of 1924-25 after I settled at Savage River. A few wolves showed up during the winter of 1925-26. By

An Alaskan wolf. Frank Glaser, in his decades of hunting and trapping in Alaska, witnessed the daily activities of hundreds of wolves and became familiar with their family life, their breeding habits, and their orchestrated stalking of caribou.

BOB STEPHENSON, ALASKA DEPARTMENT OF FISH AND GAME

the winter of 1926-27 there were noticeably more wolves, and I often saw them chasing caribou. Wolf numbers continued to increase. By 1930 during the February-March mating time they were so numerous and so noisy with their howling they often awoke me at night.

I recall one clear mid-February morning when I heard two bands of wolves howling nearby. It was breeding season, and I sensed their excitement. I dressed for a long, cold day in the hills. With binoculars and rifle I climbed a nearby ridge where I could overlook the flats where feeding caribou were scattered.

I scanned the flats with binoculars for a few minutes, but saw only caribou. Fog rose from each caribou as its body moisture condensed in the deep cold. A chill crept through my furs, so I moved to another spot. The walk warmed me. I had no sooner sat down again and braced my binoculars, holding my breath as they neared my face to keep them from fogging, when I saw a pack of eight wolves a couple of miles away. They were trotting single-file across the flats. Caribou turned and stared as they passed, but the wolves ignored them.

I swung the binoculars and was startled to see another pack of seven wolves moving single-file across the same flat. The two wolf packs were headed toward each other.

"Now I'm going to see something," I told myself. I knew wolves had territories, and that fights between packs (generally family groups) are common. Several times I found the remains of wolves killed in fights with other wolves. Often the remains had been eaten, for wolves do eat wolves.

I swept the flats again with my glasses, and was amazed to see a third band of eight wolves, trotting single-file. Now there were three packs bound for the same general area. As I watched, a low howl came from one band, to be answered by a low howl from one of the others. Eventually all three packs stopped a few hundred feet apart, appearing reluctant to approach each other. Gradually then, the three packs, a congregation of twenty-three wolves, gathered in one furry concentration on the open, snowy flat. I had a grandstand view of this remarkable phenomenon.

The wolves milled about and mixed, I heard yips and growls. Here and there it appeared that wolves were challenging one another; several appeared to be fighting. I started making big plans, thinking that eight or nine of the wolves would be killed in the melee. I had in mind sneaking in and finishing off a bunch of cripples and I imagined I was going to collect a bundle of fifteen-dollar bounties and would have a bunch of wolf hides to sell.

I dashed onto the flats and hurried to the spot. Except for tracks and a little blood in the snow, I found nothing. All twenty-three wolves had sped off. They were high in the sheep hills howling in a low, sweet chorus. I watched them for a time with binoculars, puzzled. They had seen me and left, of course.

Then I remembered that it was breeding season. Perhaps one or more females were in heat. Those wolves were just playing around at a time of excitement. All the growling and bumping each other and fussing was just posturing that didn't amount to much.

A female wolf will not breed with a member of her pack or family group, except of course with her lifelong mate. When Queenie, a female wolf-dog I owned, came into heat, none of the team could get near her. If they tried she would growl and snap at them, and sit down if they persisted. Instinct wouldn't allow her to mate with any dog she considered part of her family. The moment I put a strange wolf-dog with her, she accepted him.

One February from my lookout point I saw a family of seven wolves trotting single-file across the flats. As I watched them through binoculars the wolf in the lead stopped and moved to the last wolf in line, a somewhat smaller animal, threatening it and obviously giving it some sort of a message. The leader resumed its place at the head of the line and trotted along for another few hundred yards. It stopped again and returned to the last wolf, threatening again. But the smaller wolf refused to take the hint and continued to tag along at the rear of the column.

Finally the lead animal went back and furiously pitched into the smaller wolf, killing it within a few minutes. Then the family continued on its way.

I examined the dead wolf and removed its skin, finding it to be a young female in heat. I'm reasonably sure the animal that killed it was the mother wolf of the group. When a young female wolf comes in heat when it is about twenty-one or twenty-two months old, she is expected to leave the family and seek a mate elsewhere.

On almost any winter day I could climb one of the high ridges near my cabin and with binoculars spot a band of wolves. From December through spring, feeding caribou were scattered across the hills and flats. Almost every night wolves killed one or more caribou within a few miles of my main cabin. After they kill, and are full of meat, wolves trot off to lie down for a snooze on a good lookout point. Ravens relish wolf kill leftovers, and the coming and going of these big black flapping birds often helped me to locate wolf kills.

Occasionally during the day a bunch of wolves crossed the big flat where there were scattered caribou, and sometimes they even chased these caribou. When wolves chase caribou during the day it's usually just for fun. Most kills are made at night. Sometimes a young, foolish wolf will chase caribou in the daytime, but he's usually wasting his time. Caribou are faster than wolves. Even if a wolf sneaks to within thirty feet or so of a caribou, if the deer sees him when he makes his final dash, the wolf will pop his teeth in the place the caribou just vacated.

One three-mile by nine-mile flat I often watched not far from my main cabin lay between Savage River and Middle River. One March day from high on a ridge I watched a pack of six wolves make a rare daytime hunt there. The wolves must have been hungry, for when they are hungry they will kill any time they can. I first spotted the wolves about two miles away as they trotted single file off of a high knoll, heading across the flat, heads and tails down, looking less than ambitious. Halfway across the flat they passed downwind of a lone caribou cow. Six sniffing heads came up, and six wolves swerved to head through low willows toward the caribou. When close to the caribou, a big black wolf lay down while the other five were transformed into shadowy, stalking, cats.

As its companions sneaked off, the black wolf issued a low, musical howl and boldly walked toward the cow. She raised her head and stared at him. This was what he wanted. He trotted back and forth, howling, keeping her attention as he gradually worked closer. When the caribou seemed on the verge of fleeing, the wolf backed off a bit. The nervous cow seemed fascinated. Once the wolf ran a short distance toward the caribou then stopped and retreated before the caribou panicked; the big predator made no real effort to give chase.

With my binoculars it was all I could do to occasionally spot any of the wolves as they expertly slipped through grass and willow clumps, keeping to low ground, smoothly working their way to the cow. They formed a rough semicircle around the caribou and gradually closed in.

On their bellies, heads and tails low, they crawled and scooted ever closer. Occasionally a wolf raised up to peek at the cow, but she was so enamored with the howling black wolf she didn't notice.

Finally one of the wolves got within about thirty feet of the cow and made his dash. She wheeled and started to run. But the other wolves rushed in, and she was surrounded. In moments she was smothered by the chopping fangs of all six of the efficient killers. The downed caribou was still struggling weakly when the wolves started ripping great chunks from her hams and gulping them down.

Normally a caribou can easily outrun a wolf. A straightforward chase of caribou on an open flat doesn't work, and wolves know it. That's why a sneaky, sly conquest like this has to be orchestrated.

Wolves make their big caribou kills at night, and I could usually tell when there was going to be a big kill. One dark, quiet night in late March 1932, at about 11 o'clock as I was getting ready to go to bed, two packs of wolves were howling on the big flat. I stepped outside to listen. It sounded as if there were three or four wolves in each bunch, and I guessed they were a mile or two apart. My sled dogs were all awake and uneasy; several perched on their houses looking in the direction of the howling. Tension bristled the air.

The wolves lapsed into quiet for some time, but just as I was dropping off to sleep, they renewed the howling. This time the wolves had merged in one place. They continued to howl for a long time.

I dropped off to sleep thinking, "They're singing me to sleep." I awoke perhaps an hour later. They were still howling. I knew now they had made a kill and I was hearing post-kill howling, a behavior I'd noticed many times.

Often in winter on moonlight nights before I went to bed I scanned the ridges around my cabin with binoculars and usually could see several bunches of twenty-five or thirty caribou. Undisturbed, these deer might feed in one general area for a week. Perhaps I'd watch a bunch in the same place for several days. At daylight I'd look again with the glasses. If a group of caribou I had been watching for a few days was gone I would often go and investigate. Frequently I'd find that wolves had attacked. If the wolves were successful the evidence was there in the form of caribou carcasses.

Caribou don't see well in the dark; wolves do.

I remember one mild December night, with the temperature hovering near zero. Snow was falling. About 10 o'clock I was reading, my favorite evening recreation, when suddenly my sled dogs hit the ends of their chains, roaring and growling. I slipped my parka on and with flashlight went out and looked around. I could see nothing, but in the nearby timber I heard brush crackling.

Next morning at daylight I found fresh tracks in the snow. They printed an easily read story. Three wolves had chased a caribou down off the ridge. The caribou had run within twenty feet of my dogs' houses but the wolves detoured around them. The terrified caribou fled into the nearby forest, where it had slammed into a tree and fallen. Wolf tracks went around the trees. When the caribou hit the first tree, a wolf grabbed it. There on the snow I found blood and a piece of caribou hide as big as my hand.

The caribou escaped, and ran on. But soon it had hit another tree, again falling down. This time at least two of the wolves pounced. Bloody tracks of a staggering caribou trailed another hundred feet or so, to where the wolves finally brought it down. The three wolves had devoured almost all of that caribou, leaving the remnants about three hundred yards from my cabin.

I often found where wolves had killed eight, ten or a dozen caribou during a night kill. Usually all the dead caribou were fairly close together, perhaps within a few hundred yards of each other. Again, sign in the snow the next day told the savage tale. Wolves had encircled a bunch of caribou, spooking them. Spooked caribou in a herd have a tendency to crowd away from the edge of the herd and move toward the center, trampling one another, tripping and stumbling in the dark while wolves swiftly kill as many as they want simply by running up close and slashing.

I've watched reindeer herds on moonlit nights when I drove a dog team near them. Sometimes they panic at the sight, sound, or smell of the dogs. If bedded down they leap to their feet. They may climb over one another in their efforts to get away from the dogs so they can move closer to the center of the herd.

I've seen reindeer pile up two or three deep in such melees. I've seen fawns killed and adults severely injured in these desperately frantic getaway attempts. It has always seemed strange to me that these animals don't scatter when attacked by predators. Reindeer and caribou are essentially the same animal, and I believe their reaction to danger enables wolves to make their big kills at night.

Some nature writers claim that wolves cripple their prey by cutting their hamstring to make their kill. I've watched wolves kill caribou dozens of times. I've found many hundreds of dead caribou and reindeer killed by wolves. Only once have I seen a caribou that had been hamstrung. It had apparently escaped after what I assume was a wolf had cut a hamstring in one leg just above the hock. The caribou was dragging its leg, and I shot it to put it out of its misery.

In killing a caribou, a wolf usually runs beside it biting it in the flank. It can slash a five- or six-inch-long gash that looks like a knife-cut. One good slash and the caribou's paunch falls out. The caribou drags himself a short distance, steps and walks on the paunch and his attached entrails, and falls over within a few hundred feet. Death comes soon.

"Balance of nature" idealists love to claim that wolves take mainly the sick, halt, and lame, and that therefore wolves are beneficial to the health of their prey species. I don't see it that way. Caribou and moose cows heavy with calf—arguably the most valuable to the species—are more vulnerable to wolves than barren cows.

Calves of caribou and moose, the future of the species, are even more vulnerable. And then there are the old caribou bulls, important for breeding.

In the Alaska Range the caribou rut ends in late October. By mid-December the antlers of the adult caribou bulls are shed. These old bulls are very thin at this time, almost walking skeletons. In late December, January, and into February they are easy prey for wolves. I have often found seven or eight skinny old bull caribou in one place where wolves killed them, with only a little meat eaten from a few hindquarters. Often it seems as if it is the fun of killing that entices the wolves. The wolves weren't really hungry; they simply killed because the tired old skinny bulls were vulnerable, easy prey.

When fur prices nosedived in the late 1930s, Frank Glaser was hired by the federal government as a predator control agent. At the time, wolves were considered all bad— the only good wolf was a dead one—and the federal government and the Territory of Alaska signed a cooperative agreement to hire and pay for a wolf expert to catch wolves, and to teach trappers how to trap and snare them.

At statehood, Alaska ended widespread government killing of wolves. The wolf was classified as big game and a furbearer, and it is now managed as a valuable renewable resource.

This article is an excerpt from chapter 12 of my 1998 book *Alaska's Wolf Man: The 1915-55 Wilderness Adventures of Frank Glaser.*

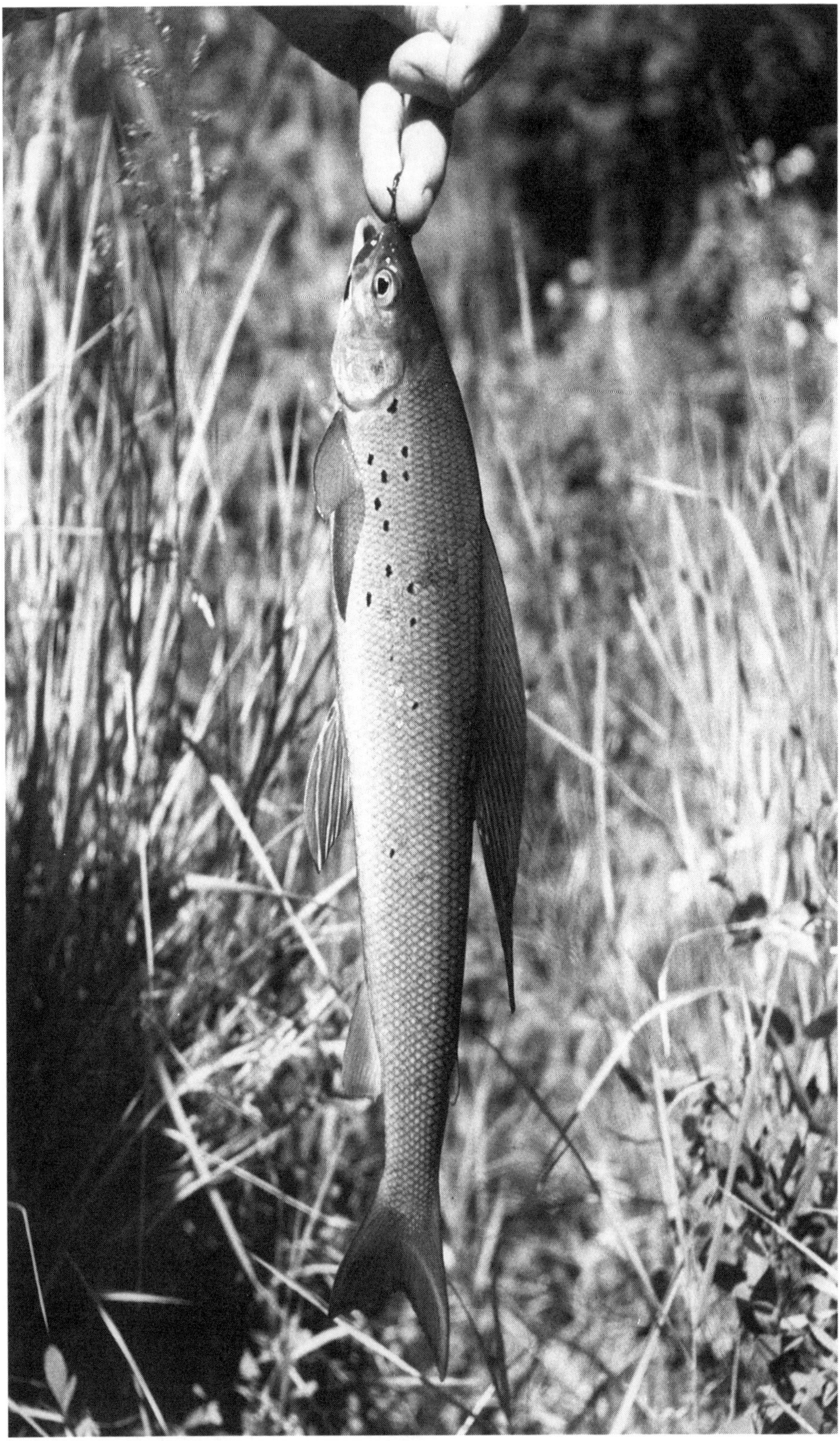

CHAPTER TWELVE

MY FRIEND THE GRAYLING

The arctic grayling, which is found throughout much of northern and interior Alaska, is a country boy with manners. He is a gentleman. He is a dry fly purist's joy, a hardware flinger's meat. He'll joyfully hit a red cranberry on a hook, a chunk of red flannel underwear, an exquisitely tied #20 fly—or a bare hook. He'll gulp down a mouse or a shrew, a barely visible midge, or an indiscreet frog.

He will patiently ignore the clumsy splashings of a tyro fisherman. His white flesh does not taste fishy. And while alive, he's one of the most vividly colored creatures found in the icy waters of the North. Sadly, he turns to a dull gray or black when dead.

And he has saved my neck on many occasions, a few of which I recount here. He's great, my friend the grayling.

The grayling conclusively proved his friendship to me during a hunt on which I guided a building

The grayling, a handsome fish that greets anglers in many Alaskan streams. If there is one fish in Alaska that is dependable, a fish you can count on for being at a given place at a given time, one that will not be temperamental when you toss a hook at him, that fish is the grayling.　　　JIM REARDEN PHOTO

171

contractor from the Midwest, a one-on-one deal, just the hunter and me. The poor guy couldn't shoot for sour owls, he couldn't climb the sheep hills, he was afraid of bears, and he was certain wolves were going to eat us alive.

Weather in the high country of the Brooks Range of northern Alaska had been perfect for three successive days. On each of those days I tried to lead the guy up the open slopes into sheep country. While climbing, my client took about three steps and stood puffing, although he was only in his mid-forties and not terribly fat. He was just plain soft. And, I thought, lazy.

"Can't we find a ram somewhere but on top of these damned mountains?" he cranked.

"Nope," I answered, "It's an easy climb, and not really far for a sheep hunt."

My unhappy client slipped one day, falling on his new .237 Whizbang Humdinger, on which was mounted a large variable scope. The rifle caliber was his own invention, he said. He'd had a gunsmith build it on a Mauser action. It was one of three odd-caliber rifles (all his own design) he had brought. He planned to use one for sheep, one for caribou, and one for moose. I don't know what he'd have done had we bumped into a bear. I guess if a bear showed up he'd have had to use my beat-up old .30-06, despite its standard caliber. He sure wouldn't want to use one of his "specially designed" sheep, caribou, or moose rifles (as he referred to them) to shoot a bear.

To make a long and unhappy story short, on his fall my luckless client bent the mounts of the scope on his sheep rifle, and when I coaxed him to crawl within 150 yards of a decent full-curl ram, his Whizbang Humdinger flung nine shots of hot lead about six feet to the right of the white ram. After about the fourth shot I saw what was happening and pleaded with him to drop the old ram with my rifle.

"No," he exclaimed. "I want to kill it with my sheep rifle. I'll compensate for it," he explained, when I told him he was throwing 'em a leetle to the right. The white hide of the Dall ram was still whole when it disappeared over a distant ridge. My hunter hadn't compensated quite enough.

I tried to compensate for the loss of the ram for the next week or so by hiking my tail off to find the ram again, or another one like it. I'd park my client in a sheltered spot about halfway up the ridge, then take off on a lope to cover as much sheep country as I could. I found a few rams with small horns, but never again on that hunt did I see a ram that could be called a trophy.

And then he missed a nice bull moose with his moose rifle.

"Too far," he grunted, when I urged him to shoot the standing animal. We were above it, prone, with no wind, the range about two hundred yards. His special moose cannon hit somewhere near the moose, for it jumped and stepped into the timber, untouched.

After about ten days of the scheduled two-week hunt my client decided I was incompetent. He hadn't killed any game. He was in daily danger of his life from wolves (we heard them howl most nights) and bears (we saw a few old grizzly tracks).

One morning we found six inches of snow on the ground. It was impossible to climb the sheep hills, and there was no point in hunting moose, at least until late afternoon. How was I to entertain the man? He didn't care to read the pocket books I had for such days. He wasn't what I would call a brilliant conversationalist; most of his talk had been complaints.

I was desperate. Every Alaskan guide I know does his best to keep happy clients, but it is impossible to get game, or even good trophies, for every single short-hunt client. Sometimes clients leave unhappy. Since my bill-paying, and the grub I fed my kids during winter, was partially dependent on hunting clients, I hated to see any of them leave unhappy.

"Let's see if we can get some fresh fish for lunch," I suggested, digging out a fly rod as my hunter disgustedly eyed the new snow.

His eyes lit up as he reached for the rod. He stepped to the bank of the nearby John River, made a few false casts, and nodded approvingly. Somehow he looked more at home with a fly rod than a rifle, and he handled it as if he knew its use.

"I'll carry the rod so you can pack your rifle," he suggested, cautious to the core (we'd seen bear tracks on the riverbank). "Which way do we go?"

I led him to a hole where a small tributary flows into the clear, icy John River and tied on a #12 mosquito fly.

"Fish it dry," I suggested.

He nodded, false cast a few times, and dropped the fly onto a slick as pretty as you please.

The fly had hardly landed when a seventeen-inch grayling arced clear of the water and snaffled it on the way down. He set the hook with finesse and gently fought the fish to shore. If he had killed a record sheep I don't believe he'd have been any happier than he was with that fish. He made me take a dozen pictures of him with it, and he was terribly disappointed when the lovely reds, purples, and blues that are so vivid in a live grayling faded to drab gray as the fish died.

Over the next few hours he became a different person. While fighting one particularly active grayling he said, "This fishing alone is worth twice the money the whole trip will cost me."

He said it, and he didn't back down. For the remainder of our time together we quit hunting while he caught and released grayling until I guess every grayling within a mile of camp had a sore mouth. But he was happy. He told me he had never hunted before but had decided it must be at least as much fun as fishing, which he had done all his life. He grimly studied books and articles about hunting, had his three super-duper rifles tooled up, and had booked with me.

When he left we were good friends, and he presented me with a bonus—the three super-duper Whizbang Humdinger Specials, with reloading dies. I soon swapped them off.

If there is one fish in Alaska that is dependable, a fish you can count on for being at a given place at a given time, one that will not be temperamental when you toss a hook at him, that fish is the grayling. And when he cooperates to the point of hitting a bare hook, well . . .

One spring many moons ago George Barfutz and I decided we wanted a couple of grizzly hides. I lived at Fairbanks in a log cabin (with plumbing) and figured a nice Toklat hide hanging on the wall would be a good way of showing folks what a great hunter I was. So George and I rode the Alaska Railroad south and had the old Moose Gooser drop us off in likely looking high country of the Alaska Range. Snowdrifts still lay on north slopes, and there wasn't much grass or other green stuff coming out yet. We each carried forty pounds of tent and vittles on Trapper Nelson packboards.

After a week of roaming ever higher into the mountains and farther from the railroad, we'd gone through most of our dried eggs, spuds, and rice. We'd seen one big, dark grizzly at a distance, had spooked a wolverine from a winter-killed caribou, but had seen virtually nothing else moving. Even ptarmigan were scarce.

We often left our food, tent, sleeping bags, and other gear and hiked off looking for bears. One day a bear found our camp while we were gone.

He left our tent in tatters, sleeping bags ripped open (perhaps he was looking for the ducks those feathers came from), our grub eaten, and other stuff scattered and ruined. We were two disgusted dudes. First reaction was to try to hunt down that damned destructive bow-legged son of a sow and slaughter him for his hide—and meat. But a couple hours of ranging around the area revealed nothing.

We had no shelter, no grub, and no bedding, and we were four days from the railroad.

My friend the grayling saved us from a hungry trip. I carried in my shirt pocket about ten feet of fish line, some leader, and a little split shot box of hooks. We salvaged half a cup of rice by tweezering it out of the carpet of tundra plants, and beelined it for the Moose Gooser line.

At the end of the first day's hike we were at a tiny clear trickle of a stream. I tied a hook and leader onto the fish line and cut a willow pole. I couldn't find any berries for bait and there were no insects about. After a bit of head scratching, I used a pocket stone to work the hook over until it was scratched silver-bright. I dropped the bright hook into a hole below an old beaver dam and worked it up and down like an ice fishing jig. Soon I had a fourteen-inch grayling. From then on it was easy, for I had bait—eyes, and strips of grayling belly. That night we had a little rice and lots of grayling that we broiled over a birch wood fire. A few pinches of birch ashes made a seasoning of sorts.

Repeat for breakfast, after alternately snoozing and keeping a couple of fires going all night; we slept on our torn-up air mattresses between the fires.

At noon we ate cold grayling we had cooked that morning. For supper next night, broiled grayling, with birch ashes for seasoning. For variety next morning, we ate birch ashes, with grayling.

We had lost weight and were sleepy, sad, but wiser hunters a couple days later when we thumbed down the rumbling old MG for the trip back to Fairbanks.

A few years later I introduced my brother Don to my friend the grayling. Anyone with an older brother knows how you're always trying to show him how to hunt and fish, and how to live comfortably in the hills with a little salt and an axe. I promised him a great Alaskan trip: we'd bag a couple of nice moose, maybe a caribou, we'd wing-shoot a few ptarmigan, and even catch a mess of fish.

Sadly, over the years brother Don had become a skeptic. Too many of his Oregon buddies had conned him into surefire elk, deer, pheasant, and steelhead trips that backfired. I learned during the first days of our hunt that he had no faith in the claims of his gone-wild Alaskan kid brother. He had bragged so much about his planned hunt with me, and then had grown so skeptical that he had arranged to borrow a lousy little 48-inch-spread moose rack from a buddy to have on hand when he returned empty-handed from Alaska. He was prepared to prove to his friends what a great hunt he had made.

His attitude began to change a bit when, high in the Alaska Range, we dumped two three-quarter-ton bull moose within sixty feet of each other, one with a 65-inch antler spread, the other with a 59-inch spread. It helped when he clobbered a fair caribou bull from the door of our tent one early morning. A little exciting wing-shooting of ptarmigan really began to convince him, but the clincher came when I took him grayling fishing.

There's no place in the world like the high country of the Alaska Range in the fall. You may have some lousy weather, a little early snow, some rain, and some wind. But the clear, calm, crisp days you do get—and they're reasonably common—make it all worthwhile.

The autumn reds and golds on the high ridges, the fresh dash of snow on the peaks, and the intense blue sky are an outdoorsman's dream. That's what it was like when Dave Lani flew us to Dickie Lake after we had hung up the meat from our moose and caribou. "You'll never see better dry fly fishing anywhere," I bragged as we took off from Summit Lake in Dave's little floatplane.

Dickie Lake, on the south slope of the range, is clear, deep, and cold. The outlet is a gurgling stream wadeable most places, with fast runs, and deep holes. It meanders through a wide-floored, deep, canyonlike place that looks like an oasis in the desert. In this high country there are few trees, but in fall the trees scattered amidst the green of the valley floor next to the stream give the place a parklike appearance.

When cool weather comes, grayling move out of the Gulkana River, up the outlet of Dickie Lake, and into the lake, where they spend the winter.

We hit that stream when it was loaded with grayling swimming toward the lake. Don tied on a dry fly. I don't know what the pattern was—and doubt it made any difference. He flipped it casually onto a slick run. He turned to me, I am sure, to ask what the delay was, and darned near lost his featherweight rod; a big strong grayling took that fly and headed downstream with it, fast.

After a scrap Don landed the fifteen-incher. He released it after admiring it for a long time as it lay in the shallows, vivid colors pulsing. He cast again and caught another. We moved upstream, and he caught a fish on about every other cast. Around a bend we encountered a young bull caribou with two cows and two calves. They eyed us calmly and slowly moved off. A flock of mallards flew over. Don was still catching grayling that averaged fifteen to sixteen inches, with an occasional larger one.

After catching the first grayling, when he whooped and hollered, he had gone silent and thoughtful. He stopped fishing to watch the caribou for a few minutes, watched the mallards whistle overhead, and slowly shook his head. Then, almost grimly, he went back to catching and releasing grayling.

In about four hours he estimated he caught one hundred grayling, of which he kept four for our supper, carefully unhooking and releasing the others. "It's hard to believe. I've never seen such dry fly fishing. It's fantastic," he finally declared.

When Don left Alaska after three weeks of hunting and fishing, I think he'd have believed me if I'd told him he could catch tuna in Lake Iliamna. He's still a skeptic about those surefire trips in Oregon, but now he's a believer in Alaska. The grayling fishing was the clincher.

In July of 1950, I fished for grayling in the Delta Clearwater, about ninety miles southeast of Fairbanks. There for the first time I saw grayling alive and in gin-clear water, brightly lit by the sun. These grayling were the fish of my imagination; spritely, and graceful, with that beautiful and colorful great flag of a fin furling and unfurling as the fish slowly moved about a deep pool. Their basic color was light gray, but their sides and fins subtly flashed all the colors of the rainbow. They were beautiful. Living gems.

This article appeared in *Fur-Fish-Game* magazine in September 1964.

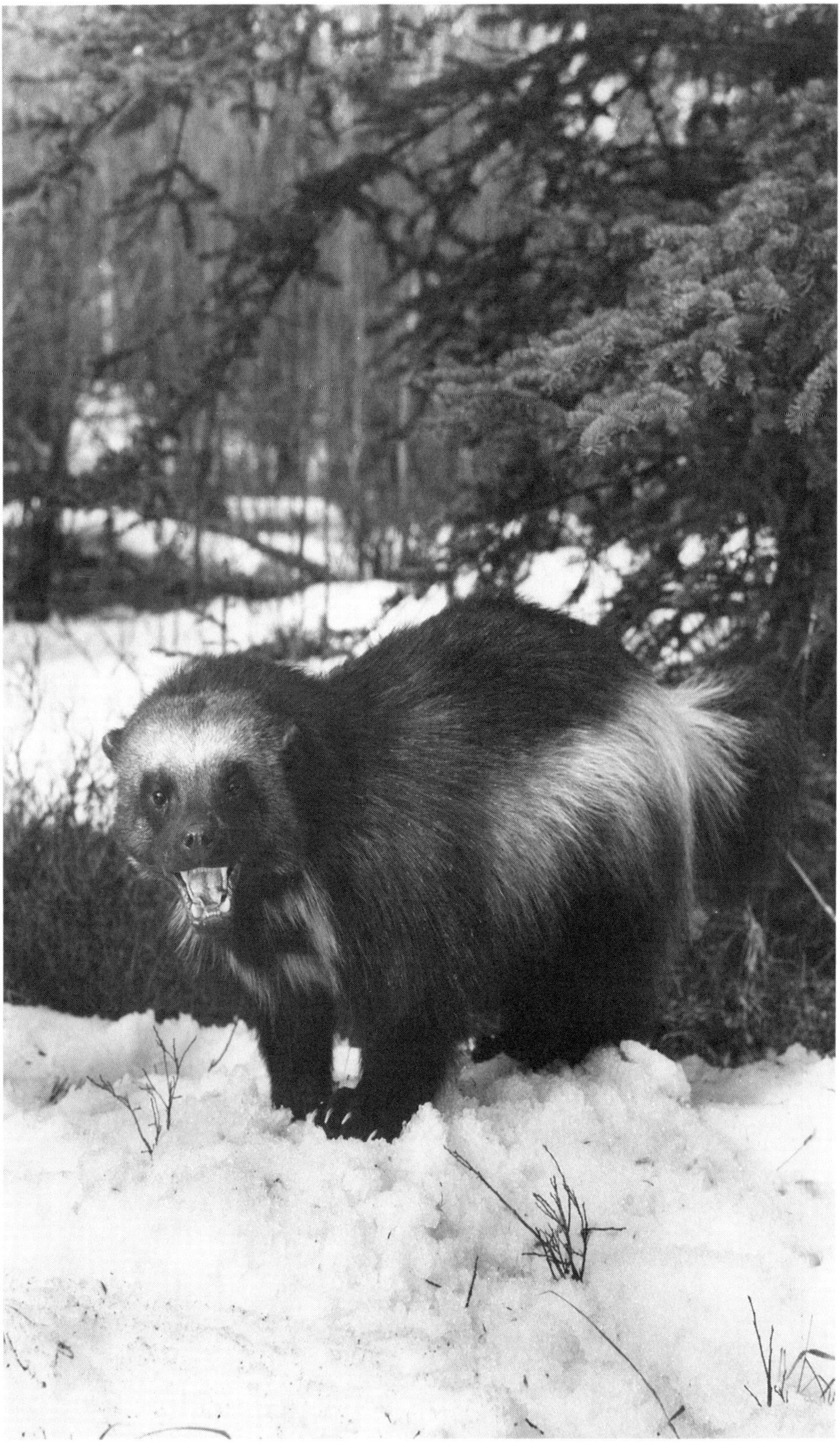

CHAPTER THIRTEEN

TALES OF THE WOLVERINE

I began to learn about wolverines in 1947 on a raw, fog-damp Alaska Peninsula day when one crashed through the alders straight toward Tarleton Smith and me, both agents for the U.S. Fish and Wildlife Service, as we stumbled in hip boots down a salmon-choked creek. I carried a .22 rifle. Tee was unarmed.

At first we didn't know what it was. The bandy-legged little black, brown and white creature burst into an opening not thirty feet away, running toward us growling loudly. We were edgy, because we were in brown bear country.

I didn't even think. I snapped a .22 bullet into the animal and he rolled into thick alders and grass. Angry roars and growls came from the tangle of alder and grass. In a few seconds, he got to his feet and fled the way he had come, still banging into alders. Their thrashing tops followed his beeline retreat over the hill and out of sight.

Why did the wolverine seem to charge us? I can only guess that he caught a whiff of our scent and was trying to escape and ran the wrong way. Or perhaps he heard us, thought we were some sort of prey he could kill, and simply charged.

The wolverine, one of Alaska's most interesting mammals. Ill-tempered and un-predictable, the wolverine had a habit of petty thievery and a well-deserved repu-tation for toughness and ferocity. This one was caught in a trap and later mounted.
JIM REARDEN PHOTO

From that time I've tried to trace wolverine yarns to their source, and in my wanderings around Alaska I've heard many. Here's a sample.

Three or four feet long, including the bushy tail, with short legs, the wolverine is the largest land-dwelling member of the weasel family in Alaska. The body is powerfully built and covered with coarse, dark brown and black hair, with white stripes along the back.

The wolverine has the reputation of being bad-tempered and capable of driving black bears and mountain lions from their kills. I regard these tales with a large dash of salt. Coyotes they might bluff. Wolves, no. Wolves can kill a wolverine with relative ease.

Frank Glaser, who trapped at Savage River in the 1920s and '30s, told me he once watched a wolverine chewing on a dead caribou. It would eat for a time, stand on hind legs and look around, run around the caribou in its nervous weasel-like way, and go back to eating.

Three wolves, trotting downwind of the wolverine, suddenly spread out and approached the feeding animal. When they were within fifty yards it stood up, looked at the wolves for an instant, then lit out for the nearest timber. The wolves caught it within a few yards, one running on either side, the other following. All Frank saw was a rolling mass of fur and flying snow.

It wasn't much of a fight. The wolves got up, the wolverine didn't. The three wolves walked stiff-legged around the dead wolverine, splattering it with little bursts of urine. They finally scratched snow over it and trotted off.

On another occasion, two of Glaser's big sled dogs ran down and quickly killed a wolverine. Neither dog was injured.

A persistent but incorrect statement about wolverine fur appears in countless references, to the effect that frost won't form on it. Nonsense. Northerners like to use wolverine fur as a liner for a parka ruff. A long-haired wolf ruff breaks the wind and protects the face in deep cold. Wolverine fur is commonly sewed on the wolf fur immediately next to the face where, in deep cold, frost often forms from one's breath.

Frost will form on wolverine fur just as it does on any other fur. However, wolverine fur is durable. When frost does form on it, the wearer can peel if off and the wolverine fur doesn't break and the guard hairs do not pull out. Thus it is long-wearing. But, believe me, frost does form on wolverine fur.

Here's a wolverine yarn I stumbled onto at Fairbanks. Someone who knew I was interested in wolverines told me that one had attacked Dave Tucker, a Fairbanks garage owner and mechanic.

Tucker, quick-moving and slim, a pleasant man of forty-five or fifty, pulled his head out of an open car hood and shook hands when I introduced myself. I ignored the grease.

"So, you heard a wolverine attacked me?" he grinned. Then thoughtfully, "I guess one could have, all right. Let's have some coffee and I'll tell you about it."

Tucker had a hunting camp near Indian Pass, high in one of the most beautiful reaches of the Alaska Range. In May 1952 he walked alone to the head of a broad valley and sat there sweeping the magnificent scenery with binoculars, looking for a grizzly bear. Suddenly he became aware of something behind him. He whirled to see a wolverine, about fifteen feet away, slowly bellying along a big snowbank toward him. Beady, dark eyes met his startled look.

Dave leaped up, snatching his rifle. At this the wolverine stopped, stood on hind legs for a moment like a miniature bear, then dropped to all fours, snarled once, and bounded away into the valley.

Tucker concluded the story with the remark, "Yeah, I think he'd have jumped on me if I hadn't seen him. He wasn't stalking me for the fun of it."

Dick Ragle, who was the Air Force officer in charge of search and rescue in Alaska during World War II, was a geology professor at the University of Alaska, Fairbanks, when I knew him as a fellow faculty member. Here's Ragle's story:

One fall during the war a training plane with a student pilot and an instructor crashed among the steep, glacier-studded Alaskan peaks. Under Ragle's direction, search planes spent days looking for it. Winter snows covered the plane before it was found. It lay there all winter with the bodies of the two men still inside.

A wolverine, traveling above timberline, found the wreck with its two occupants. It dug a tunnel through the snow to the crumpled fuselage, clawed its way inside, then lived on the bodies for much of the winter.

The wreck was found in the spring. Only bones were left of the two men, and there were still wolverine tracks near, with wolverine hair snagged in the jagged metal fuselage of the plane.

All wolverine tales aren't so grim. This one came to me from Jim Brooks, one of my former wildlife students and a frequent hunting companion.

Bill White, an old-timer, ran a trapline in the Bristol Bay region. When marten season opened one mid-November, he and a cheechako (greenhorn) boy set traps in the cubbies, or shelters, hanging a lure nearby, generally a feather, so it swayed about to attract the curious little creatures. The cheechako, who had never seen a marten, wanted to know how to kill one in a trap.

"That's easy," Bill grunted. "Ya just step on 'em with your snowshoes and squeeze their heart until they stop moving. But don't worry about it. Most of them'll be dead when you find 'em anyway."

When they first went to check traps Bill took off one way, the cheechako the other. The boy found the first four or five traps undisturbed, then came upon one of the larger traps, which held a ferocious, growling victim.

If the cheechako thought anything, it must have been that he had an all-fired big marten. Boldly, he jammed one of his snowshoes on top of the threatening animal. Powerful jaws ripped at it, and it took some time to wrench the shredded shoe free.

A couple of hours after dark the boy came staggering to the home cabin. His snowshoes were wrecked, and his pants were in shreds. He was cut and scratched. And he was angry.

"Bill," he burst out, "I'll take your word for it that you don't have any trouble killing your marten when you find 'em alive in your traps. But, by gosh, I'm carrying a rifle after this when I run my half of the line."

With that he shrugged out of his packboard and dumped a dead wolverine in front of the gawking Bill.

Northern Indians and Eskimos, who for generations before Columbus proved their ability to survive in the Arctic, have many legends about the wolverine.

A bush pilot friend of mine was winging his way along the bleak arctic coast, accompanied by a young Eskimo named Robert. Suddenly they spotted a wolverine on the snow beneath. They buzzed the animal, and it buried itself into a deep drift.

My friend landed the ski plane near the wolverine and, envisioning a new lining for his parka ruff, told Robert to go shoot it while he kept the engine running.

Robert, an intelligent young Native, stared at him in horror. "I don't want anything to do with that wolverine," he said, shaking his head.

My friend was amazed. He had seen the young Inuit hunt walrus from a frail skin boat and shoot polar bears from close range. The danger of sea ice was nothing to him. But a thirty-pound wolverine: that was different.

Finally, Robert cautiously approached the half-buried wolverine and shot it. Even then he was nervous when he picked up the dead animal to return to the plane.

The Koyukons, a branch of the Athabascan Indians, live along the Koyukuk and lower Yukon Rivers. The Koyukons call the wolverine Doyon, which is derived from the Russian Toyon, which means chief, or great man.

Jimmy Sam, a Koyukon, was trapping marten when a wolverine showed up on his trapline and started to beat Jimmy to the animals in his traps. Jimmy found mostly shredded fur and a few bones where the wolverine had robbed his traps and eaten the catch. Until the wolverine was trapped, Jimmy knew he wouldn't get many furs.

Cutting the head from a recently killed caribou, Jimmy tied it firmly several feet off the ground to a tree. In the snow beneath it he buried three #4 traps.

The wolverine soon found the head, circled suspiciously, carefully stepping around the traps. He then stood on hind legs to grasp the caribou head. It wouldn't move. He yanked and pulled, becoming more angry by the minute. Finally he forgot where he was putting his big ivory-clawed feet. In moments two of the traps had him in their cold grip.

When the trapper arrived, a quick rap on the nose with a stout club finished the wolverine. Jimmy returned to his village with his catch, skinned it, and then well away from the village, he carefully and respectfully burned the carcass.

The wolverine has a well-deserved reputation for being powerful for his size. A big wolverine might weigh thirty-five pounds; most adults weigh from twenty-five to thirty pounds. It is largely because of the wolverine (and bears) that trappers, miners, and others who live in the Alaska wilderness must build a cache—a safe place to store food, furs, and other items. Many caches are built atop four stout logs wrapped with slippery tin to keep wolverines from climbing. Unoccupied log cabins must be stout. Bears as well as wolverine like to break into cabins that smell of food.

Warren "Tillie" Tilman, a Fairbanks guide, once trapped with Old Bill Crow in the Chugach Range up where the foaming Matanuska River roars into being. This was around 1925 or 1930, and when Tillie told me the story in the mid-1950s, he clearly remembered details of Bill's wolverine experience.

At the start of one trapping season Old Bill left his base camp and snowshoed to one of his line shacks. He knew something was wrong almost as soon as the little cabin came into view. A hole had been gnawed in the lower corner of the door. Several long brown-and-black guard hairs were stuck to the wood at the hole.

Inside, the once-neat cabin looked as if it has been turned upside down. Pots and pans, chewed-open cans of food, flour, coffee, tea, and cornmeal littered the floor; the stove was pushed on its side, as were the table and benches. A mattress, caribou hide, and sleeping robe that had hung on a wire from the ridgepole had been pulled down and systematically shredded. Waterfowl down from the expensive robe was scattered throughout the cabin, along with caribou hair and mattress stuffing.

To cause such destruction the wolverine had to first claw through a foot of sod on the roof, then gnaw through a layer of three-inch spruce poles. Since he was unable to climb out where he had entered, he finished up by gnawing his way out the door.

Further inspection showed Bill that the wolverine had also managed to climb into his nearby pole-cache, despite the tin-wrapped legs. It, too, was a mess.

Bill got his revenge three or four days later. He returned from his trapline to find a spitting-mad wolverine hanging from three huge fishhooks halfway up one pole of the cache—a trap he had set, hoping for a return of Mr. Wolverine.

Ray Woolford, enforcement chief for the U.S. Fish and Wildlife Service in Alaska in the 1950s, told me about Edwin, an Indian trapper in the arctic Koyukuk country. Edwin had a bush pilot fly him to a lake along the Koyukuk River. The ski plane landed on crusted snow of a lonely spruce-rimmed lake, where Edwin and the pilot unloaded a trapping outfit of grub, clothing, sleeping bag, traps, and dried salmon dog food. Edwin placed his rifle on top of the pile. Then he and the pilot flew back to his village for Edwin's dog team.

As the plane landed next to the pile of gear left earlier, the men discovered a wolverine had been there. Its tracks were everywhere around the pile where it had ripped a sleeping bag open, and where it had clawed or bitten into a few other items, but apparently everything was still there.

But wait, where's the rifle?

The wolverine had carried it off. And though Edwin tried trailing the animal, he lost the tracks in a maze of caribou tracks. He searched for several days, but never found the rifle.

I've never heard of a bear or a wolf or any other wild animal packing things off as wolverines occasionally do. One of the strange aspects of wolverine vandalism is the items they sometimes lug off. Sprung traps, a compass, a sheath knife, tools, and pans have all been packed off and cached by various wolverines I've heard of. His behavior gives the impression of a tough little devil-may-care bandit. He's different. Perhaps that's why legends grow in his wake.

George Bishop, a long-time big game guide, once watched two wolverines on the Alaska Peninsula for several hours as they teased an old brown bear sow and her two cubs. He saw the two cubs legging it for ma, wide open, with two wolverines chasing them. The mother stood up and leaped toward the pursuers a few times, and they hightailed it, but not far. Soon they were back, hounding the bears. Several times in the next few hours the wolverines actually got themselves between the mother and her cubs. When that happened they really had to scoot to escape to thick alders ahead of the old lady.

Were they playing? Teasing? Did they think they could catch and kill one of the cubs for food? What were two wolverines, generally antisocial creatures, doing together in the spring, anyway, when it isn't even their breeding season?

The behavior of most of our large mammals is fairly predictable. Not that of the wolverine. He's different, and hard to understand. That's what makes him so interesting. My fix on it? Any animal that would tease a quarter-ton brown bear has to be crazy—or it just doesn't give a damn.

This article appeared in *The Star Weekly Magazine,* Toronto, on November 29, 1958.

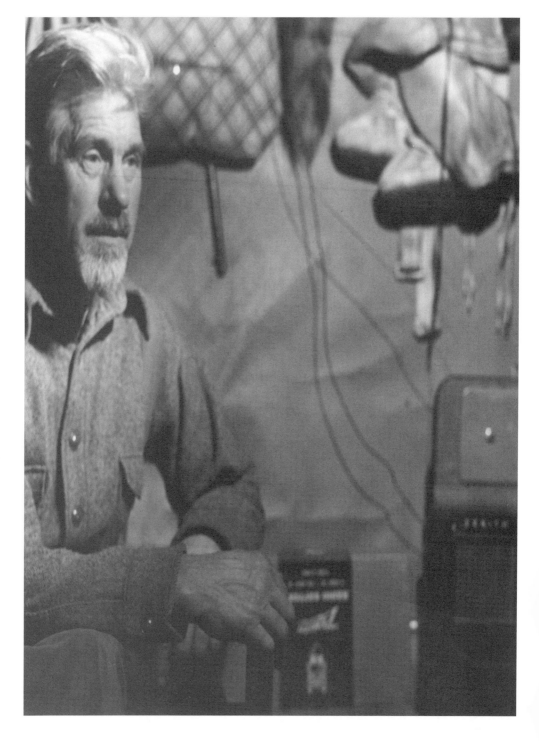

CHAPTER FOURTEEN

VOICE IN THE WILDERNESS

For many years beginning in the 1940s, few people in any village or lonely trapping cabin within range of radio station KFAR's 10,000-watt transmitter ever missed the program called Tundra Topics. *This ten-minute program, aired six nights a week on the Fairbanks station, was the bulletin board, mailbox, and newspaper to thousands of isolated people living in subarctic and arctic Alaska.*

On the program, listeners might hear birth announcements, news of a death, word that groceries would be flown to someone's solitary cabin soon, or simply that a traveler from the bush had reached Fairbanks safely. Anything and everything that might be of interest or importance to residents of the lonely Alaska wilderness was broadcast over this interesting and intimate program.

It was 45 degrees below zero on a black night on Christmas Eve 1954 when thousands of Alaskans in remote villages scattered from the arctic coast to the Alaska

Trapper Slim Carlson in his cabin with his beloved radio. He often listened to foreign stations, comparing their reports of news with the American version. He never missed "Tundra Topics" if he could help it. JIM REARDEN PHOTO

Range heard a familiar voice on their radios make an urgent request: "Will the people at Manley Hot Springs put some lanterns on the airstrip at 10:30? Bob Byers expects to be over the village at that time and he will need lights in order to find the strip and land. Also, please have the sick man at the landing strip. Byers will fly him to the hospital immediately."

A shortwave message from the little village telling of a sudden illness had reached Fairbanks. Byers, who provided air service for Manley Hot Springs, had immediately requested Fairbanks radio station KFAR to make the announcement over the one program he knew everyone in the village would be listening to.

Then he ordered his airplane warmed for the dangerous flight, confident the dark airstrip would be lighted.

The lanterns were there. Byers made his landing, and in a few moments thundered off the snow in his ski plane. Through the pitch-black, frigid darkness he flew old-timer Pete Johnson, who had suffered a stroke, back to the hospital at Fairbanks.

The radio program over which the emergency message had been broadcast was *Tundra Topics.*

"*Tundra Topics* reflects the most colorful life of Alaska. It is close to nature, and we try to keep it that," said Alvin O. Bramstedt, who was manager of the Midnight Sun Broadcasting Company in the 1950s. When the program was inaugurated in 1943, with a local bank as sponsor, no one envisioned the importance it was to assume to people in the vast bush country of interior Alaska.

At first the program consisted of a few news notes, such as, "Pat Savage was in town today" or "Lobo Houston is wintering at Circle Hot Springs again this year." Gradually, more helpful personal items were added, and many bush residents began to depend on the program for help in delivering messages that might not otherwise be delivered for weeks, or even months.

Federal Communications Commission regulations forbade a commercial station to send personal messages from point to point, so a bush pilot's message to a resident would come out like the following actual transmission: "Ole Olson's generator has broken down again, and pilot Frank Jones has dropped the needed part on the river ice above the bridge at Ole's place. A red streamer is attached to the box." A legitimate news item had been made of the message—and Ole Olson learns that his part has been delivered, and he knows where to look for it.

In the isolated villages and lonely cabins where mail delivery was slow at best, the popularity of the program snowballed. Soon, at 9:30 each evening, six nights a week, bush country talk ceased, potlatches were recessed, and for ten minutes careful attention centered on battery-powered radios. Trappers hurried their dog teams home in time for the broadcast, and if they missed a program they worried about it, sometimes for weeks, fearing they had missed news of personal interest

Bill Eiseinminger, a trapper on the Goodpaster River, came in from his trapline late one night and heard the last part of a message about a cabin in Fairbanks that had burned. The more he thought about it the more convinced he became that it was his cabin. He worried and thought about it all winter. When spring came and the ice went out, he built a raft and hauled enough household goods from his remote trapping cabin to set up housekeeping in town. He was amazed to arrive in Fairbanks to find his cabin still standing, as good as ever.

It would be impossible to estimate how many lives were saved directly or indirectly by *Tundra Topics.* Requesting villagers to furnish emergency lighting for lonely airstrips when illness strikes was not unusual.

Sometimes it was the faithfulness of the listeners that saved their own lives, such as the case of the family that bought potatoes at a trading post on the Yukon River and soon departed by boat to return to their remote cabin. The clerk who had sold the potatoes was horrified to learn, a day later, that they had been poison-treated seed potatoes.

A shortwave radio message was sent to KFAR, and that evening the family learned, in time, how close they had come to serious illness or even death.

One winter listeners heard that a flying missionary, the Reverend Walter Hannum, had called KFAR, informing the station that he had flown over the John Larson cabin that day and was unable to see any signs of life— no tracks in the snow, and no smoke coming from the chimney. He said he expected a dog team from Rampart to be sent to the cabin immediately to see if Larson was all right. The people in Rampart got the message, a dog team was sent, and Larson was found to be all right. But it could have turned out differently.

Sometimes a life-giving message for a tuberculosis-afflicted Indian was transmitted, informing him that a bed was awaiting him at a sanatorium and that he was to immediately fly in, at the Territory's expense, to report for treatment.

Some items were heartbreaking. Edwin Simon, an Indian trapper at Huslia on the Koyukuk River, near the Arctic Circle, once told me he heard via *Tundra Topics* that his tubercular son, 130 miles away at the Tanana Hospital, was failing and that if Edwin wanted to see him again, he should get there soon.

Next morning, early, two different bush pilots who had also heard the broadcast arrived to fly Edwin to the hospital. He saw his son once more before the boy died.

Another message that must have caused listeners to look at each other sorrowfully was, "Here is a news item of interest from Dr. L. L. Disoway at Fort Yukon that will sadden Joe Netro and Mrs. Kirk at Old Crow village in Yukon Territory. Little Billy's condition became worse and he passed away on December 12th."

Most of the broadcasts dealt with everyday matters:
"Mrs. Red Anderson is having twenty-five pounds of salmon strips, a keg of salmon bellies, and a shipment of dried fish flown to her by Byers' plane tomorrow. Peter Evans will be putting the fish on the plane for her." Peter Evans takes the hint, and Mrs. Anderson gets her fish.

"Albert Pitts at Big Lake will be interested to know that Jack has received the spare parts OK." Everyone in the area of Big Lake knows what the message means, though it probably piques the curiosity of other listeners.

Bush pilot Frank Barr flew over a tractor train crawling across the wintry Alaskan wilderness toward the arctic village of Wiseman and noticed that the driver had taken a wrong turn. He notified *Tundra Topics.* The cat skinner heard the broadcast, turned his train around, and went back to take the correct trail.

One woman wanted her husband, on his trapline, to "please come home to cut some wood so she and the kids can stay warm."

And this message during a spell of minus 50-degree temperatures: "Mrs. Rita Scott, of Fairbanks, informed us today that her husband, a pilot-biologist with the U.S. Fish and Wildlife Service, is weather bound at Hughes. Mrs. Scott added that she, the furnace, the house, and the child are getting along fine, but the car needs Mr. Scott quite badly at this time." Scott heard the message all right, but he couldn't do much about it.

"Mrs. Margaret Williams of Galena is feeling much better in St. Joseph's hospital." The message eases a village family's worries.

"Pilot Frank Barr would like to pass along to the people at Caribou Creek that he was unable to land on his way back from the Fortymile today because of mechanical difficulties." The message is likely greeted with sighs of relief, for the bush pilot is a solid link with the world to countless residents of the bush. When he doesn't arrive on schedule and the weather is good, apprehension mounts about his safety.

"Our friend Fred Pitts at Big Lake is probably wondering about his mail. Wien Airlines has tried to get there three times, but has had to return each time because of weather." The message explains something that Pitts probably was worried about.

"The dentist will be at the Tanana hospital on the fifteenth. Those wishing dental care should come to the hospital." This message could be good news for an isolated trapper with an aching tooth.

"Bob Rice Air Taxi will be in Wiseman Thursday afternoon at four to pick up Joe Ulen and bring him to Fairbanks. Ulen has an appointment with Dr. Hugh Fate at 9:30 Friday morning." This could be the first news that Ulen has of the appointment. Such arrangements were often left to the bush pilot, the doctor, and not infrequently to KFAR.

"A plane will arrive at Minto tomorrow morning to pick up a group of children coming in for the clinic. The plane will leave Minto sharply at eight o'clock, so the children can keep their nine o'clock appointments." The message no doubt causes excitement among the Native children in the tiny village fifty miles west of Fairbanks.

Other important functions of *Tundra Topics* were to keep listeners posted on fur prices, movements of the freight-hauling sternwheel riverboats on the big rivers, fishing conditions, location and movement of caribou herds, and road and airstrip conditions.

Travelers were cautioned to dress warmly while riding bush planes in extremely cold weather. Important national and local news was aired, but politics, murders, and non-pertinent unpleasant news was not. The weather forecast was given immediately following the program.

Perhaps a city dweller doesn't understand the feeling of joy of a couple far out in the bush when they hear, "A grocery order has been filled for Al and Lila Kinz, at Tibbs Creek, and it will be dropped by plane in a day or two."

But other bush residents do. *Tundra Topics* is truly a voice in the wilderness.

KFAR no longer broadcasts Tundra Topics. *Almost every Alaska village now has modern telephone service, and the need for programs like* Tundra Topics *has decreased. However, several stations still broadcast similar programs that isolated bush residents without regular telephone service continue to rely on.*

This article appeared in *The Alaska Sportsman*
in September 1956.

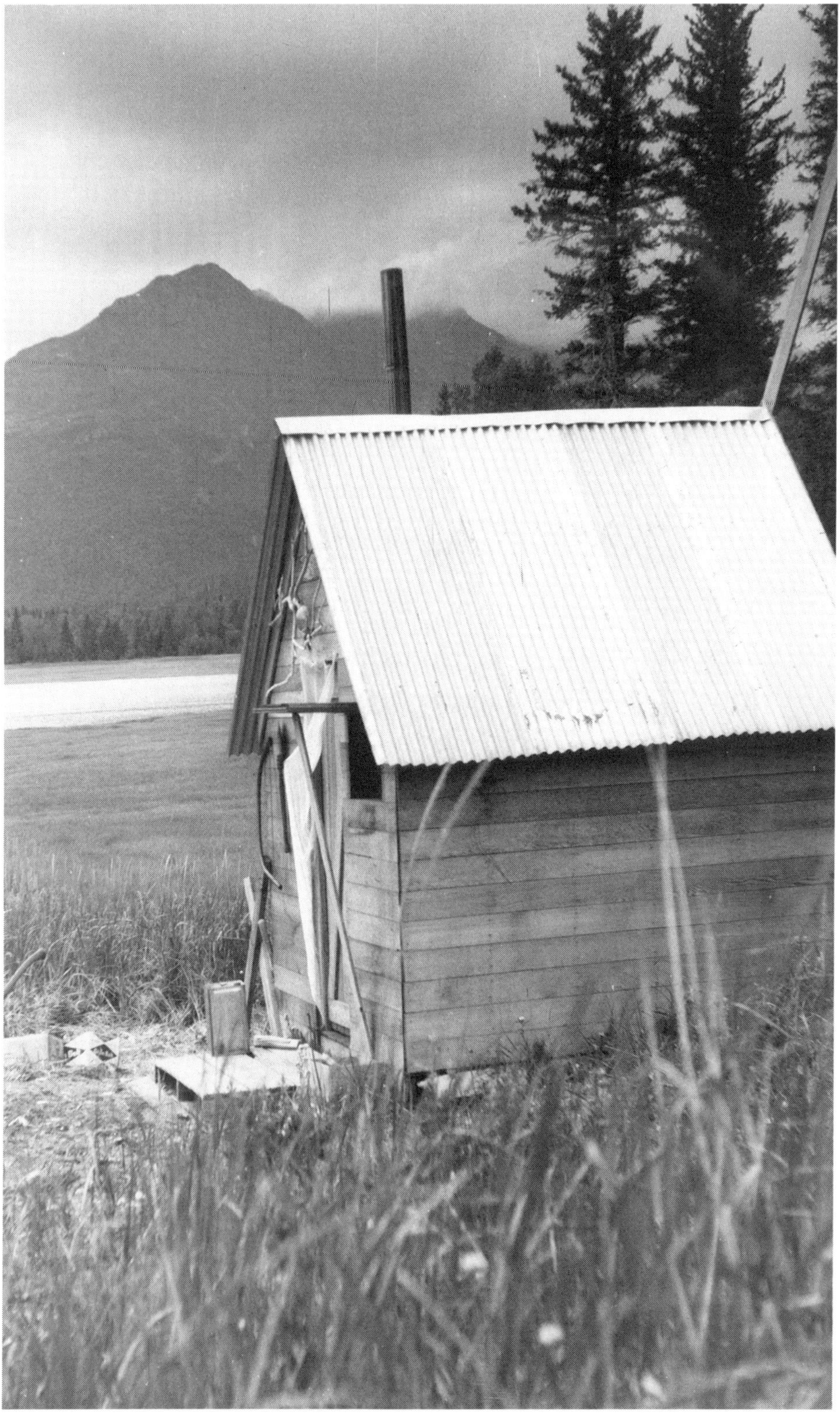

CHAPTER FIFTEEN

STREAM GUARD

This story is based on events experienced over a period of several years by a number of different stream guards— individuals who were hired by the federal government and, later, the state to prevent illegal fishing at the mouths of salmon streams in Alaska. The names of people and places are fictional, including that of the flying Russian Orthodox priest, although there were and are such priests in Alaska.

The young hero of this story is based partially on an actual stream guard who earned the nickname Dirty Neck because his cabin was always dirty, his clothing was dirty, and, of course, his neck was dirty. This wasn't unusual; some of the young stream guards the state hired were on their own for the first time in their lives with no mother to nag them into cleanliness.

In the 1960s when I wrote "Stream Guard," my first work of fiction, I was area management biologist in charge of Cook Inlet's commercial fisheries for the Alaska Department of Fish and Game.

A stream guard shack at Chinitna Bay, on the west side of Cook Inlet, about 1959. These tiny shelters were sturdy and easily warmed with a small woodstove. The federal government built shacks like this one near the mouths of many salmon streams throughout the Territory.   JIM REARDEN PHOTO

The inlet was too rough for Jerry to patrol, so he was sitting on a hillside watching with binoculars when the gray boat bucked weather up the inlet to Kamaluk River. He saw her pull into the stream, then a net was dropped over, and pursed. The two fishermen—he could clearly see the red beard on one—were hoisting salmon aboard.

It happened so quickly that Jerry didn't realize what happened until the boat was a speck down the inlet, heading toward a cannery, her hold full of illegally caught salmon.

Jerry was of average height, skinny and thin-faced, with serious blue eyes. His eyes became even more serious as he brooded over the raid, for his job was to protect salmon in the river, and he had failed. Despite the rough water he should have taken the outboard-powered patrol skiff and at least tried to catch the boat.

He doubled his efforts, often patrolling the choppy water all day, pushing the big state skiff until he was soaked and chilled. Often it was near midnight with the sun dipping from sight, with winds from the glacier-studded peaks burning like ice, before he returned to the warmth of his cabin.

When he had applied for the job it looked like a featherbed, a paid vacation. The Alaska Department of Fish and Game was paying him—a nineteen-year-old from Oregon—to guard salmon in Kamaluk River. They were the spawners, the future of the species in that river. There were two big orange-and-white signs a mile each way from the river mouth, and no commercial fishing was allowed between them or in the river. He was instructed to enforce that regulation by patrolling Kamaluk River and the inlet around it with the twenty-foot skiff.

He had quickly learned that nothing was easy at Kamaluk River. The stove was ancient and wouldn't burn properly for him. Either the wood fire went out, or it roared as if to engulf the cabin. He ate burned eggs, and his coffee was either watery or it tasted like turpentine. When he tried to patrol, he often found his skiff aground where dropping tide had left it and he had to wait for high tide for it to refloat.

His dishes always seemed to be dirty, his sleeping bag was cold and clammy. Mornings, his new hip boots felt like wet sponges. His clothing became grimy.

He didn't sleep well because it was light most of the time. No one had told him that the summer sun in Alaska hardly sets. The noisy gulls and eagles feeding on spawned-out salmon along the river never seemed to sleep.

He was homesick, tired of poor food, tired of being dirty, tired of sleeping cold. Days he fought the tide and the big skiff, nights he endured his loneliness and discomfort in the tiny cabin.

The floatplane landed on the afternoon of his tenth day and taxied ashore. The man who had hired him (Jerry thought of him as the warden; Alaska called him a protection officer) climbed out. His tanned face looked tired, but the crow's-foot-wrinkled eyes were pleasant, the slow smile friendly. "How's it goin', Jerry?" he asked, looking at Jerry's dirty clothing, the high-and-dry skiff.

"I'd like to leave," Jerry answered. It was hard to say, but he managed it.

The warden showed no surprise. He opened the cabin door and looked at the dirty dishes, the cluttered floor, the scattered clothing.

Jerry suddenly felt ashamed.

"You mean you want to quit?" The warden's voice was impersonal.

"Yeah, that's it," he answered in a subdued voice.

The warden nodded thoughtfully. Year after year cheechako (newcomer) kids like this showed up in Alaska and were hired as stream guards because most Alaskans were already occupied. It was difficult to find good men for the jobs.

"OK, Jerry. But I'd appreciate it if you would stay until I get a man to replace you."

Perhaps he hadn't intended to emphasize the *man* so much, but it came out that way, and Jerry understood.

"I think I could do the job all right," he said. "I guess I'm not the type for it is all," he finished lamely. He couldn't remember all the reasons for quitting now.

"It may take a few days," the warden said. And then, grimly, "In the meantime I'd clean up that pigpen you're living in. Camping isn't bad if you do it right. Cut a pile of dry firewood, and wash dishes when you finish eating. Air your bedding on good days, and for heaven's sake put some soap and water in a bucket and boil those dirty clothes. Maybe things'll look different to you then."

Jerry didn't change all at once; his bad habits were too strong. But he tried. He washed dishes, scrubbed the floor, and aired his sleeping bag so that he slept warm. After a few days he shaved a bar of soap into a bucket of water and boiled the clothes he wasn't wearing.

When rinsed his underwear looked more gray than white, and there were stains left on the jeans, but at least they didn't smell bad. They certainly felt better.

He started sawing dry wood daily. Eventually he was forced to clean ashes out of the stove, after which it began to behave. Finally he tied a rope across the river and fastened a pulley he found in the cabin to the middle of it so he could stand on the beach and pull his skiff into deep water and still retrieve it when he wanted. That way it was always afloat and ready for him to go on patrol.

One day he took the rifle the warden had left with him ("Don't use it unless you have to, but there are big bears here," he had said) and walked upstream to count spawning salmon as he had been instructed.

He found huge bear tracks and remnants of salmon upon which they had fed. The river was alive with salmon; they swirled in pools at his approach, fins and tails plunking the water. He estimated their numbers by counting groups of twenty-five, as the warden had instructed. He came to a quiet stretch and sat to watch.

Fish were paired. Males were brick red and yellow, their backs humped, big teeth showing. They little resembled the fat, silvery fish that had skittered noisily into the river near his cabin.

A female digging a nest in the clear water industriously scrubbed at the bottom with her bleeding tail. Her mate hovered near. Jerry watched fascinated as finally she turned on her side and in an agony of effort extruded the orange eggs, most of which adhered to the gravel in the nest. The male beside her quickly fertilized them, the white milt from his body appearing briefly and then sweeping away with the current.

The female started to cover the now fertile eggs.

The adults, after spawning, would drift off and die; salmon that would hatch from the eggs would return to the Kamaluk River in four years. Future runs of salmon lay with the eggs.

Back at his cabin the sight of half-a-dozen fishing boats anchored nearby came as a shock. But they were all within the legal fishing area. He sighed with relief. Not yet would he have to test his courage with lawbreakers.

After supper he sat on the stoop looking at the boats. Smoke curled upward from heating and cooking stoves, skiffs bobbed at their sterns, and he faintly heard men's voices and music from a radio. It was companionship of sorts, but he was too shy to take his skiff out to visit. Next day they were gone.

Jerry was shoving off in the skiff when the warden's plane appeared, circled, and whistled in for a landing. He was alone. "I haven't found anyone to replace you yet," he said. "How're you doing?"

"Pretty good I guess. I was just leaving to patrol," he answered.

Jerry realized he had been dreading the return of the warden, and suddenly he knew he didn't want to leave.

"I wonder if I could change my mind. I think I'd like to stay now," he said.

The warden didn't answer. Instead he tied the airplane and walked to the cabin. The dishes were clean, the bed neat, the floor swept. Dry wood was piled near the door.

"Things look better now, huh?" he said. "Sure, I'll be glad to have you stay. It's tough to get good men for stream guard jobs," he answered.

He hadn't emphasized the word *men,* but the kid could have sworn he did.

The days shortened, with more dark at night, and salmon ceased running into the Kamaluk. Jerry had come to like his work, and even the solitude didn't bother him much now. No fisherman had been near for several weeks when one day a boat ran into the river, dropped anchor, and a man rowed a skiff ashore.

"Allo," he greeted. "I'm Eric Johnson. "I'm s'posed to take you 'cross inlet to Port Chugach. Your boss wants you to go to anot'er crick where some late pinks are runnin'."

Eric helped him nail shutters over the windows, grease the stove to keep it from rusting, and hang the mattress with wire from the ceiling to keep mice from it. Last, they barred the door. "That'll keep bears out, I t'ink," Eric said.

A howling norther caught them halfway across the eighty-mile stretch of open inlet, and Jerry got seasick. He fell into a bunk, but was pitched onto the deck where he remained, his emptied stomach tied in knots, his head whirling.

Eric didn't laugh. "I us't get seasick as a boy."

Jerry awoke in a bunk, covered with a blanket, sunlight streaming through a porthole. They were in port, tied alongside another boat.

The warden soon arrived in his plane. "We're short of boats," he explained. "I've got to find you a ride to Humpy Bay."

They found a grubby little tub that belonged to Jimmy Petrofsky and his fat wife. "Yeah, we go Humpy Bay," Jimmy told the warden. "Sure, we take stream guard wid' us. Glad to help."

Jerry piled his duffel into his state skiff, tied it behind Jimmy's boat, and rushed to a general store for groceries. He hurried back, for Jimmy had said he was leaving in an hour or so.

The hour dragged into three as Jerry sat on the dock. Jimmy and his wife had sauntered down the board sidewalk of the fishing village after telling Jerry, "We get grub."

It was late afternoon when the Petrofskys returned, Jimmy with a box of groceries and half a jug of wine. He and his wife staggered aboard and settled like dirty seagulls on the afterdeck, where they silently passed the jug back and forth. The red stuff trickled off their chins and dribbled slowly down their necks.

The jug empty, Jimmy crashed it violently against a barnacled piling and growled, "Le'sh go fish'n."

He stumbled into the cabin and started the engine. It roared loudly. Jimmy yelled to his wife, "Turn 'er loosh." She clumsily threw the lines off and Jimmy slammed into reverse, backed into another boat, bounced, rammed forward as he spun the wheel, ricocheted off another boat, narrowly missed a dock, skinned by a buoy, and headed out the bay. Yells of anger and amusement floated in their wake.

Jimmy waved Jerry inside, but when he whiffed the combination of boozy breath, hot engine oil, and cooking odors in the cabin, his stomach rebelled. He chose to stand near the open door, watching Jimmy guide the boat carelessly out the bay. It was a sunny afternoon and the day breeze had kicked up a lively swell. The old boat rolled and pitched spiritedly. Jerry got seasick again, and clung to the rail, feet braced, spray drenching him.

He wondered why he had been so stupid as to keep this stream guard job.

Toward evening a gentle rain started. The wind dropped, the boat plowed over gentle swells, and Jerry recovered. Jimmy had unearthed another jug of wine and while piloting the boat had managed to swig a fourth of it. He was literally clinging to the wheel to stay upright. His wife snored loudly from a bunk.

Jerry rummaged and found a marine chart, located Humpy Bay. "Jimmy, is that Indian Island?" he asked the drunken fisherman, pointing.

He had to repeat the question. "Yah, Ind'n Island there," Jimmy agreed. And pointing, "Humpy Bay over dere."

"Jimmy, I'll steer," Jerry suggested. "You get some sleep."

"OK," the sodden man agreed, releasing the wheel and collapsing in a bunk.

Two hours later Jerry nosed the old tub into Humpy Bay, dropped the anchor, and turned the engine off. He then sat leaning against the pilot house bulkhead and dozed off with the snoring of the drunken Petrofskys and the drumming of rain in his ears.

Someone stumbled over his feet, and he awoke to find Jimmy's wife standing over him, looking at him with bleary eyes.

"Who you?" she grunted.

He came to his feet and started to walk past her when Jimmy stumbled toward them and saw Jerry apparently standing in his wife's arms. He swung wildly at the kid, missed, and fell against his wife. Both rolled in a heap on deck, cursing.

Jerry fled to his skiff. By the time Jimmy and his unlovely spouse had reached deck, he was headed up the bay toward the salmon stream he had been sent to guard.

He found the stream markers, pitched the tent the warden had left with him, cut firewood, and prepared for his stay. Later that afternoon, as smoke poured lazily upward from the tent stovepipe and he was cutting more wood, a plane circled, landed on the bay, and taxied ashore.

Jerry thought it was the warden, but the man who climbed out was dressed in black, with a white collar. "I'm Father Kozminof, the Russian Orthodox priest," he said. "My good friend the warden told me he had sent you here with, ah, the Petrofskys. I learned they were drinking when they left Port Chugach, so I stopped to see if you had any trouble getting here."

"No trouble, Father. Thanks for stopping. Would you care to have supper with me?"

The priest joined him in his simple meal, sitting on the canvas cot inside the tent as Jerry prepared it. He knew more about the habits of salmon than anyone with whom Jerry had talked, and Jerry asked dozens of questions.

"Salmon are the mainstay in the economy of my people, and I've made it my business to learn as much as I can about them," the priest explained.

As he left he promised to try to stop for another visit. He often flew over Humpy Bay, he said. Many small floatplanes flew over, Jerry soon noticed, for it lay between Port Chugach and another fishing village.

Days passed. Salmon swam upstream, spawned, and died, and gulls, eagles, crows, and ravens quarreled over their rotting carcasses. A few boats caught fish legally outside the stream markers and went on. Nights lengthened and became darker. A fresh run of pink salmon schooled off the mouth of the stream, awaiting the mysterious signal that would send them splashing upstream. They constantly leaped and skittered across the quiet green waters of the bay.

One day a gray boat nosed into the bay and ran up the stream, scattering the salmon. A huge red-bearded fisherman leaned over the side, watching the fish.

Jerry pushed his beached skiff into the water, started the outboard, and ran to the fishing boat. "Would you please move outside the markers?" he requested.

"We have as much right to be here as anybody. Those your fish?" Redbeard sneered.

Jerry's face went white with anger. He had been fairly certain this was the boat he had watched rob Kamaluk River. Now he was sure.

In answer Jerry recorded in his notebook the name *Flo* that appeared in tiny letters on the boat, then rowed to the port side, where he could see the license plate required of commercial fishing boats in Alaska. He wrote down the number, pointedly ignoring Redbeard, who stood watching.

"I'll ask you again," he said in a level voice. He was shaking, and afterwards he wasn't sure if it was from nervousness or anger.

"And what'll you do, sonny, if I don't move," Redbeard challenged. But somehow Jerry sensed the man was not as sure of himself as he had been.

"I'll cite you into court for harassing salmon," he said firmly.

Redbeard blustered and finally sneered, "We'll move, all right. But not because you tell us to. This is a lousy place to anchor."

With that he moved the boat a few hundred feet away and splashed his anchor overboard. He and his helper, a sallow-faced boy of about fifteen, disappeared into the cabin for the remainder of the day, where they apparently slept.

Once, late in the day, a small floatplane buzzed over, circled the anchored boat once, then went on. Jerry thought it was the warden, but he wasn't certain.

The *Flo* was still anchored, no lights showing, no sign of life, when darkness came. It was now August, with a few hours of darkness at night. Jerry was suspicious. Instead of going to bed he quietly sat near a dark spruce tree, his sleeping bag thrown over him to ward off the chill. The prickly needles of the tree urged him awake from time to time.

Near midnight a muffled rattle drifted across the water. The shadow of a mountain darkened most of the water, but nearby star reflections glinted from the pulsing sea. He saw the seine skiff, then shortly the *Flo.* It was high tide and the fishermen were rowing and towing the *Flo* into the stream mouth.

"Make sure they get a few fish aboard," the warden had told him, in giving instructions on how to handle a violation. "They can claim they were doing practically anything if they don't have fish aboard, and you'll be laughed right out of court."

He waited, shivering with excitement—or was it the cold?—as the two outlaws worked the *Flo* into position and pulled the long seine out with the skiff, worked it around the fish and pulled it alongside, bulging with splashing salmon. Fishermen call this the money bag.

The outlaws started the engine of the *Flo* and idled outside of the markers into open fishing waters. When they passed the markers all attempts at silence stopped. Deck lights went on and the two men began dipping a huge brailing net into the quivering mass, hoisting it with the deck winch and cascading the flopping fish into the hold.

When three brail loads were aboard, Jerry raced to his skiff and sped to the *Flo.* He tied alongside and stepped aboard.

"Turn the rest of 'em loose," he said, his voice loud and steady.

The two fishermen were dipping the brail into a mass of fish in the money bag as he spoke. They stopped and Redbeard, looking surprised, asked, "Why? We're outside the markers."

"You weren't when you seined those fish," Jerry said levelly.

"You're dreaming, punk. Now beat it."

"I said release those fish, and I meant it," Jerry repeated firmly, but wondering if the outlaws could hear his heart pounding.

"Well, now, I don't believe we will," Redbeard said, and he deliberately dipped the brailing net into the fish and signaled his partner to hoist away. The rigging creaked, and the net moved upward a foot.

Jerry yanked out his sheath knife, stepped across the deck, and slashed the line to the brailing net. It dropped and the heavy handle struck Redbeard's belly.

"Now turn them loose," Jerry's voice was firm.

"You little punk, I'll . . ." Redbeard yelled, starting across the deck. Jerry crouched, white-faced, stern, his sheath knife still in his hand, waiting.

Redbeard stopped.

Jerry had the advantage; he must keep it. "You," he said, looking at Redbeard's partner, "get over there and help him release those fish."

Sallow-face moved slowly, but he moved. He fumbled with the lines holding the net, and Redbeard helped.

"You'll regret this," he growled. "We caught these fish legally."

Finally the fish were released. Jerry made them pile their seine on the stern of the *Flo,* where he put a state seal on it—a seal that could only be removed by a law officer or the court. He cited both fishermen into court at Port Chugach for three days hence.

Before leaving the *Flo* he counted 193 fresh salmon in the hold. "When you unload tell the buyer to credit them to the state," he instructed.

He shook for three days. Again and again he drew his sheath knife to look at it, and he lived again the moment when he slashed the line to the brailing net and crouched, waiting to meet Redbeard.

The warden whistled when Jerry told him of his midnight tangle. "You were lucky. He's a nasty one. Gives us problems every season," he said.

"Think my case'll do any good, Warden?" Jerry asked anxiously.

"We'll see," was the smiling answer.

The tiny courtroom was crowded with fishermen. The judge had Jerry stand and swear to tell the truth and describe what had happened.

Redbeard glared across the courtroom as Jerry talked. He told everything he could remember. Once Redbeard shouted, "He's lyin', Judge," but the judge told him to shut up.

The judge asked Jerry a few questions and released him. Redbeard swaggered to the stand.

It was Jerry's turn to feel like yelling, "He's lying," for Redbeard told a convincing tale of having a couple of hundred fish in the hold of the *Flo* when he stopped at Humpy Bay to get some sleep. He had been awakened in the middle of the night by the crazy kid accusing him of catching fish in the creek.

Sallow-face repeated the story convincingly.

The judge said quietly, to himself, "Two against one."

Just then Father Kozminof stood and asked, "May I testify, your honor?"

The judge's eyebrows shot up and his voice was respectful as he said, "Of course, Father."

Jerry looked at the warden, who grinned and looked smug.

The priest was sworn in. He spoke calmly, with a trace of his forefathers' Russian accenting the words.

"It is my understanding that this, uh, incident, occurred last Tuesday."

"Yes, Father. Tuesday night."

"And the vessel *Flo* was the only boat in Humpy Bay late Tuesday afternoon?"

"That is what all three parties have testified."

"Then I believe the stream guard is telling the truth," the priest said.

A sudden buzz of voices flooded the room, and the judge rapped his gavel for silence.

"Please go on, Father."

"I flew from the lower inlet into Port Chugach late that afternoon. I flew over Humpy Bay and saw the *Flo*. I was interested enough to circle, looking to see if there were fish aboard. The hold cover was off, and the hold was empty. I'm afraid our fishermen friends here," a gentle nod toward Redbeard, were not telling the truth when they claimed to have fish aboard when they arrived there."

The verdict was guilty; sentence was loss of the boat and six months in jail for the man who had been stealing fish for years. Sallow-face got three months.

That evening Jerry and the warden sat companionably on the dock. The gulls were quiet. Water chuckled around bobbing fishing boats.

"Warden, you knew Father Kozminof was going to testify, didn't you?" Jerry accused.

"I had a hunch," was the only answer. But the warden grinned.

An eagle sailed over. Gulls perched on pilings turned heads and silently studied it. Jerry and the warden both watched with interest. Smoke from the warden's pipe drifted upward.

"Warden, I like Alaska. I like watching salmon, and, well, I've kind of changed in the last few months. I've been wondering: do you think I could come back and work for you again next season?"

"I've been hoping you'd ask," was the answer.

The federal government, which managed Alaska's fisheries through 1959, used stream guards to watch salmon streams throughout the Territory for many decades. Alaska as a state assumed management of fish and game in 1960, and the stream guard program was continued for five or six years, then it was dropped.

Many professional biologists who worked for the Alaska Department of Fish and Game in the 1960s first came to Alaska to work as stream guards. That was my route to Alaska. In 1947, when I was twenty-two years old and studying fish and game management at Oregon State College, I was hired for the summer by the U.S. Fish and Wildlife Service to be a fishery patrol agent, a position akin to that of stream guard, and I arrived in Alaska from Seattle aboard the FWS vessel Crane.

This article appeared in *Boys' Life* in August 1966.

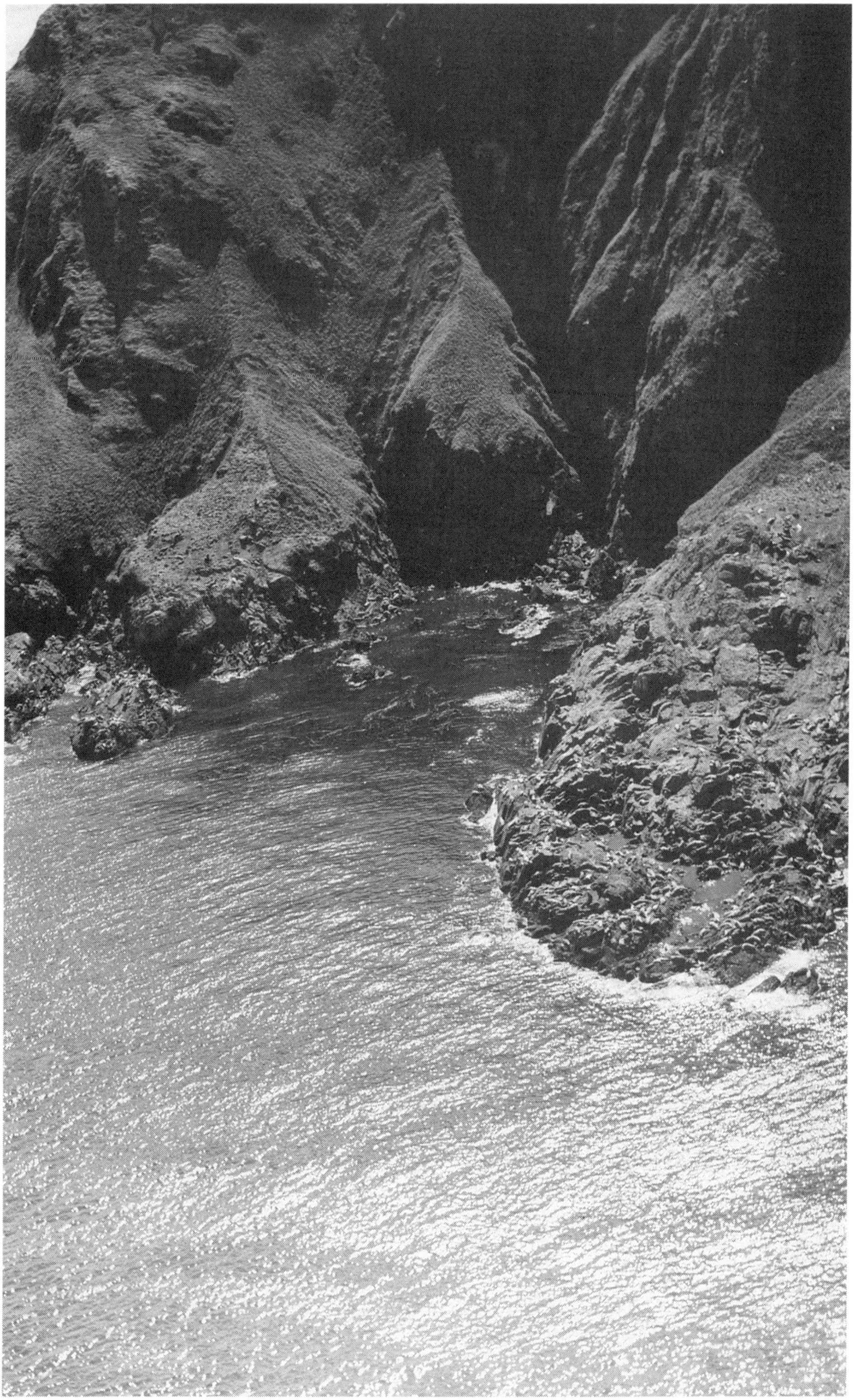

CHAPTER SIXTEEN

HELL ON AN ISLAND

Frank C. Johnson, the subject of this remarkable story, was born and raised at Steubenville, Ohio. After a hitch in the Navy, he married and he and his wife, Cathy, settled in northern California, where he worked as a police officer for five years.

In 1959 he and Cathy moved to Ketchikan, Alaska, where he soon joined the Alaska State Police, serving one year at Anchorage and three at Homer. In 1964 he resigned from the state police and worked as a commercial fisherman, in construction, and as a seal hunter (in the days before the Marine Mammal Act of 1972, which halted all harvesting of marine mammals except by Natives).

This story of his hell on an island is related in his voice.

The hunt started badly. Neither of the two outboard motors on the cabin boat *Eight Ball* would start after I launched. I had to use oars for twenty minutes to push

West Amatuli in the Barren Islands group south of the Kenai Peninsula. It was on nearby East Amatuli that Frank Johnson and his boat were tossed ashore by a vicious storm that trapped him on the uninhabited island.   JIM REARDEN PHOTO through ice floes along the beach of Kachemak Bay, near Homer, at the tip of the Kenai Peninsula, where I live. I finally got one motor started and traveled about eight miles before anchoring for the night. I had tried to find someone to go with me, but the cold, discomfort, and danger of winter hunting had discouraged others. I didn't have enough sense to stay home myself.

Next day, at Seldovia, twenty-five miles across the bay from Homer, I met my friend George Johnson, owner and skipper of the seventy-foot *Jeanette F.* George fishes commercially for king crabs off Kodiak Island in the Gulf of Alaska, and he delivers his catch to Seldovia. As a favor, he had agreed to haul me and my twenty-eight-foot boat across the stretch of storm-racked waters between the Kenai Peninsula and Shuyak or Afognak Island, just north of Kodiak Island.

The *Eight Ball,* built of three-quarter-inch plywood and coated inside and out with fiberglass, was so heavy the winches of the *Jeanette F.* couldn't handle it without assistance from a dock winch. We finally got it aboard, lashed it on the afterdeck, and left Seldovia about 8 o'clock that evening, January 20, 1965.

Seven hours later we were passing through the six Barren Islands, where the twenty-foot tides of Cook Inlet meet the storm-whipped waters of Shelikof Strait and pour together into the Gulf of Alaska. This is a violent storm center; winds in excess of one hundred knots are common. The Barren Islands were named by Captain James Cook in 1778, and he named well. Trees on the islands are stunted or lacking, beaches are mostly precipitous and rocky, tide rips are among the most vicious in Alaska. The islands are uninhabited.

We were going through the pass between the islands of Ushagat and West Amatuli when a sixty-knot nor'easter hit. Within moments we were being rolled violently. The ropes holding the *Eight Ball* broke, and it slammed back and forth, held only by lines tied to the bow. The three crew members and I tried to retie it, but it was all we could do to keep from being swept overboard. All three of us got cuts or smashed fingers. We finally gave up and joined George in the wheelhouse.

The wind and huge waves made it impossible for George to turn the *Jeanette F.* into the weather, so we rolled and pitched in the trough, listening to the *Eight Ball* banging about the stern. I didn't own the *Eight Ball*, but I had promised the owner to make good if I lost it on my hunt. Aboard it I had two outboard motors, a twelve-foot aluminum skiff, six hundred pounds of salt for sealskins, ten plastic garbage cans to keep hides in, a .222 Sako rifle equipped with a 6X scope, a scoped .22 Magnum, a couple of extra rifle scopes, about a thousand rounds of ammunition, 168 gallons of gasoline in two drums, and various outboard tanks, tools, radios, sleeping bags, first-aid kits, and grub. I had spent six hundred dollars for supplies for the hunt, and in all I had about four thousand dollars wrapped up in the boat, equipment, and supplies.

So here I was in danger of losing boat and equipment before I even got started. The *Eight Ball* swung back and forth, threatening for forty-five minutes to go overboard. Then we left the rips and came to some big swells. George could turn into the weather, and we managed to lash *Eight Ball* down again. The only damage was inside the boat: two cases of outboard oil had been smashed, and the oil, mixed with salt water, was spread liberally throughout my gear.

Six hours later we pulled into Perenosa Bay on the north side of Afognak Island and unloaded *Eight Ball.*

"Thanks a lot, George," I said. "I certainly wish I could pay you."

"Not for that trip," he replied.

During the next three weeks I hunted around Shuyak Island, but with only fair success. The wind blew constantly ten to fifty knots, and on some days snow flew by me for hours.

I lived aboard the *Eight Ball* comfortably, with my two-burner gasoline camp stove and single-mantle gas lantern keeping the cabin warm. A few minor incidents marred my hunt, like the day I got careless and dropped my rifle after shooting three seals with it. The eyepiece of the scope was dented, and a chip of glass came out of the ocular end. Several days later I missed five easy shots, then checked the gun on a target and found I was two inches high and three-quarters of an inch right at fifty yards. That's too far off when you're shooting at a bobbing seal's head at ranges up to one hundred yards.

I've never seen a more beautiful place than Shuyak Island with its dozens of inlets and coves. I saw sea and land otters, deer along the beaches, bald eagles, and so many mallard ducks you could have lived on them with a slingshot.

On February 3, I went to Port William and used the radio at the cannery to talk with my wife at Homer. While there I hastily jammed the hides of a dozen seals into one of my plastic garbage cans and had just enough time to get it onto the mail plane. When I arrived home there'd be a check for $198 from those twelve hides—the only income I would have from the trip. During the next week I had my best day, shooting eight seals from one rock and retrieving them all. It was the first calm day in three weeks.

On the morning of February 11, it blew a blizzard, and I holed up. I had about eighteen prime hides aboard that would have averaged twenty-five dollars or more. With the dozen I'd sent from Port William, my expenses would have been covered. Still, hunting had been far from my expectations, so I planned to ship the rest of my hides from

Port William next day, then perhaps hunt my way to Kodiak Island, sixty miles south.

However, on the evening of the eleventh, after a day of blizzard, it suddenly calmed. By 8:00 p.m. the wind had stopped, and the silence was almost unbelievable. The Barren Islands, 20 miles to the north, loomed clearly. I observed the sea carefully. It was calm, with a long, low swell. Suddenly I decided to go home. The *Eight Ball* could travel at about twelve knots, and the twenty miles to the Barren Islands and the remaining twenty miles to the tip of the Kenai Peninsula on the mainland looked like a cinch.

I have never been so wrong.

It was 9:20 p.m. when I left Shangin Bay and headed for the Barrens. The eighteen- and ten-horse motors pushed me along nicely, and we climbed over and dipped between the smooth swells with scarcely a ripple. I reached Ushagat, the main island of the Barrens, around midnight, and I was tired and sleepy. I looked for a place to anchor, found none, and decided to run the five miles to East Amatuli Island. I pulled into Amatuli Cove about 3:30 a.m., dropped anchor, and lay down for a few hours.

I was awakened by the wind screaming through the mast guy lines.

I hurriedly got up, fired up both outboards, pulled anchor, and got out. That nor'wester blew straight into Amatuli Cove. I headed into the wind and went to West Amatuli Island, about a mile and a half away. There I found the wind pouring straight down off the 1,200-foot mountains, and whirlwinds were twisting on the sea's surface. I could find no shelter. The water was beginning to get wild, so I turned and hightailed it back to Amatuli Cove. On the way my eighteen-horse motor stopped, and I had to go the rest of the way with the ten. When I finally dropped my thirty-five-pound anchor in the cove it was daylight.

The wind continued to howl, the air grew colder, and snow started whipping by. I suppose there are a lot of places in the world where it snows horizontally, but I'll bet few see as much horizontal snow as the Barren Islands. The anchor line iced up, and ice started to build on the boat. The swells rolling into the cove splashed water onto the *Eight Ball*, where it froze instantly.

I was about three hundred yards from the beach, but after the snow started I couldn't see it. The wind grew stronger and it swung the boat back and forth in a huge arc. The aluminum skiff, tied astern, followed. At the end of one arc, the wind caught the skiff and flipped it over, dumping my extra survival gear. It was then I first felt fear and realized how helpless I was.

It would have been suicide to face the wild outside waters in the *Eight Ball*. I couldn't safely beach the boat, yet I couldn't leave. I had to stay put and try to hang on. My log entry for that day read, "Blowing 50 to 70. Sure giving me hell."

Throughout the day, the anchor held as the boat swung back and forth over surging waves as I watched the streaming snow and listened to the scream of wind. Once each hour I crawled around the outside of the cabin, clinging to the icy boat, trying to beat the ice off with a hammer. Once I decided I simply had to find a safer, more sheltered anchorage. I started the one good motor, crawled forward, and tried to pull the anchor. I couldn't budge it.

I had a four-channel, twenty-five-watt, two-way marine radio powered by a twelve-volt battery, but I had no way of charging the battery, so I had reserved the radio for emergency use only. Now I punched the mike button and called for any station to answer.

The battery seemed dead. I didn't get an answer.

Shortly after dark I started the ten-horse motor and let it run in neutral at a fast idle. It was fed by a forty-gallon tank, and I knew I could run it all night if I wanted.

Each swell jerked on the anchor line, and the terrible wind kept a continual strain on it.

About 11:30 that night the anchor line snapped.

I'll never forget the horror I felt when the *Eight Ball* surged loose, driven by wind and swell. It lay in the trough, moving toward the beach.

I left the cabin like a shot, frantically leaped over junk in the cockpit, slammed the idling outboard into gear, and twisted the throttle wide open. At the same instant I yanked it around, trying to turn the bow into the wind.

The boat wouldn't turn. Weighed down with hundreds of pounds of ice, the twenty-eight-footer stubbornly remained broadside to wind and sea, drifting inexorably toward the beach.

That ride was absolutely terrifying. The wind screamed, snow blinded me, and the night was black.

I'm sure the Lord takes care of fools. Why else should I go aground on the only sandy beach on East Amatuli Island? There are jagged rocks along every inch of shoreline of the two-mile-long island, except where I landed. To cap it off, the tide was dropping. Each wave picked the boat up and pushed it higher onto the steep beach. Half an hour later I was high and dry.

As soon as the boat quit pounding I fell into a bunk and slept.

I awoke as the tide started back in, Saturday morning, February 13. The swell was bound to swamp the boat, so I removed the motors and took ashore food, tools, rifles, stove, lantern, and virtually everything aboard except two 55-gallon drums of gasoline, plastic garbage cans, and the seal hides.

I tried the radio again, calling "Mayday" several times on each of the four frequencies. I heard no answer.

221

The tide reached the *Eight Ball* and filled it with water and sand. I watched helplessly from the beach.

The seal hides and the two drums of gasoline washed overboard and drifted down the beach. The water slammed into the boat with such force it tore the bunks loose, and the cabin also started to break loose.

Among the emergency equipment I carried was a sheet of lightweight black plastic. And the last item my wife, Cathy, handed me before I left home was a construction-type staple gun. "Just in case," she said.

I searched the beach and found a couple of water-soaked two-by-six boards in a tiny draw between two humps of ground. Placing the boards between the tops of the humps, I stapled the plastic to the boards to form a shelter about five feet long, four feet across, and two feet high. I weighted the edges of the plastic with canned food and chunks of drift.

That day I emptied the boat of sand. I filled a fifteen-gallon can with sand and lashed a couple of big rocks to it, hoping to use it as an anchor and kedge myself off the beach. I lugged the can and rocks out at low tide and planted them as firmly as I could. But as the tide came in again that evening, the "anchor" skidded ashore and water again filled the boat. I had worked all day for nothing.

I tried the radio once more. I tried the Coast Guard frequency of 2182 kilohertz, calling "Mayday" to any station. No answer.

I tried 2450 and 2512, frequencies commonly used by vessels in Cook Inlet. No answer.

Then I tried the fourth and last frequency, 2638, a between-ships channel commonly used by tugs and many larger commercial vessels. Miraculously I got an answer. The 110-foot *King and Winge* was fishing for king crab only six miles away. I detailed my location and my plight. The boat had a full load of crabs and was having heavy going;

the skipper doubted that he could help me. Since my life was not in immediate danger, he understandably didn't want to poke around the tide-ripped, rock-strewn Barren Islands on a black howling night in a blizzard.

I requested that my wife be informed of my location, and I said if the wind should die at high tide next day, I thought I could refloat my boat and get out without help.

Cathy got the message next day. She didn't know if I had gotten off the island, but she waited a day or two, then called the Coast Guard at Kodiak. They put out an alert, with a description of my boat and my last known location.

Daily then the Coast Guard put twin-engine amphibious SA-16s into the air and flew over the Barren Islands, trying to spot me. But the weather was hideous, and it was a wonder they could fly at all. Within another couple of days, the Coast Guard cutter *Balsam* was sent to the islands to search for me.

Later I learned that three different king crab boats in the Kodiak Island vicinity headed for the Barrens to try to help. One was the *Bainbridge,* another I still don't know the name of, and the third was the *Success.* But by then the *Balsam* was in the area. This unselfish attitude, and the obvious risks that people were willing to take to try to help a fool in trouble, is typical of Alaska. I saw it again and again while I was with the Alaska State Police.

Once I got the message off to the *King and Winge* that wild night of February 13, I had to get busy to keep from freezing to death. It was dark and snowing hard. My boat was full of water and sand. I was hungry, wet, and cold, and my sleeping bag was wet. I had started the hunt with a dozen pairs of gloves but had lost them all when I swamped on the beach. Both of my flashlights became soaked with salt water, corroded, and within hours were useless.

I put my air mattress on ice- and snow-covered ground inside the tiny shelter, crawled in with the two-burner stove and lantern, and lit them. I got dry and dried my sleeping bag and socks. I got into the bag and tried to sleep, but I could stay warm for only two or three hours. Then I had to dry the sleeping bag again by putting it in a high, dry spot in the shelter.

Next day, February 14, I refloated the *Eight Ball* using as an anchor the fifteen-gallon drum with three huge rocks tied to it. But the fierce wind blew the boat back onto the beach, and it swamped again.

That day I found my two drums of gasoline ashore in a drift pile. Thereafter I had about thirty-five gallons of usable white gas for my stove and lantern. This was fine for a few days, but then carbon formed in the generator of the stove. I had to refill the stove frequently, and each time I shut it off I feared I might never get it relit. The stove and lantern meant heat; my life depended on them.

Day after day, temperatures were near zero. It snowed almost constantly, and I could seldom see more than a hundred yards. On Wednesday, February 17, the cutter *Balsam,* lying about a thousand yards from me, recorded the wind at ninety knots and the temperature at 14 degrees below zero.

I couldn't remain out of my shelter long because my hands got cold. I wore insulated underwear, a warm parka, and my insulated hip boots. I would dash out of the shelter and hustle the five hundred yards to where my gasoline drums were, fill a five-gallon can, hurry back, then spend the next hour shivering and trying to get warm again in my little shelter.

I finally stopped trying to refloat the boat. It was just too cold to work. I realized my battle now was just to stay alive. The wind literally seared me with cold, and it sapped my strength. Between the cold and wind, I think my reasoning was affected. I started talking to myself as I never had before.

From the day I had talked to the *King and Winge* I heard airplanes almost every morning. They seemed to be searching, and I was pretty sure it was for me. This kept hope alive. One day, through a cloud layer during a brief lull in the snow, I saw a Coast Guard plane at about fifteen hundred feet.

I decided to light a fire, hoping it would be seen by a plane. I piled dry driftwood and poured outboard oil and gasoline on it. My hands were so cold it was difficult to hold a waterproof match and strike it. When I did manage to get one to ignite, the howling wind snuffed it out.

I crawled under the plastic to warm my hands, and then got out the blowtorch that was among my tools. It was a regular plumber's torch. I got it lit and generating properly, then crawled out and headed the few feet to my pile of wood. Before I got there, the wind snuffed the torch out. I tried again, this time carrying the lit torch along the ground where I thought wind wasn't so strong. Again it went out. It was so cold and windy the heat was pulled away from the torch so fast that it stopped generating.

I had some railroad flares, but they were wet. I carefully dried one over my stove, lit it, then hustled to the pile of driftwood, threw on a fresh gallon of gasoline, and dropped the flare into it.

The wind blew it out instantly.

I said to hell with it and crawled back under my little shelter.

The wind continually whipped and popped my plastic covering, and after a few days it began to wear out. Pinholes developed, then nail-size holes, then larger ones. At the end it was perfectly light inside from all the holes.

I'm six feet, two inches tall, and since the shelter was only about five feet long, I had to lie with my knees bent. This became excruciating.

There were no trees, no caves, no shelters among the rocks. There wasn't enough driftwood to build a shelter. I thought of chopping the boat up with my axe, but I knew my hands would freeze if I tried to work very long.

Then the stern of the boat was knocked loose from one side, and seawater froze inside. Swells slammed into the aluminum skiff and popped the rivets, and it froze down. I didn't have the strength to do anything with either the skiff or the *Eight Ball.*

I had a twelve-transistor radio, and each night at seven and nine o'clock I tuned to the marine weather forecast. Wind was predicted for the Barren Islands each day, and it got to be such a nightmare hearing the forecast and knowing the wind was to continue that I decided not to listen. Then I'd wonder about the forecast and turn it on again.

On the Thursday following the Friday I was blown ashore, I hustled down the beach for five gallons of gasoline, and decided to fix a good meal. I put a can of frozen chicken on the stove while I thawed myself out in my sleeping bag. I dropped off to sleep.

I awoke to odd noises. The plastic was popping in the wind and, since I knew my mind had been tricking me, I decided I was hearing things; it had sounded like human voices.

Moments later someone picked up the flap of the plastic, stuck his head in, and asked, "Hey, how you doin'?"

Three men from the Coast Guard cutter *Balsam* were standing beside the shelter. They were Ensign F. M. Kien of South Bend, Indiana, Engineman second Jesse J. Findley of Dinsmore, Florida, and Seaman Raymond B. Webb Jr. of Phoenix, Arizona.

The *Balsam* had been within a thousand yards of me for twenty-four hours, continually blowing her whistle. I hadn't heard a thing. The men had come ashore in a motor cargo boat after spotting my white, ice-covered boat. They had thought they would be picking up a corpse. The ship's weather records showed that a full gale had blown during my entire stay on East Amatuli Island.

I've never been so glad to leave a place. I had gone aground Friday, February 12, and the Coast Guard picked me up the following Thursday, February 18. So many things happened, and I was awake and asleep so often, it seemed more than a month to me.

Within an hour I was on the radio of the *Balsam* talking to my wife on the radio at Homer. The Coast Guard picked up all my personal gear, but I left the *Eight Ball* and my aluminum skiff behind, items worth thousands of dollars. But I came out of it alive, without even frostbite. Who worries about money?

After his ordeal in the Barren Islands, Frank became serious about commercial fishing and obtained his own boat, working it from Homer for the next twenty years or so.

In the late 1980s Frank retired from commercial fishing. He and Cathy sold their home and their fishing boat and, with their two children, moved south to warmer climes. I haven't heard from Frank since they left. I miss seeing him. He was universally admired and liked, and he was one tough guy.

This article appeared in *Outdoor Life* in September 1965.

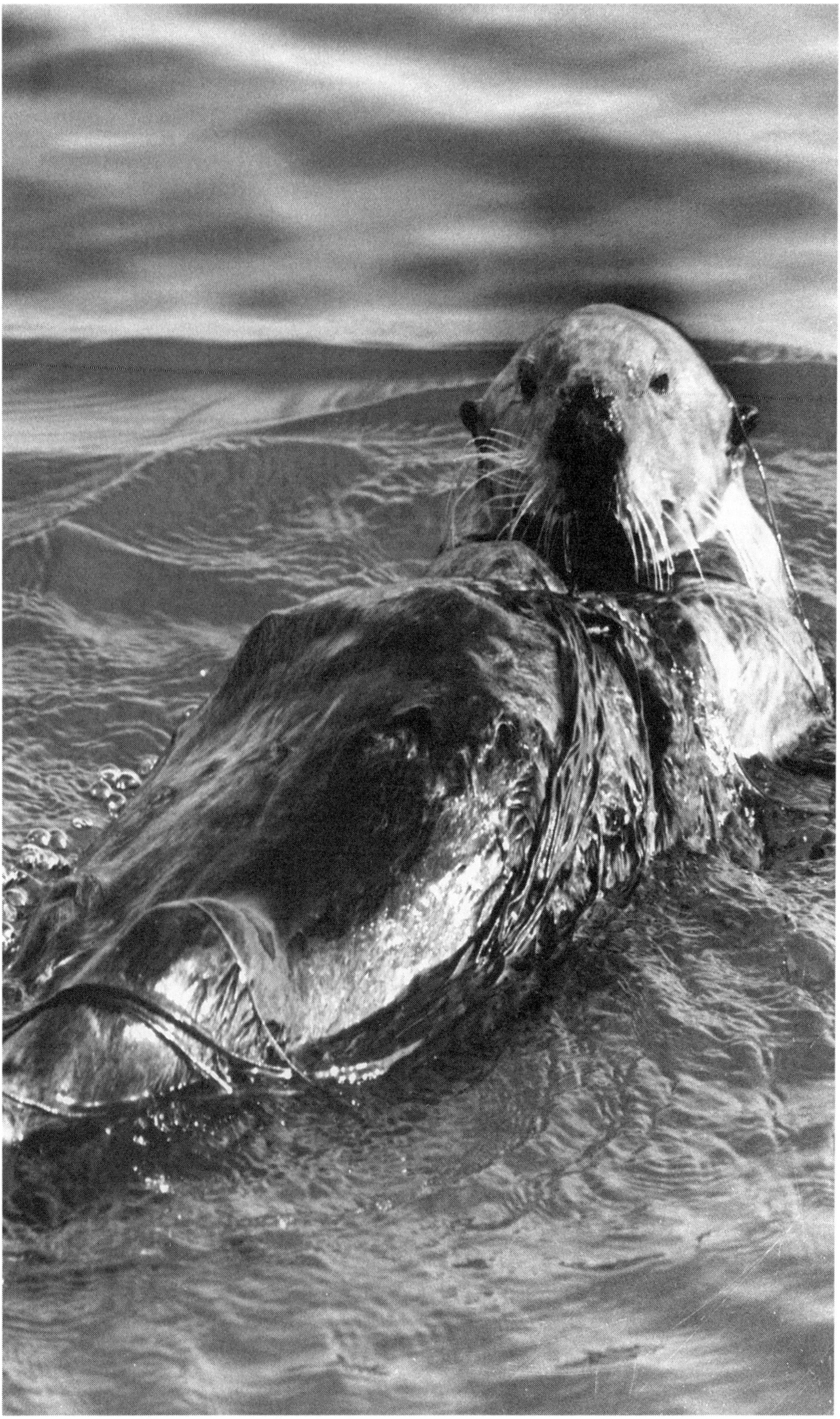

CHAPTER SEVENTEEN

RETURN OF THE SEA OTTER

The electrifying news that Alaska was going to market a thousand sea otter furs in 1968 came like an announcement that the passenger pigeon was back, or that buffalo could again be hunted on the Great Plains. Long a rare species, the sea otter had been protected since 1911. But by the mid 1960s, the population had rebounded with a vengeance, and there were too many sea otters for the food supply, principally at Amchitka Island in the Aleutians.

The announcement from Alaska's governor, Walter J. Hickel, said that five hundred otters had already been harvested and another five hundred were to be taken by Department of Fish and Game biologists from the fog-shrouded Aleutians. John Vania, the marine mammal biologist in charge of the hunt, was a longtime friend, and it wasn't difficult for me to wangle an invitation to accompany the hunters.

A sea otter, draped in kelp. A sea otter commonly swims on its back, as this one is doing. The animal often drapes kelp or seaweed over its body to anchor itself in place while it sleeps or rests. JIM REARDEN PHOTO

In 1947 I talked briefly with a wrinkled old Aleut who, at the turn of the century, hunted sea otter from English Bay, near the tip of Alaska's Kenai Peninsula. He described for me his last hunt, which must have taken place in the early 1900s, when there were then few otters left.

"I paddle bidarki to Flat Island, where I camp wit'out fire for one week, two week, almost t'ree week, in September mont'," he told me. Many of his words were Russian, and his accent was Aleut-Russian, and I had difficulty in understanding everything he said. A *bidarki,* or *bidarka,* is the seagoing Aleut skin boat, somewhat like the Eskimo kayak. Flat Island lies off the tip of the Kenai Peninsula amidst violent tide rips that spook even today's well-equipped fishing boat skippers.

The slightest whiff of smoke frightened sea otters, the old man explained. So did man tracks and scent on a beach. An otter that sighted a hunter would never be seen again, he solemnly avowed.

After nearly three weeks he saw an otter swimming near the island. He hurriedly launched his bidarka and paddled to intercept. The otter surfaced, he shot, and missed. The bullet splashed close to the animal's head.

"I hunt otter no more," he sighed.

Statehood in 1959 gave ownership of sea otters to Alaska, for they are creatures of the tidelands and of the three-mile strip of coastal waters owned by the state. At statehood it was apparent that sea otters at Amchitka were fully as numerous as they had been in pre-Russian days.

Each winter dead otters had been washing ashore at Amchitka—a sign of lowered vitality and inability to meet the stress of lowered temperatures and winter storms. Amchitka otters began to diminish. It became clear there were too many sea otters and not enough food. Good management called for thinning, and the best way is by selective harvesting. This is why John Vania and his crew were hunting the otters.

At that time, an estimated thirty thousand to forty thousand sea otters were in Alaskan waters. Harvest was justified only at such islands as Amchitka and Adak, where the animals could not spread into their old range. Sea otters will not move great distances across deep open water, regardless of population pressure.

"We won't harvest sea otter where the animals can spread naturally into unoccupied but formerly used sea otter range," Vania told me.

Late September 1967 found me on stark, treeless Amchitka Island, three-fourths of the way out the Aleutian chain, and more than fifteen hundred miles from Anchorage. I was so far west that the longitude of Honolulu lay a thousand miles east of me.

With athletic, wind-bronzed John Vania, who was thirty-three years old, were fellow biologists Ed Klinkhart, thirty-one, and Karl Schneider, twenty-seven. Innokenty Golodoff and his nephew, Nick Nevzoroff, Aleuts with bronze skins and snapping black eyes, from Atka Island three hundred miles away, were boat handlers, skinners, and general tigers. Aleuts are among the world's finest seamen.

"Worst weather in the world, this," John Vania facetiously said of our unusually mild day, momentarily watching the bright sun dance on a gently heaving sea and the light breeze ripple the brown grass of the island. We were loading hunting gear into a sixteen-foot skiff, preparing for a day's sea otter hunt.

John was backhandedly referring to the U.S. Coast Pilot's statement that no area in the world has worse weather than the Aleutians. At Amchitka, visibility is less than three miles with a ceiling of less than a thousand feet during 60 percent of the year. Winds average twenty to twenty-five miles an hour in summer.

Nick nosed the skiff through the kelp, heading a mile offshore to parallel the island's coastline.

"How many otters will we see today?" I asked.

"Plenty," John answered. "Why don't you count them?"

Clear of the kelp, Nick turned the eighteen-horsepower outboard loose, and we spanked across the glittering sea, roller-coasting over the vast swells that must have swept up from somewhere around the Hawaiian Islands. The boat answered quickly to Nick's sure touch.

Within ten minutes we saw sea otters riding the great waves along the jagged coast. There were singles, pairs, females with pups, and pods of up to a dozen, as far ahead as the eye could stretch. As we neared, slim necks thrust high as the animals peered at us, wet fur shining in the sun; when we got close, they rolled under the clear water, then surfaced astern. At least half were females with pups.

Nick approached a house-size rock, half a mile or more offshore, and John, rifle in hand, leaped out at the top of a wave surge. Nick backed off as the boat dropped about eight feet when the wave moved on, then maneuvered the boat into perfect position again for me to jump after John as another wave lifted.

John stood squinting through his variable-power Weaver scope at a pod of twelve to fifteen sea otters, about a hundred yards away, all floating on their backs, asleep. Several lay with kelp draped over their bodies to keep from drifting, a common sea otter habit. Hurriedly I snapped pictures with a telephoto lens while John selected an animal. He killed only adults without pups.

The little .243 Husqvarna rifle spit out its factory load of eighty grains of pointed lead, and spray flew as survivors hurriedly came awake and submerged, leaving the animal John had shot floating quietly on the surface.

Most wild creatures lose their grace in death, and the sea otter must be the extreme in this regard. When dead, it is probably the least attractive animal in the world. Nick retrieved it. I stared at what appeared to be a near-shapeless fur sack, half full. It was an Al Cappian schmoo, a blob. It had the head of a giant rat, with stiff white whiskers, flat lusterless brown eyes, tiny ears. The short front legs were out of proportion: they were mere stubs appended to loose fur. The great webbed flippers of the hind legs, which projected almost straight astern, were the most obvious part and the only truly symmetric feature.

"Pick him up," John suggested, perhaps noticing my disappointment. I grasped the loose skin with two hands and lifted. And I continued to lift as the hide stretched, but the sixty-pound carcass remained firmly on the boat's bottom. I had to stand and lift in order to raise the carcass, so elastic was the thick-furred skin.

"Now do you understand how we get a seven-foot-long hide from a four-foot animal?" John asked, grinning.

I parted the inch-deep, velvety fur, which was wet on the outside, and found the down-like underfur to be perfectly dry. Air is trapped there, adding to the insulating value. In calm water, John commented, a submerged otter can be followed by a chain of bubbles released from his fur.

The male was slightly larger than the average of about fifty pounds for Amchitka males. Females weighed about ten pounds less. The largest males there weighed about eighty-five pounds, while the heaviest sea otter John recorded was a 101-pound giant male live-trapped in Alaska's Prince William Sound for transplanting.

The purple-stained teeth of John's kill were small for such a large animal. The molars were flat, more fit for grinding than tearing. They were vastly different from the teeth of the remainder of the family, of which the sea otter is the largest member. Its close cousins, including the weasel, mink, marten, fisher, wolverine, and river otter, have sharp-cusped teeth, adapted for tearing meat and holding squirming prey.

Nick had been speeding down the coast. A few hundred feet ahead a small otter appeared. Nick ran to it, and we found a several-week-old pup, too young to dive, pushing its head beneath the surface and spanking water futilely with ridiculously large hind flippers. He could drive himself under momentarily, only to pop up like a cork, water draining from his fur, as off a duck.

The mother timidly circled seventy-five yards away while I snapped pictures of the pup. When we got close, the baby otter threatened with his tiny white teeth, screeching *eeeeeeee* at us. In a few minutes he tired, and floated quietly on his back, watching us.

We could easily have taken the pup aboard, and I once reached to touch its warm fur. But there was no point to it, and we sped on. Behind us the female surfaced, took the pup in her mouth, and submerged.

On that bright day at Amchitka, the Aleut boatman Nick worked us from rock to rock, often following channels threading offshore reefs, as we hunted the sleek otters. The roar of waves pounding rock and the cries of seabirds followed us. Bald eagles were always in sight. There were black oystercatchers, as large as bantam chickens, feeding on the rocks. Their scarlet bills and black bodies were visible for hundreds of feet. Harlequin and scaup ducks, an occasional emperor goose, cormorants, kittiwakes, fulmars, guillemots, and others were constantly in flight about us.

Nick eased us onto dozens of rocks, most of which were slippery. John and I would ease to the tops and peer over at swimming or sleeping otters. John always squinted carefully through his rifle scope, making sure there was no pup, and that an animal was adult, before he fired. The older and larger the animal, the lighter-colored is the head. Really big old males' heads seem almost white. A front view, with white whiskers resembling a crisp beard or mustache, made clear why some call the sea otter "old man of the sea." Whiskers are tactile organs and help in the search for food on the bottom of a deep and dark sea.

The two little Husqvarna rifles used by Vania and Klinkhart for harvesting the thousand sea otters for the state weigh just over six pounds each. They're battered from contact with rock and boat, and salt water has discolored them. Yet they still have pinpoint accuracy for the hundred yards they are sighted for. Almost all shooting is done with the scopes set at four power.

Every shot is a head shot. Although most shots are between seventy-five and one hundred yards, it is still tough shooting. A hit in the body can ruin a thousand-dollar fur. The animals invariably bob with the waves, or they may be swimming, when shot. Out of the last five hundred killed, only three were known to have been crippled and lost.

No shots are attempted from a boat, for the risk of crippling is too great. A jacket, a life preserver, any kind of pad, is always used to rest the rifle on while shooting from rocks.

After a day or two of shooting an area, otters become wary and difficult to approach. When John told me this, I remembered the old Aleut and his claim of the wariness of sea otters on his hunts at Flat Island in the early 1900s. Sea otters do not exhibit the curiosity of the common hair seal, hunted so extensively in coastal Alaska. A seal will surface to look at a boat or a man, and move closer for a better look. Not a sea otter. They seem to have little or no curiosity—except, sometimes, for taking one good look before leaving, which is sometimes a fatal mistake.

We had eight otters aboard when we returned to our landing place at the end of the day. I had counted nearly three hundred sea otters. The place teemed with them.

Next morning, we had twenty-three sea otters to skin, the eight John had collected and fifteen that Ed and Innokenty had taken on the opposite side of the island. It took five men less than two hours to complete the skinning.

All skins are cased; that is, turned inside out like a sack as they are pulled from the carcass, and then heavily salted for later fleshing and processing in Anchorage. All manner of scientific data and specimens were collected from the otters by Karl Schneider as the naked carcasses were turned over to him. Growth rates, reproductive information, age data, and food habits were a few of the things Karl was studying.

The shapelessness of the dead otters disappeared with removal of their thick pelts. The skinned carcasses were lean and hard with the powerful muscles that give members of the mink family their great strength and agility. There was virtually no fat on the bodies, for these animals depend upon their magnificent fur for warmth.

On another day I accompanied Ed Klinkhart and Innokenty Golodoff. Using one of the few autos on the island, we drove to within half a mile of the beach, following an old wartime jeep road, left the car, and walked into a forty-knot wind.

The fine rich smell of the sea was in that wind. The surf was up, and the thunder of waves battering the island drowned our voices as Ed led the way to the beach. Eagles fought the wind overhead as we stepped over rotting kelp piled in windrows by the sea. Glass floats from Japanese fishing nets glittered along the high tide line. Five-inch diameter sticks of bamboo from some unnamed warm land behind the heaving horizon were scattered there, as were metal trawl floats from Russian vessels that fish nearby.

We climbed a point overlooking the raging sea and settled into the deep grass. A fine mist flew horizontally at us from offshore. Water streaked my camera lens, Ed's rifle, and his covered rifle scope. Fat drops trickled down our necks, wet our faces, and dripped from noses and chins.

An occasional strong gust actually shook the point we sat on. It was comprised largely of grass roots and a sort of half-formed peat.

As we watched the boiling water, a sleek sea otter head bobbed between the breaking waves, moving easily. It smoothly disappeared moments before the surf thundered down where it had been. Another sea otter appeared, swimming into the waves. As I watched through quick-misting binoculars, it corkscrewed into a roaring wave, turning over and over apparently in play, to reappear on the far side.

Another otter swam into a channel between offshore rocks; a wave picked it up, but just before the wave slammed whitely against the rocks, the otter gracefully rolled out of sight only to surface in calmer water a few feet away.

Otters frequently swam directly under the bluff where we sat. However, today they remained offshore. Ed decided to climb out a rocky point to get closer. I remained with Innokenty on the point, fascinated by the roaring sea, the driving moisture, the frolicking otters.

Ed soon disappeared in the swirling mist. Innokenty and I sat silently, watching the fury of the sea and the fluid grace of the animals among the waves. A huge bald eagle with feathers missing from both wings swooped within six feet of us, unaware of our presence. His wings roared as he passed, even over the sound of the wind and waves; he turned to breast the wet wind, then climbed with clumsy flappings until he nearly disappeared in the sky.

Half an hour passed, and the dull boom of a shot sounded. Innokenty roused, and his rain clothes rustled. "I guess I go fishing," he grinned over his shoulder as he left to help Ed retrieve the otter he had probably shot. There was little danger of losing the shot animals: the wind and surf were sure to toss them onto the beach within minutes, the reason Ed had selected this spot in such weather.

I sat alone for another half hour, watching wind kittens dance on the leaping water, enjoying the curl of foaming breakers, the deep roar of water hammering rocks—and seeing the agile form of sea otters as they played and fed amidst bedlam.

Ed collected three fine big males that afternoon. Each of us carried an otter wrapped around our necks as we climbed to the car. The soft fur warmed our wet skin. Talking was difficult. This was the Aleutian weather so often spoken of with curse and awe. The grassy and treeless slopes rippled in the damp wind, and we were frequently staggered by violent gusts. I knew then that I could never think of sea otters again without recalling that murderous surf, the swirling Aleutian mists, the spume flung far inland by the howling wind, and the agile otters diving, feeding, and playing.

On yet another day, with the winds still whooping steadily, while John and Ed, with their Aleut helpers, hunted down-island, I sought out a sheltered cove with an overlooking bluff, crawled to the grassy edge, and spent three hours watching a female otter with a half-grown pup as they swam and fed within 150 feet.

They floated on their backs, heads together, drifting, resting, the position in which sea otters spend most of their relaxed time. With large hind flippers held high, short forelegs on their chest and bodies floating high, a resting sea otter appears much larger than it actually is.

The female rolled over and plunged smoothly under water. She surfaced a minute later and lay on her back with four or five two-inch-diameter green sea urchins on her chest. She ate rapidly of one, and then, holding the others tightly with her forelegs and in a fold of fur on her chest, she gracefully rolled over to wash away debris from her feeding. She repeated this regularly, feeding, and washing her fur clean as she fed.

I timed her dives at from fifty to eighty seconds. The water was shallow; she probably chose it so her pup could also feed. At Amchitka, adult males and single females normally fed farther offshore.

Once she surfaced with a flat rock that she placed on her chest, and against which she dashed some sort of a shell. Perhaps it was a mussel. She used her forelegs to hold the shell. John Vania told me that sea otters also slam clams together in order to break them open.

The pup started to feed, duplicating its mother's actions. Once, after they had fed for an hour, the pup nursed on one of the two prominent nipples far to the rear of her body. She continued to feed as the pup nursed, rolling to clean her chest from time to time. The pup clung tightly as she rolled, turning with her, plunging through a complete somersault.

Whenever they became separated, one or the other called in a loud birdlike screech, *eeeeeeeee,* repeated until the other replied with a similar sound. They swam to each other, the mother examined her pup carefully, and then both resumed feeding.

Both animals continually cleaned their fur. Matted or dirty fur allows cold to penetrate. Captive sea otters kept in dirty water where they cannot keep their fur clean usually die from exposure. Sea otters apparently have no external parasites, such as lice, for none were found by the state biologists.

After nearly three hours both ceased feeding, the female lay on her back and clasped the pup to her chest, and, floating high, bobbing on the waves, she swam off, occasionally twisting and looking over her shoulder to see where she was headed.

That afternoon as I watched the two otters I could look offshore at the heaving sea named for Vitus Bering, where he and his Russian crew had sailed when they discovered sea otters in these Aleutian Islands. I was curled beneath a strand of barbed wire, strung by our troops during World War II. During that war the Japanese occupied and fortified American-owned Kiska, forty miles northwest of Amchitka, and Attu, two hundred miles beyond Kiska, to the west.

All about me were deserted coastal gun mounts, thousands of Jamesway huts, jeep roads, wind-wrecked hangars, and one lone, battered and forlorn P-41 Warhawk fighter plane. The weathered letters IHTFP appeared with regularity on hangars and other buildings on the island. One ambitious soldier had cut foot-high letters out of plywood, painted them red, and nailed them high on a power pole. After a week it dawned on me that the letters meant, approximately, "I hate this foul place."

Amchitka Island, treeless, windy, foggy, cool, thirty-four miles long and three wide, with no town or village, with only recreation that was provided by the military, could be Endsville to a bored GI. However, the island has a singular, stark beauty. In some ways it resembles the grassy alpine meadows of the high Alaska Range. It is a biological melting pot, with birds from both North America and Asia. It is an island with a past, and while I was there I could hardly help but muse on that past.

In 1741, when Bering was searching to determine what land lay to the east of Kamchatka, probably 100,000 to 150,000 sea otters were scattered along the coast from Attu, westernmost of the Aleutians, to southern California. Bering discovered Alaska and the sea otter in the Aleutians on the same voyage. (Also see the next chapter in this book, "Alaska: The Russian Connection.")

At the time, discovery of the sea otter seemed by far the most significant.

Bering sighted Amchitka in October 1741 as he and his scurvy-weak and despondent crew were trying to sail back to Kamchatka. Their ship grounded in the Komandorski (Commander) Islands, five hundred miles west of Amchitka, where Bering died. The following fall, the forty-six survivors of the seventy-five who had set sail with Bering limped home in a small boat constructed from parts of the ship they had wrecked on Bering Island. With them was a collection of sea otter furs, and they vividly described the abundance of sea otters in the Aleutians.

The 170-year-long hunt started immediately. At first there were plenty of otters in the Aleutians. As they were killed, the hunts extended to California. The fabulous furs soon attracted British, Spanish, French, and American hunters and traders who poached the animals or traded the Natives for the fine skins, and smuggled them out of the sparsely settled Russian colony.

We celebrate the adventures of our American mountain men—Kit Carson, Bill Williams, and others who daringly penetrated our unknown far West for beaver. The exploits of the early Russian fur hunters who sought the sea otter were even more dangerous. The crews were mostly ruffians from the Kamchatka frontier. Leaders organized bands of these toughs, who then built a *shitika,* a simple flat-bottom sailing ship of green timbers lashed together with leather thongs.

In such crazy craft the *promyshleniki* (paid fur hunters) braved the stormy Okhotsk Sea, dodged through the chain of sunken rocks that line the Kamchatka coast, and crossed to the specks on the vast sea that are the Aleutian Islands. There they hunted and traded for skins and food, for they lived largely off the sea. Their trips lasted from one to four years. For the first thirty years, one third of the vessels leaving Kamchatka on sea otter hunts were lost.

These rugged Russians found perhaps sixteen thousand Aleuts, who skillfully hunted the stormy seas around their stark islands in bidarkas. The Aleuts killed sea otters, seals, and sea lions with spears and bows and arrows. Innokenty and Nick, John Vania's helpers, came by their sea skills honestly.

The promyshleniki enslaved the Aleuts, forcing the men to hunt otters. Villagers were transplanted when local otters were wiped out. Murder and rape were common. Feodor Solovief, leader of one expedition, is said to have "experimented on the penetrative power of musket balls" by tying twelve Aleuts together and discharging his rifle at them at short range. The bullet lodged in the ninth man. Solovief reportedly killed three thousand Aleuts on one campaign.

After 125 years of Russian reign, there were but about six thousand Aleuts left, and most had some Russian ancestry. The Russians called them creoles.

Sea otters became decimated. The Russian fur companies, seeing their profits drop, set quotas for harvest, and in about 1850 sea otters slowly started to recover from the heavy kill. By 1867, when the United States bought Alaska, an estimated 600,000 to 800,000 sea otter skins had been taken from the Northwest Pacific coast and the Aleutian Islands.

After the United States purchased Alaska, American hunters slaughtered sea otters recklessly, eager to get the furs that brought such high prices from wealthy orientals, from Russian royalty, and from the rich of Europe.

By the 1900s the hunt was clearly over. In 1906 the schooner *Challenge* hunted Amchitka for many weeks, but killed only four sea otters. In 1910 a crew of forty Aleut hunters on the two American vessels in the sea otter trade obtained only sixteen otters during a summer of hunting. Individual pelts brought $1,000 to $1,500.

Finally, in 1911, the sea otter was protected. Between 1911 and 1967, when John Vania and his crew harvested a thousand of the animals, no sea otters were legally hunted in North America.

Experts have calculated that perhaps five hundred wary, man-shy otters were left in 1911. These were scattered nearly two thousand miles from Attu to Prince William Sound, on the north rim of the Gulf of Alaska. Somehow, a few managed to survive near Monterey, California. None survived in British Columbia; the sea otter is the only mammal ever completely wiped out there. None were left in Washington, or Oregon, or in Southeastern Alaska.

A few illegally taken pelts sold around 1920 for a reported $2,500 each.

The nearly seventy-island Aleutian Island National Wildlife Refuge, made up of all but seven of the islands in the Aleutian chain (Amchitka is in the refuge), is the "sea otter belt" of yore, and of today. Here is where the greatest concentration of sea otters was found by Russians, and here is where the greatest number live today. Why here? Probably because of the thousands of square miles of clear shoal water, where sea otters can easily dive to the bottom to feed.

The violent history of sea otter hunting passed through my mind as I lay watching the female and her pup feed in that sheltered cove while the strong Aleutian wind dashed great combers against the rocks of this treeless brown island, so far from the metropolitan centers of the world.

After two weeks at Amchitka the otter musk on my clothing was, well, redolent. I wore clean clothing on the flight home; nevertheless I carried a faint otter aroma.

The state sale in January 1968 of the sea otter furs taken by John Vania and his crew brought a total of $141,000. Highest price for a single fur was $2,300, paid

by Neiman-Marcus of Dallas, Texas. All one thousand furs went in two hours of spirited auctioning to more than one hundred fur buyers who traveled to Seattle for the sale.

The 1972 federal Marine Mammal Act seized control of all marine mammals in the United States. Management of the sea otter became a federal responsibility, and the state of Alaska no longer had authority over the animal. The only harvest allowed since 1972 has been by Alaska Natives, and they have taken very few.

According to the U.S. Fish and Wildlife Service, which has monitored the animal since 1972, there were perhaps 150,000 sea otters in Alaskan waters until about 1992. At that time the Aleutian Islands sea otter population started a precipitous decline. Fish and Wildlife Service biologists estimate the Aleutian population dropped 70 percent during the last eight years of the twentieth century. This left perhaps 18,000 of the animals in the Aleutians—down from 50,000 to 100,000. The Aleutian sea otter population had been considered the largest and most secure in North America until this sudden decrease.

Fish and Wildlife biologists suspect the sharp decline of Steller sea lions (and possibly harbor seals) in the Aleutians and Bering Sea may have deprived killer whales (orca) of their normal prey species, forcing the whales to feed on sea otters. For the first time ever, killer whales were seen preying on sea otters in the Aleutians during the late 1990s.

In November 2000, the Fish and Wildlife Service took the first step toward listing the northern sea otter in the Aleutians as threatened or endangered, declaring it a candidate species for protection under the Endangered Species Act. This designation may or may not lead to listing the animal as endangered. It does begin the pro-

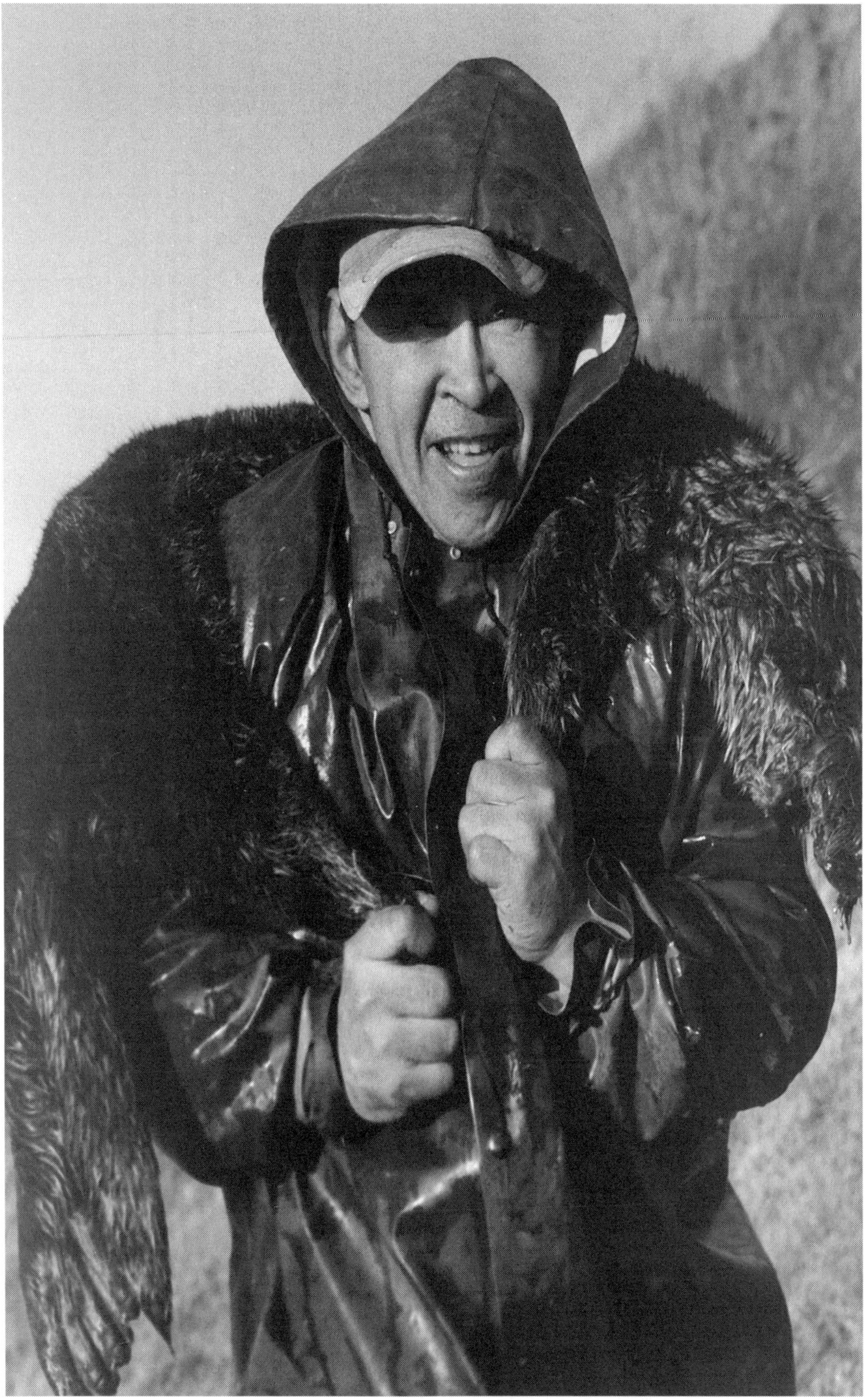

cess of collecting data so biologists can determine the extent and cause of the decline.

Sea otter populations in the rest of the state are healthy, even increasing in some localities.

This article appeared in *The Alaska Sportsman* in January 1969.

Innokenty Golodof, with a sea otter collected in 1967 at Amchitka Island. During that period of great sea otter abundance in the Aleutian Islands, the state government hunted hundreds of the animals in order to thin the population.

JIM REARDEN PHOTO

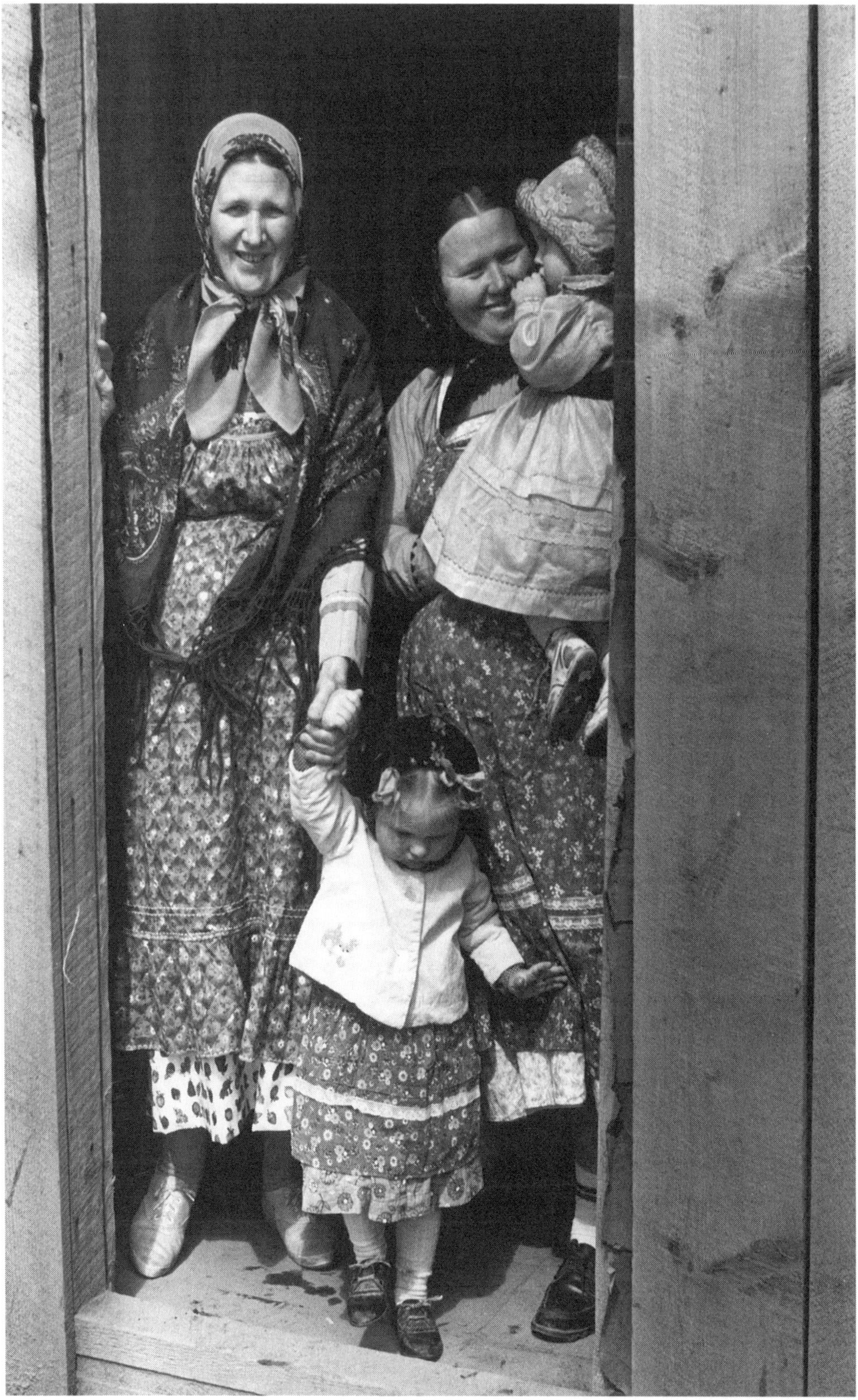

CHAPTER EIGHTEEN

THE RUSSIAN CONNECTION

Spire-topped spruces brood over the snow-blanketed village of Nikolaevsk on Alaska's Kenai Peninsula, the home of Russian-expatriate Old Believers, a splinter sect of devout Christians whose beliefs extend back hundreds of years. Fleeing communist Russia, for fifty years they wandered the earth—Manchuria, Hong Kong, Brazil, Oregon—to end their journeys in 1968 at this village they carved out of the Alaskan wilderness.

While visiting the village in the early 1970s for a celebration of Russian Easter, I reflected on the centuries-old bond between Russia and Alaska.

I enter a simple cabin, and waves of excitement, bright colors, noise, warmth, tantalizing food odors, and good cheer greet me.

Two Old Believer mothers in a cabin doorway in their new village of Nikolaevsk on the Kenai Peninsula, in 1971. Once the new Alaskans were settled and prospering, the rough cabins were replaced with modern homes. These women wear the traditional clothing of their sect.   JIM REARDEN PHOTO

"Christos voskrese (Christ is risen)," I am joyfully greeted by bearded men, some wearing black cassocks from all-night church. Others wear colorful hand-embroidered rubashka (shirt-blouses).

"Voistinu voskrese (Indeed he has risen)," I respond, as they have taught me, my voice lost in the hubbub.

Women in vivid peasant dresses and head scarfs are setting a table for the first non-Lenten meal in seven weeks. Chatter and laughter mingle. Excited children swirl underfoot.

Braga—fermented from fruits, yeast, and sugar— flows freely. After several cups I feel as one with these colorful Russians who revere tradition, trappings, and the language of their homeland.

The singing starts. The harmonies are true, the words Russian. The songs express sadness and longing, and revive old memories. I notice an occasional tear: the alcohol and the old songs stir deep emotions.

The nostalgic songs, the dress, the language, and the spirit of Old Russia are at home here among the towering spruces and snows of Alaska. As the clear voices soar and the braga flows it seems to me that history has come full circle, with Russians again pioneering amidst the forests and mountains of Alaska.

It is appropriate, for Alaska's Russian connection extends back more than 250 years. As I enjoy the songs and sip the fiery drink my thoughts bridge those years as I recall the cruel but colorful past, when other Russian voices resounded in Alaska.

Czar Peter the Great and the Empress Anna started it. To learn what lay between Asia and America, then a blank on maps, they sent Danish-born Vitus Bering across cold northern seas on one of the last great sea voyages of discovery on our planet. (Also see the previous chapter in this book, on sea otters.)

Bering's first voyage, in 1728, was a failure. East Cape Siberia lies but fifty-four miles from Alaska's Cape Wales, and Bering sailed between these points through the strait that now carries his name without ever seeing Alaska, although he did see and name Alaska's St. Lawrence Island. He also sighted one of the two Diomede Islands. Only three miles apart, Big Diomede became Russian, Little Diomede American.

Fourteen years later Bering again sailed in search of the northwest coast of America. He commanded the *St. Peter,* with seventy-five men; Alexei Chirikof commanded his other vessel, the *St. Paul,* with seventy-six men. Both vessels were eighty feet long, with a beam of twenty-nine feet.

Within days the two white-winged brigs lost each other in fog, and never rejoined.

Chirikof sighted the Alexander Archipelago of Southeastern Alaska and sent ashore a longboat with eleven men. It disappeared. He sent a small boat to search for the longboat. It too disappeared. To this day no one knows what happened to the boats or the men. Without going ashore on the newly discovered land, Chirikof returned to Kamchatka. Twenty of his men died of scurvy.

Huge, kindly, moon-faced Bering was ill after sixteen years of struggle. He had had to build his ships from local timber after hauling iron, tools, and rigging across more than five thousand miles of mostly wilderness Russia. He sailed on after losing contact with Chirikof. His first view of Alaska, on July 16, was of the great snowcapped St. Elias mountains, above which towers shining 18,008-foot Mount St. Elias, named by Bering.

At sight of the great Alaskan mountains the ill and worn-out Bering shrugged his shoulders and ordered sail set for return to Kamchatka. He sent a longboat ashore for water at fifteen-mile-long Kayak Island. Aboard was naturalist/physician Georg Wilhelm Steller who, with the crew of the longboat, became the first-known Caucasians to leave footprints in Alaska.

In ten hours Steller carved himself a niche in history by swiftly collecting and describing what he found on Kayak Island. He discovered evidence of humans, saw foxes and sign of sea otters, magpies, ravens, and other birds, and identified and collected many plants. A jeering, brilliant blue-crested jay came near. Steller must have smiled then, for he shrewdly realized he was really in America; years earlier he had seen a hand-colored plate of the similar eastern America blue jay. Today that Alaska jay carries Steller's name.

Scurvy, lack of drinking water, and constant storms bedeviled the expedition on its return voyage. The Shumagin Islands off the Alaska Peninsula, where they again stopped for water, were named for a crew member who died and was buried there—the first Caucasian to be buried in Alaska.

More gales, more deaths, and even fiercer storms. Lines carried away, sails wore thin. Green water rolled across the decks. It became bitterly cold.

Bering anchored his battered ship in the lee of an island, and that night a huge wave lifted it over a reef and it came to rest in calm water. Forty-nine men were down with scurvy, twelve had died. Another score were yet to die of the disease. The *St. Peter* blew ashore, a wreck.

They wintered there in the Komandorski (Commander) Islands of Russia, sheltering in dugouts constructed from old fox dens. Foxes swarmed, a pestilence, nipping at food, chewing shoes. Steller, with an axe, killed more than seventy in three hours; for every one killed, two seemed to replace it.

Bering died on the island that now bears his name, little knowing that he was to become one of the giants of Alaska's history and that historians would rank him among the world's greatest explorers.

Fifteen months after they had departed Russia, forty-six survivors of the *St. Peter,* toothless from scurvy, clothing in rags, hair and beards matted, came ashore at Kamchatka in a boat built from their wrecked ship.

There is irony in the immediate reaction to Bering's last voyage: the discovery of abundant sea otters proved of more immediate interest than the finding of Alaska and the northwest coast of North America. The survivors described the Komandorskis, and they told of the Aleutian Islands, those volcanic, summer-green jewels that sweep across the North Pacific toward Kamchatka. On the Komandorskis and Aleutians, tens of thousands of sea otters swarmed, so tame they could be killed with clubs.

The men had proof: about nine hundred fine sea otter pelts they had collected at Bering Island. For these skins Chinese buyers paid roughly the equivalent of half a million dollars in today's currency.

Why is sea otter so valuable? Simply, it is the most durable and the warmest fur known. Inch-deep and velvety, the underfur is so dense you can part it with your breath and not see the skin. Shake a sea otter pelt and silvery, bronze, or gold light shimmers from the guard hairs. Some furs are dark brown, others are nearly black. Cased skins may be seven feet long, and three skins make a large coat.

The *promyshleniki*—frontier fur hunters of the Siberian taiga—went wild. In crude vessels of timber lashed together with rawhide they sailed for the Komandorskis and, after that, to the Aleutians. Within twenty years they were sailing to mainland Alaska, exploring, hunting. Dozens of vessels were swallowed by storms, but those that returned carried furs worth fortunes. To these crude Russians the risk was worth it. It was the sea otter, then, that brought the Russian legions to Alaska.

How did the *promyshleniki* treat the gentle Aleuts, the aborigines who lived in the Aleutian Islands?

"God was high in His heaven, and the Czar was far away."

The Russians raped and stole. When the Aleuts fought back it was called an uprising. In retribution, promyshleniki wiped out eighteen villages, killing men, women, and children. The cruelty defeated the Aleuts, who became slaves and concubines.

The Russian-American Company built settlements at Kodiak and Sitka, origins of those Alaska cities of today. Resident company managers between 1799 and 1867 were also the governors of Alaska. Of the fourteen Russian governors, the first—flaxen-haired Alexander Baranof—was the giant, although he was physically small and slim.

He built ships, established trade, and defeated Alaska's Natives in battles. From his imposing log "castle" at Sitka, he was the power from the Aleutians to California. When Baranof summoned, Aleut sea otter hunters came, often by the hundreds and for hundreds of miles, paddling across violent northern seas in tiny skin bidarkas (kayaks).

Baranof was a lusty, tough, self-taught merchant with vision. He left an estranged wife in Russia, and also had an Alaska Native "wife," as well as alliance with at least one other. "I sin," he once reported to owners of his company, "sometimes from weakness and sometimes from necessity, as I did during my long stay at Chugach when the Chugach people gave me a girl for a hostage. On account of that, the Chugach became more attached to me and more confiding."

Subsequent governors explored, charted, and further secured the Russian presence in Alaska. Over the years Alaska's Natives became Russianized as they embraced the language, foods, clothing, religion, and other trappings of Mother Russia. Then fur became scarce and profits dwindled. In 1867 the United States purchased Alaska from Russia for $7.2 million.

To modern Alaskans the Russian Bear loomed large, especially during the years of confrontation between the United States and the Soviet Union. In 1986, as the Cold War started to thaw, a sixty-seven-member Alaska Performing Artists troupe spent three weeks on a fourteen-performance tour of the Soviet Union. "We received a tremendous welcome," former Alaska Governor Jay Hammond, a member of the troupe, told me. Performers included Eskimo dancers, gospel singers, and others.

Hammond said the Soviet people appeared grim and unfriendly on the streets, but inside concert halls, "They stood with arms above heads, clapping, and joining in Russian versions of 'Moscow Nights' and the English version of 'We Are the World.'"

"It became a lovefest. People hugged and there were tears," Hammond said.

American Eskimos in the troop met children of friends from Siberia they hadn't seen in forty years. A young Russian Eskimo woman approached the Alaskan Eskimos, spoke in Eskimo, and learned she was a close relative.

"There wasn't a dry eye in the house," Hammond said.

Alaska's Russian connection from the distant past includes a legacy of hundreds of Russian place names—Shelikof Strait, Bering Strait, Baranof Island, Shumagin Islands; an attenuating strain of Slavic blood, mostly among Aleuts who adopted Russian names—Golodoff, Lekanoff, Tutiakoff, Zaharoff (my wife, part Eskimo, born on the Bering Sea coast, carries a middle name, Anecia, that echoes her probable Russian ancestry); and a history of often-despotic rule that resulted in near annihilation of the Aleuts (sixteen thousand Aleuts at discovery, six thousand at the U.S. purchase).

A few Russian words are part of Alaska's language: *chi* (tea), *bidarka* (kayaklike skin boat), *barabara* (underground house), *pushki* (cow parsnip). Some descendants of the original Russians at Kodiak and on the Kenai Peninsula, in the Aleutians, and at Sitka still speak a halting, archaic Russian.

The connection is still seen in picturesque blue-roofed, diagonal-cross-crowned Russian Orthodox churches, and in museums crammed with early Russian memorabilia. Costumed "Russian" dancers still perform at Sitka; a balalaika ensemble plays old Russian tunes at Kodiak; and for many years performances were given at Kodiak of *Cry of the Wild Ram,* a play about Alexander Baranof.

Alaska was considered Russian for 126 years. The United States has owned Alaska now for roughly the same length of time. The blood of Russia flows in the veins of many Alaskans, and the early Russian influence is still felt. Since the end of the Cold War, relationships between our farthest north state and Mother Russia have once again become close.

What goes around comes around, as the saying goes, and I thought of this and Alaska's turbulent Russian connection while I drank braga, ate Russian foods, and listened to sentimental songs, celebrating Russian Easter in the Russian way in that tiny cabin surrounded by the snowy spruce forests of the Kenai Peninsula.

I first wrote about the Kenai Peninsula village of Nikolaevsk in an article that appeared in National Geographic *magazine in September 1972 (*"A Bit of Old Russia Takes Root in Alaska"*). When the Cold War began to thaw, I wrote the article published above, after talking with Alaska Governor Jay Hammond about his trip to Russia and after rereading several Alaska history books and reviewing notes I had taken for the National Geographic piece.*

The raw cabins originally built by the Old Believers in Nikolaevsk are now gone, replaced with modern homes, and the population has more than doubled from the two hundred residents who were there when I visited for that Russian Easter celebration three decades ago.

This article appeared in the October 1988 issue
of *Alaska* magazine.

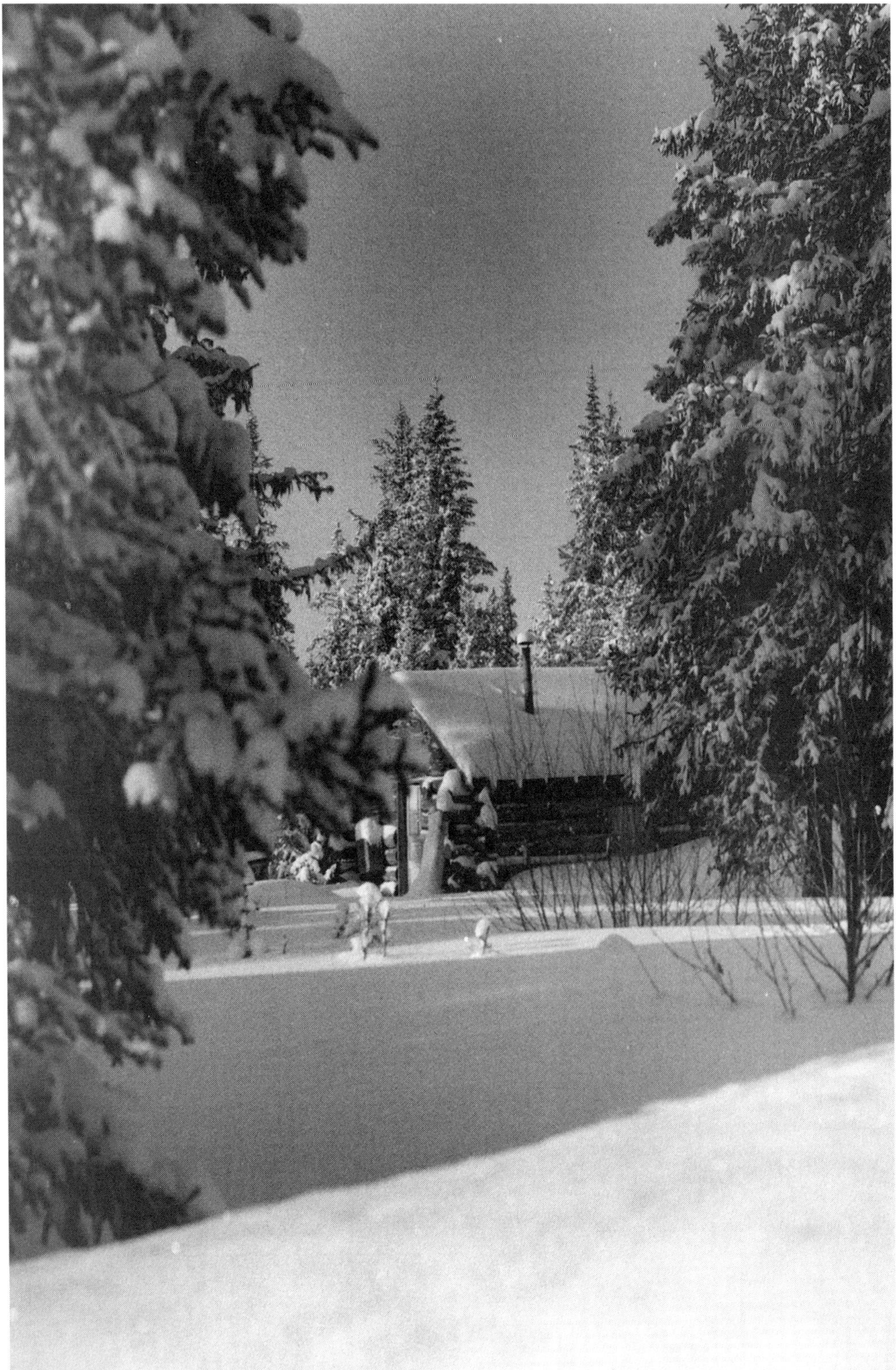

CHAPTER NINETEEN

AT HOME IN THE WILDERNESS

The Alaska wilderness is a natural home for bushrats—those people who choose to live isolated in the bush and to provide for themselves from the bounty of forest and stream. Most people who arrive in Alaska from elsewhere to live as bushrats have romantic ideas about what it is like to live off the land—and most leave after a short trial. I've known of a number of these who didn't survive; sometimes their bodies were found, sometimes not.

The state of Alaska has occasionally opened land to settlement, offering cabin sites in the wilderness. I am aware of one offering in a remote, offroad area, in which thirty cabin sites were claimed. Within five years only one of the people who had signed up for the sites was still there.

I've also known half a dozen successful bushrats, and have heard of many others—people like Wesley Hallock and his family. Wes permitted me to tape-record and interview him for the story of his family's life in the wilderness, and it is told here in his voice.

An Alaska cabin in the snow. Wesley Hallock was among those adventuresome Alaskans who built a cabin in the wilds where he could share life with his family, far from the pressures of the modern world.   JIM REARDEN PHOTO

I wanted to believe the freshly dug hole was a wolverine den, but somehow it didn't add up. There were no tracks in the fresh snow, yet some animal had recently been there, for there was no snow on the mound of new dirt that ringed the hole.

I circled, looking for tracks, and found none. I approached the den from uphill, chambering a cartridge in my .270, feeling a bit foolish about being so cautious. Yet, caution had become second nature because of where I was, and because of our lifestyle.

When I was twenty feet from the den the silence was shattered by a loud woof, and I jumped in surprise. Moments later a black animal bounded out of the den, headed downhill. It was a black bear, and I had found his winter quarters just as he was settling in. The sound of my footsteps on the crunchy snow had caused him to bolt. Now my caution didn't seem so foolish.

My rifle came up, the crosshairs of the scope settled behind a shoulder, and I fired. Tracks and a bloody trail led me to a nearby clearing where I found the bear, dead. It was fat, and superbly furred. Still, my sense of gain was touched with a feeling of regret, a feeling that all who love animals have when they bag their quarry. I killed because there was a purpose in the death of that black bear. My family needed the meat, the fat, the fur, of this animal.

I hesitated to dress the animal where it fell, knowing it would be difficult to keep twigs, mud, leaves, dead grass off the meat and fat. He weighed about 150 pounds. I'm over six feet tall, and strong, so I shouldered the bear whole and packed him the mile or so to our cabin. By the time I got there that little bear weighed about a ton.

My wife, Cyndi, who had never eaten bear meat, made no comment when I dropped the animal in front of our cabin, but our four-year-old son, Russell, was soon rubbing the glossy fur and watching as I skinned. The bear was covered with fat up to three inches thick, and Cyndi filled pans with chunks of the white stuff. She cleaned, trimmed, and rinsed them in cold water, and put them on the woodstove to simmer. For twelve hours the fat bubbled over low heat with an occasional stirring, giving off a slight baconlike aroma. It rendered into two gallons of amber oil and a hard residue (cracklings) that settled to the bottom of the kettle. Cyndi strained the oil through a clean cloth into coffee cans, where it cooled and thickened into an opaque white product that resembled vegetable shortening.

I hung the quarters of meat from a pole outside the cabin, where it froze, and we ate the rich, fat-marbled meat all winter, alternating with caribou.

What led me at the age of twenty-five to abandon civilization and challenge the wilderness with my little family? I don't hate people, and I'm not hiding from something in my past. The answer is simple. Like many Americans today, I was seeking something. I wanted to live closer to nature. I wanted to control my life. I was looking for a challenge.

I moved to Anchorage from Morrison, Colorado, with my parents, eighteen years ago, and quickly came to love Alaska's wilderness. Cyndi and I were married while I was on a trip visiting Colorado, and I told her about my hope to live in the wilds. She grew up near Chicago and had had little outdoor experience.

In a canoe, Cyndi, baby Russell, and I explored many wild rivers that can easily be reached from Anchorage. I killed a moose and a lot of small game, which we ate and enjoyed. But where we lived in town there were barking dogs, the sounds of traffic and roaring snow machines. When we explored with the canoe, others whizzed by us in powerboats. I had a compelling urge to move to some wilderness spot where we could be alone.

After a couple of years of exploring rivers, hiking, hunting, fishing, and running traplines in areas I could reach from Anchorage, where I worked for a moving company, Cyndi was convinced. "Let's pick a spot and go build a cabin," she suggested.

It took us a year and a half to decide where to go in the Alaska Range and what kind of a cabin to build, and to accumulate the equipment and supplies we needed.

After studying maps, books, and many reports, I flew into the country we had selected. It was a remote spot where there was game, trees I could cut down for a log cabin, firewood, good water, and a place where I could trap. It was near a lake large enough to land on with a floatplane. Our spot is at about 1,100 feet elevation in the Alaska Range in an area where timberline is at 2,000 feet. Moose live throughout the area, there are occasional caribou, bears, and small game, and it is fair fur country.

In mid-July 1977, our chartered bush plane landed on the lake we had chosen. The plane was so heavily loaded that water almost covered its floats. With us was Knik, our husky dog. We had a tent and camping gear, dried food, tools, traps, summer and winter clothing, snowshoes, bedding, dishes, lanterns and fuel, insect repellent, first aid supplies, a 12-gauge Remington 870 pump, a Marlin .22 automatic, and a .270 and a .30-06, both in Remington Model 700 with 4X scopes.

For the cabin we planned to build we had nails, clear plastic for windows, spikes for the logs, a stovepipe, and hinges for the door. We splurged on a heavy plate-steel, airtight stove with a firebrick lining and detachable oven.

I took a day to pitch our insect-proof umbrella tent where we could live while I built the cabin. We had about six weeks before snow flew, and I wanted the cabin finished by then.

Spruce at our elevation are sharply tapered and stunted. This dictated the size of our cabin, which turned out to be 12 by 14 feet. Sound small? Try moving and lifting green logs by yourself for a bigger cabin. Butts of our cabin logs averaged nine to twelve inches in diameter. My goal was to fell, limb, and peel ten logs a day. I floated them in the lake to our cabin site, and in five working days I had fifty logs ready to start building.

Using a shovel, in a thickly timbered area I stripped moss from the ground and packed gravel under the sill logs to retard rotting. For the first two years the cabin floor was hard-packed dirt. In our third year, I flew in plywood and built a floor, a real luxury.

Cyndi gathered sphagnum moss for chinking. When I had a log notched and ready I raised it and poked it tight with moss, knocked the blocks out, and let it settle, then spiked it into place. On a good day I managed to build two complete rounds. I had the walls up in about ten days.

I worked twelve to fourteen hours a day, and we soon realized that the flour, rice, powdered eggs, dried beans, and other foods we had brought were too basic, for I lost about twenty-five pounds, and my endurance decreased during the six weeks it took to build the cabin. During that time we lived partly on lake trout, which I caught from the lake with rod and reel. The lakers were very cooperative, and we had all of them we wanted to eat.

To make tight-fitting corners in the logs I used a large half-round gouge chisel to cut where I scribed for my saddle notch, and I hacked the interior out with my double-bit axe. I cut the doors and windows out after the logs were all up. For the roof I used 117 ten-foot-long, three-inch-diameter spruce poles. Over the poles I put a layer of six-mil Visqueen plastic, then over that we laid squares of insulating sphagnum moss. The roof drains well, holds heat in, and doesn't leak.

The new cabin, with its sweet-smelling spruce logs, seemed luxurious after those weeks in the small tent.

The cabin's dirt floor became drier and drier during the winter. Dust became a problem, so we sprinkled snow on the floor at night before going to bed. The snow melted and laid the dust. It was a fine art to know how much snow to use to make it damp, but not muddy.

While building the cabin we saw black bears and an occasional moose wandering the opposite shore of the lake. One day an old sow blackie with three cubs swam to our shore, the little ones bobbing along in her wake. I wasn't concerned, for I was sure she would sense us and leave. As a precaution, however, we took Russell to the partly finished cabin and waited for her to realize we were there and to leave. That was a mistake. I should have instantly let that sow know we were there.

We stood quietly, me with rifle in hand. We heard a twig snap. Knik raised his nose and his hackles went up. The sow stepped out of the brush twenty yards away, saw us and the cabin, and froze. For a moment I thought she was going to charge. She didn't know what to do.

Knik started for her, but returned when I yelled. The sow turned and sent her cubs up a tree. She was so close that I fired a round over her head. She ignored it, and, to my relief, went up the tree with the cubs.

We got out of sight and finally the sow came down and started snooping. I was glad then we had taken the precautions to leave no food scraps anywhere; we had even buried fish cleanings in the lake bottom so there was no scent. After she walked through camp and satisfied herself that there was no danger, she called her cubs and they left.

I had to hand-rip boards for the cabin door because the spiral-grain spruce in the area will not split straight. As I laboriously sawed, I'd have paid fifty dollars for a simple board. Finally the door and windows were done, and the stove was installed. I made three-legged stools from log slabs, using brace and bit to make the leg holes.

Firewood was my next concern. There were plenty of dead spruce near the lake and I cut what we needed and floated it to the cabin. Our cabin is snug and warm. The heavy stove holds heat well, and it will burn all night with a couple of good chunks of firewood. In three years, I doubt that we've burned more than three cords of wood a winter.

Cyndi keeps a sourdough pot going and bakes bread, cake, and cookies every five days or so. She and Russell pick wild cranberries (lingonberries), rose hips (rich in vitamin C), and blueberries. The cranberries and rose hips keep without special care, and she freezes the blueberries when weather permits. By mid-October our entire outdoors is a freezer.

The first year, I started hunting meat in September, making long hikes from the cabin, getting acquainted with the area. I wasted a lot of time because I didn't know local places most frequented by big game, but I learned quickly.

One day a bull moose stepped out of the timber a rock's throw from the cabin. The season was open, and I ran for my rifle. By the time I got to it and returned, the moose was gone.

In October I was edgy because I hadn't killed any big game, and we badly needed meat. We had killed a few spruce grouse, and during the September migration, I had shot many mallards, scaup, and wigeon that stopped on the lake. They were fat and delicious.

Moose season closed, and I just had to get some caribou. I sat by the lake one quiet morning, rifle across my lap, and glassed a nearby ridge. After days of watching that ridge without seeing anything, it came as a jolt when I spotted a herd of eight or nine caribou.

I slipped on my packboard and headed out. The caribou were traveling. They would grab a bite and move on in their seemingly slow walk. I was lean and tough, but it took an hour for me to get to where I expected to intercept them. I climbed higher and circled until I spotted two small herds bedded down. They were well out of range.

I had to walk in sight of one herd while approaching the other. Surprisingly, I moved within easy range without the animals spooking. I shot a dry cow and the others in that herd left.

I ran to the top of the ridge and found the second herd still bedded, picked a young bull, and shot him behind the ear. He slumped in his bed, and the rest of the herd wasn't even disturbed until a fidgety cow smelled the fresh blood. Then all of them left.

A few days later I shot the black bear at his den, Caribou, the bear, ducks, grouse, and ptarmigan fed us through the first winter. With meat to eat, my weight and endurance immediately increased.

Since then I've killed a bull moose each fall. The farthest I've had to pack a moose was about a mile. We now have our canoe at the cabin, and I can pack moose anywhere to the shore of the lake and paddle it home.

I have also killed caribou early in the fall, before it was cold enough to freeze. I cut it into strips, salt and pepper it liberally, and air-dry it into jerky, which I like to eat when on the trail.

I had two dozen traps that first winter. I had to keep moving them, for at first I didn't know where the fur was. Like most North Country trappers, I fought the weather. I would set traps and it would rain and freeze the traps, so I would have to reset them. Or a heavy snow-fall would bury traps I had set in the open, or it would bury the cubbies (shelters) in which I had set some traps.

I had never trapped marten, and I had to learn their habits. I was delighted to learn that the marten in our area are large, dark, and finely furred. I started to trap marten with a basic ground set under a tree. Since then I've gone to various pole sets and have used Conibear traps, which kill the animals instantly. Marten are full of curiosity and will investigate a ptarmigan wing swinging on a string in the wind near a trap, or the various scents I use.

During the first winter I found lynx tracks in the snow along a riverbank. I set a pair of #4 traps in a natural cubby in some driftwood and willows. They went untouched for three weeks. Then one day they held a wolverine. For a thirty-pound animal, he had a very deep growl, and was, simply, ferocious. He lunged at me with a roar when I neared. My hair stood on end and I'm sure my eyes looked like saucers. I dropped him with the .22. Since then I've heard of trappers who wade in with a club to finish a wolverine. They can have it: I prefer the .22

I hand-sawed most of my fur-stretching boards and took great care with my furs. That first winter I caught thirty-eight marten, a wolverine, and several beautiful red foxes, which stepped into #4 traps I set next to my ridgetop caribou kill gut piles. I've since caught more fur each winter.

In order to trap more efficiently, I cut about thirty miles of trail in three ten-mile loops from our cabin. I use snowshoes, although most commercial trappers in Alaska use snow machines or even airplanes. Somehow I don't like the idea of snow machines on a trapline. They're noisy even when they work well, and they can get you into trouble by taking you a great distance and then quitting. With webs I know that even if I'm slow I can walk home.

At times it is lonely on the trapline. I leave the cabin before dawn, walk at a good clip on snowshoes all day, and return after dark. I see a lot of interesting things: where a horned owl has caught a rabbit; tracks of a passing wolf pack; a cow moose and her calf; signs of a river otter family.

Our life is adventurous, I suppose, because we are totally on our own. There is no nearby doctor, no hospital, no drugstore. We can't run to a supermarket if we've forgotten something. We don't have a two-way radio to call for help. Some people think of adventure as a succession of narrow escapes. To me that's poor planning. I take every precaution to avoid trouble. We have never had what I consider a close call.

The greatest danger I face is crossing ice on a good-size river and on large creeks. If I'm doubtful about a crossing, I carry a spruce pole. If the ice breaks I can bridge the hole with the pole and pull myself out. I'm always prepared to shed my snowshoes and my pack quickly if I break through, and I carry matches in a waterproof safe so I can build a fire to dry out.

I prefer constant cold once winter arrives. When it warms to above freezing, my snowy trails get soft, our meat starts to thaw, and ice crossings get tricky.

During deep winter when I am busy trapping, Cyndi reads the books she collects during the summers when we visit town. She cooks, does her housekeeping, and listens to our battery radio. Cabin fever has never been a problem. Sometimes we go for days without much talk, then suddenly, we explore some subject in great depth. Though we know a lot about each other, it seems we always learn more. We get along better in the wilderness than we do in town.

During our first season, relatives in Anchorage became worried and sent a plane for us in March. We returned to town on that plane, and I sold the fur I had trapped and got a temporary job to earn needed cash. By fall we were back home in the wilderness. That has set the pattern of our lives.

As a result of our living in isolation most of the year, Russell, now nine years old, has learned to think for himself, and he is unusually independent for his age. He watches my every move, and I'm careful to explain things that he finds difficult to understand.

I have considered buying a small plane for travel to and from our cabin, but somehow that would change things. We want to live in the wilderness like the Alaskan old-timers did.

My greatest satisfaction often comes after a long, cold day on the trapline. Dark has fallen, and I slog along on squeaking, hissing snowshoes. There is fresh-caught fur in my pack. Then I get a whiff of wood smoke, and through the dark spruces I see lantern light shining from the cabin's windows. That welcoming cabin, a tiny haven in the wilderness, a lonely pinpoint of warmth, with Cyndi and Russell waiting, is, to me, true happiness.

I tape-recorded Wesley Hallock's story in Anchorage, where he and his family lived in a small apartment while briefly in town. Since the story was published, I've lost track of the Hallock family. I'd like to hear from Wes Hallock to learn how he and Cyndi are doing. Are they still out there in the boondocks? Or did they get their fill of it? How long did they last? When I interviewed him I was impressed by the thoughtful and careful way he went about moving from Anchorage into the bush. He went prepared mentally, and with the right

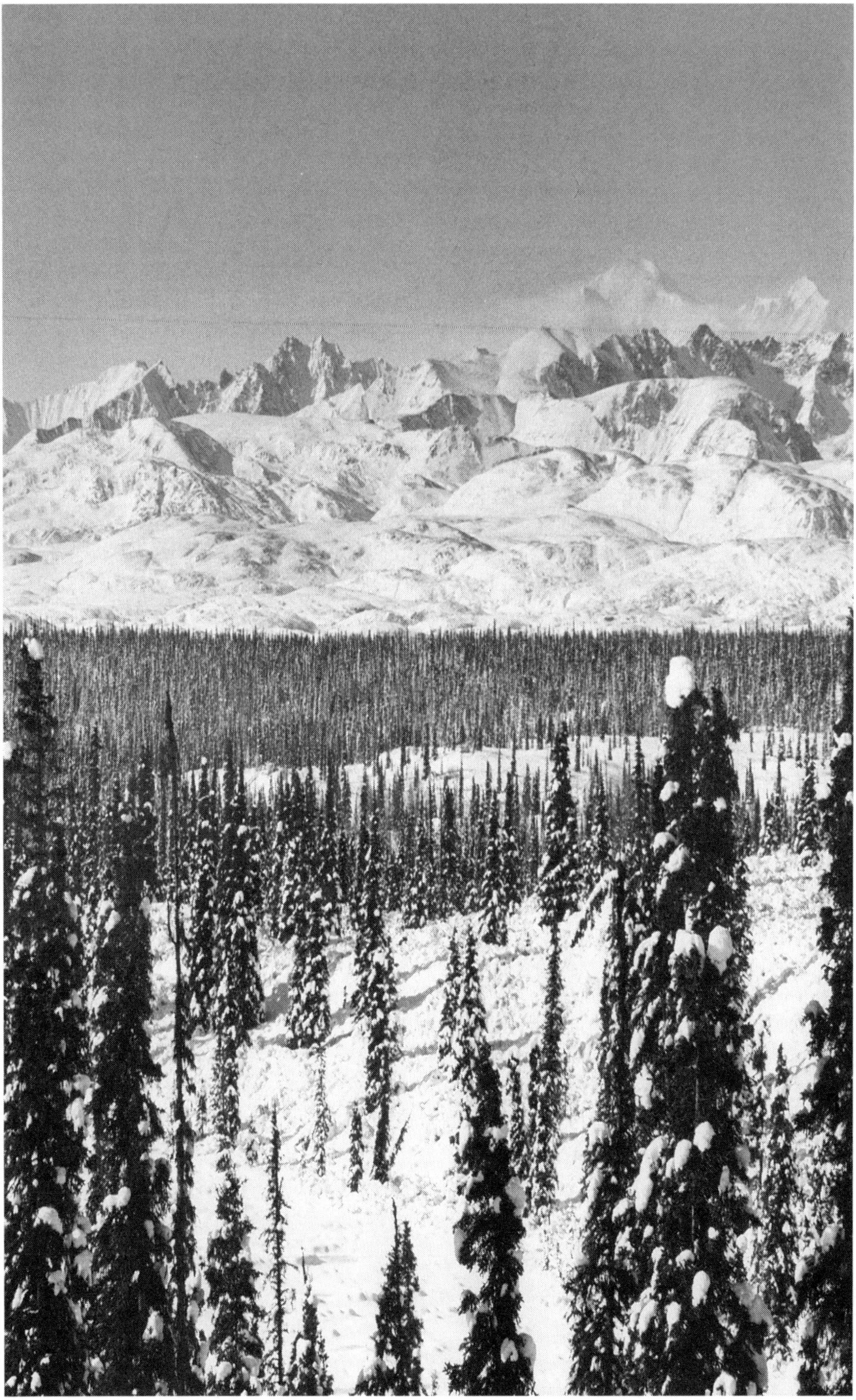

kind of equipment for safe and comfortable survival.

I have often wondered about Russell Hallock, Wes and Cyndi's son, who was nine years old in 1982. Does he still live with his parents, or has he chosen another way of life?

I usually don't mention the names of bushrats because anonymity often goes with the lifestyle. Most people I have talked with or written about who live alone in the wilderness request that I not use their names, or at least change their names.

Wes Hallock was an exception. The only request he made was that I not disclose the location of his chosen paradise, a request I have honored.

This story appeared in *Outdoor Life* in January 1983.

Wesley Hallock built a cabin at elevation 1,100 feet in the Alaska Range in an area where the timberline is at 2,000 feet. Moose live there with occasional caribou, bears, and small game, and it is fair fur country.   JIM REARDEN PHOTO

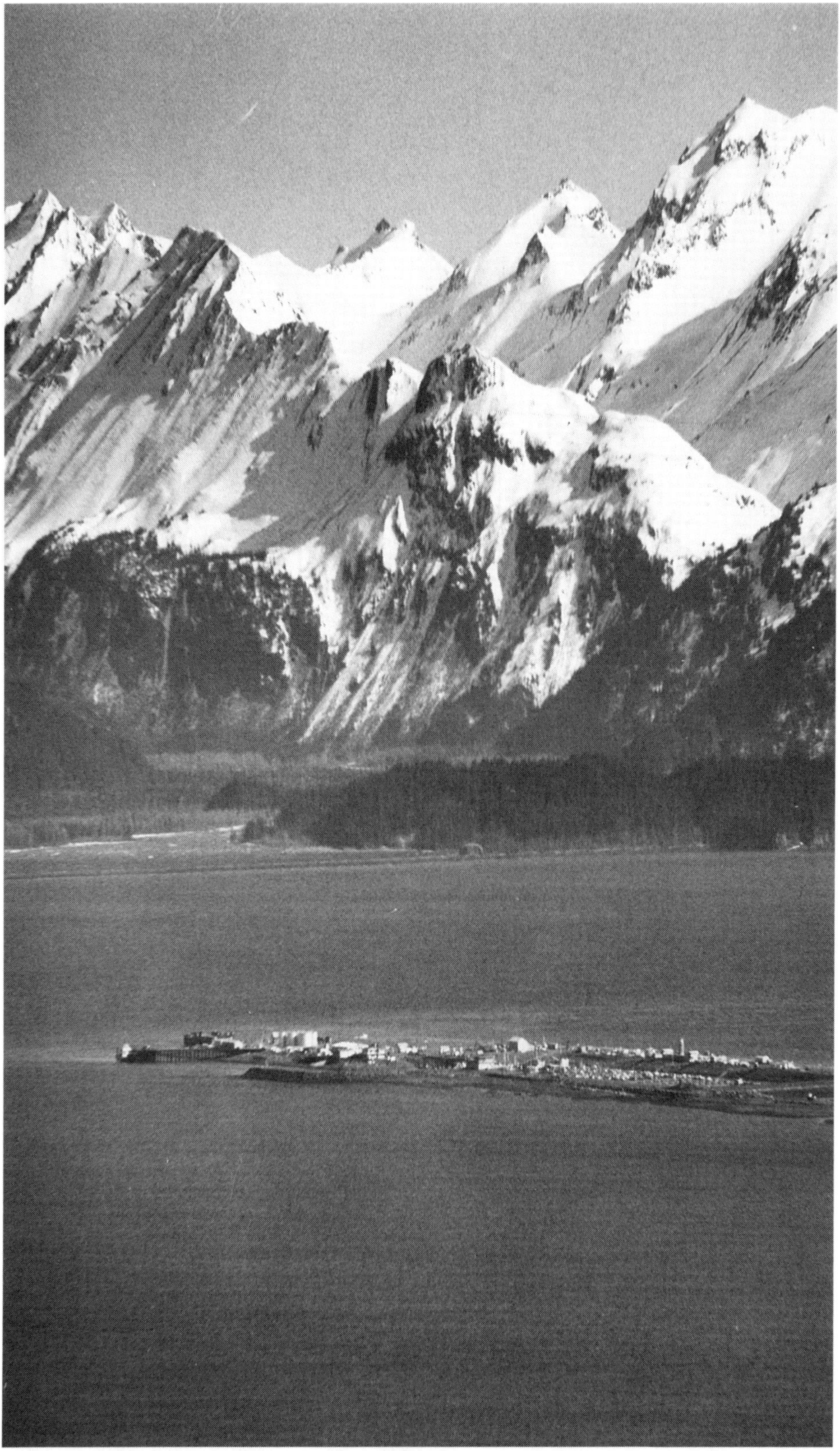

CHAPTER TWENTY

AT HOME ON KACHEMAK BAY

In 1977, Bob and Phyllis Henning, then owners and publishers of Alaska magazine, traveled abroad for several months. Bob wrote the "Main Trails & Bypaths" column for the magazine each month, but he asked me to write the May 1977 column. Bob prefaced my article this way:

"Jim Rearden, Alaska magazine's Outdoors Editor, lives at Homer on the Kenai Peninsula, where oil and moose, and in the opinion of some local residents, 'too damn many tourists,' make for a graphic example of the 'old' Alaska jammed up against the new. We asked Jim to use 'Main Trails' space this month to tell it as it is for him and his family in this time of change—to give you a thumbnail assessment of what has happened in the past few decades, and what he surmises the future might hold."

The *Sea Lion* plunged and leaped as huge foam-crested waves battered her. I spun the wheel again and

An early 1960s photo of a portion of the four-mile-long Homer Spit in Kachemak Bay. The spit is now a popular center for recreation, shopping, and tourism; the towering Kenai mountains are within Kachemak Bay State Park.

JIM REARDEN PHOTO

again to meet the fury of the seas that roared into lower Cook Inlet from the turbulent Gulf of Alaska. My wife Audrey, knuckles and face white, hung on grimly. Neither of us thought the twenty-seven-foot boat would survive.

We were struggling to reach Kachemak Bay at the tip of the Kenai Peninsula, on the east side of the inlet.

After nine hours of fighting the sea and our panic, we pulled into the shelter offered by the Kenai Mountains that forever defend Kachemak Bay from the furies of the gulf.

As I often do when I return to this bay, I thought then of my reasons for settling here twenty-two years ago. Like the *Sea Lion,* I was seeking shelter—a place where the furies of a frantic world might pass me by.

In 1947, on my own Cook's quest of discovery, I followed the track of that great explorer to Alaska as a summer employee of the U.S. Fish and Wildlife Service. Aboard the eighty-foot FWS *Crane,* I had a royal tour of the Inside Passage of Southeastern Alaska, after which we crossed the stormy Gulf of Alaska and stopped at Seward. Next, the *Crane* rolled her white wake across the tranquil blue waters of forty-mile-long Kachemak Bay. Parrot-beaked puffins and quick-winged murres arrowed past, herring gulls and kittiwakes quarreled on nearby rookeries, and white-headed bald eagles soared above.

We docked at Seldovia on the south shore, where I watched fishermen readying boats and nets for the salmon season. I explored the boardwalk that overhung the lapping waters of Seldovia Bay. It tunneled through stores that overflowed with frontier-taming tools, clothing, pilot crackers, canned food, boat parts, fishing gear, hardware.

I hiked into the mountains and sat on a high grassy hillside. Few houses were visible. The nearest highway, which was gravel, was one hundred miles away. Kachemak Bay glistened like a blue, translucent jewel, with deep, clear waters, bordered by thrusting glacier-encrusted mountains and pungent spruce forests. It was a virtually untouched land, with a beauty I had never before experienced.

But change was on the wind. At the very moment I sat on that grassy hillside, a survey crew was laying out the route of the Sterling Highway, which by 1952 was to become a dusty link between Homer, on the north shore of Kachemak Bay, and Anchorage, 235 miles away.

In 1947 Seldovia, with 450 residents, was a major hub of commerce on the Gulf of Alaska. All mail and freight came by boat. Most ships that were headed to the westward—Kodiak, the Alaska Peninsula, the Aleutians, Bristol Bay—stopped at Seldovia. The stores of Seldovia were the banks: a fisherman would hand his pay over to his storekeeper at the end of the salmon fishing season, keeping enough for a party or two. Annual "jawbone" (credit) was the rule; customers were expected to pay after the fishing season, and salmon was almost the sole industry. With poor seasons the bill might go unpaid for several years.

When one of the small freighters of the Alaska Steamship Company arrived each week, most Seldovians came to the dock to watch and to greet the ship. At Christmas the crew always had a bag of oranges, candy, and nuts for every kid in town. The kids were allowed to explore the ship, and each child was allowed to blow the whistle. There wouldn't be another ship until April, when the salmon cannery tenders arrived from Seattle with supplies.

Each year at the end of fishing, the cannery tenders hauled fishermen and homesteaders to Seldovia from all around lower Cook Inlet so they could buy a year's supply of groceries. Stores worked twenty-four hours a day at this time, with clerks hauling tons of boxed groceries and bags of flour along the boardwalk on hand-pulled wagons. There were few cars in Seldovia then. Tenders, jammed with supplies, would leave on the morning tide, and the homesteaders and fishermen often wouldn't return to Seldovia for another full year.

I left Seldovia reluctantly that year, for the friendly, relaxed, pioneering spirit was contagious.

Three years later I was back in Alaska, a faculty member at the University of Alaska at Fairbanks, in Interior Alaska. But teaching wasn't for me. In 1955 I became a freelance writer, which was the excuse I needed for moving to the shore of Kachemak Bay, the beauty of which still haunted me.

Now in 1977, more than twelve hundred people live at Homer, where I settled, with about five thousand in the trading area. There were fewer than five hundred in 1947. The Sterling Highway, which winds through the spruce forests, tundra, and mountains from Homer to Anchorage, is now paved.

Commercial fishing is still the foremost employer, but tourism and farming and a half-subsistence-from-the-land kind of life sustain many residents. Some who live at Homer work in the oil industry, commuting to offshore platforms in upper Cook Inlet, and for the past few years, some have worked on the trans-Alaska oil pipeline.

Seldovians still depend largely upon fishing, but the great earthquake of 1964, combined with the building of the Sterling Highway, which doesn't reach Seldovia, bumped that village into a kind of limbo. Changes that occurred on the shores of Kachemak Bay as a result of the earth's great convulsion were almost as violent as the quake itself. With the quake Seldovia settled about three feet, and high tides soon washed over the boardwalk and into canneries and stores.

After a bitter fight, a slight majority of Seldovia residents voted to allow a federal urban renewal program to rebuild the town. It did so by first destroying all the canneries, the boardwalk, and most of the homes and stores, and cutting down a midtown landmark hill. At the same time a fine new ice-free boat harbor was constructed.

It was, and still is for some, a bitter experience. "The bastards destroyed my home and my town," Jack English, a fifty-four-year resident of Seldovia, told me. Jack has been a marine surveyor, a U.S. commissioner, and a state magistrate. His wife, Susan, was Seldovia postmaster for forty-nine years.

At the destruction of their town, many Seldovia fishermen fled to the lucrative Kodiak fishing grounds; few have returned. Crab has become king to Seldovia, and an old Alaskan crab-processing firm, Wakefield Fisheries, constructed a modern processing plant there even as urban renewal was being completed.

Seldovia today in 1977, with about the same population as in 1947, with loggers now included among the citizenry, is recovering and growing. But the old-time atmosphere is gone, and the town has an entirely new character.

Homer, on the north side of the bay, is where the action is. Here ends the paved road from Anchorage. A four-mile-long gravel and sand spit projects into the bay, the tip of which was the site of the original town because it was a convenient boat landing. Today the town spans several miles of upland at the base of the spit; the spit is the industrial section, with several fish canneries, and recreational center.

Old-time Homerite Stanley Nielson was six when his parents brought him here from Denmark in 1919. "There were no roads then—nothing but moose trails," he recalls. "We bought groceries in Seldovia once a year. Once my brother and I counted eighty moose in one herd. We practically lived on moose meat. We burned nothing but local coal and wood for heating and cooking, hauling it with a wagon and a team of horses. We used coal-oil lamps."

The big 1964 quake gave Homer a boost, although the event itself was frightening. I stared in amazement as seventy-foot spruce trees whipped like fishing poles, waves rippled the ground, parked cars skittered and leaped, and power poles and wires dipped and whipped crazily.

The most serious damage at Homer was loss of the new harbor breakwater at the tip of the spit. It was constructed of auto-size boulders; all were swallowed by a submarine landslide. One moment there was a breakwater, next moment it was gone.

The boost for Homer came with the fine new boat harbor constructed at the end of the spit by the Corps of Engineers to replace the destroyed boat haven. It has provided a safe home for a large fleet of salmon, shrimp, halibut, and crab fishing boats, as well as a swarm of summertime pleasure boats. Seldovia and Homer fishermen earn several million dollars annually from Kachemak Bay for their efforts, as this glistening, deep, clear-water bay has proved to be one of the richest marine environments in the world.

A lot of boat wakes crisscross Kachemak Bay, with the commercial fishing fleet and the hundreds of sport boats. Another kind of wake results from the approximately three hundred oil tankers and freighters that annually jog into the bay to pick up or drop off the marine pilots they need to negotiate the waters of the upper inlet.

The moose are still here, but not in the numbers they once were. Fire protection has allowed much of the Kenai Peninsula to grow into dense spruce stands— poor habitat for moose. Hunting pressure is great, and the only big bull moose are in hard-to-reach distant mountains. However, when snow is deep in the hills, a handful of moose are pushed to the lowlands, and many spend their winters in and around Homer, feeding on remnants of vegetable gardens and on yard plants and scrub willows.

There has been more human change and development on the shores of Kachemak Bay in the three decades since I first viewed it in 1947 than in all previous history. Greatest impact has resulted from the highway. With it have come unkempt drifters, sportsmen, tourists, serious young people looking as I did for a place to make their home, and many Alaskan retirees.

During summer, dust billows high from graveled side streets and outlying roads as traffic builds. Daily I see the pinprick sparkle of great jets high overhead in the clear Alaskan sky, contrails inked to the horizon, as a reminder of the nearness nowadays of other lands and other ways. Small planes and helicopters constantly buzz overhead.

Old homesteads are being subdivided so that new homes can be built on the resulting small lots, and land prices are high; thousands of dollars for an acre for remote plots isn't unusual. Few have water or sewage facilities or are near a road.

Local spruce trees are being cut as never before. Most logs are shipped to Japan, and it is difficult to buy even rough-sawed local lumber at about two hundred dollars for a thousand board feet.

The state, in a frenzy for income, leased the bottom of fish-rich, lovely Kachemak Bay to oil companies for $25 million. The howl that arose from local residents and fishermen who love the bay, and who derive their income from it, with resulting court action and pressures, caused Alaska's legislature to authorize the governor to buy the leases back, and oil drilling in Kachemak Bay itself appears indefinitely postponed.

These impacts of civilization, and the summer Coney Island atmosphere of Homer Spit, with the Chamber of Commerce drive to "develop" the area and to promote "progress," are not what I sought when I first viewed this lovely bay.

But one mellows with age. I must admit I appreciate the paved highway when I want to visit Anchorage, the modern phone system that has replaced the voice radio I first knew here, the modern hospital, the volunteer fire department, and varied services and stores.

The chill waters of the bay are still clear and clean, despite an occasional minor oil slick, and the great mountains and glaciers still glisten as they did at my first view, while the spruce forests along the south shore—now largely a state park—still march essentially unmarred to the restless waters. Seabirds still quarrel at their rookeries, and sea otters reappeared about a decade ago, returning to Kachemak after nearly a century of absence.

The ultimate refuge for the Rearden family—wife Audrey, thirteen-year-old Tamara, fourteen-year-old Michael, and me—is the log home I built with my own hands. The logs were cut on the south side of Kachemak Bay and floated to the Homer Spit, where they were sawed on three sides. I lifted each eight-inch-by-eight-inch-square log into place on the two-story building and installed the plumbing, wiring, and heating systems.

When winter storms rage and snow rattles against windows, there is a near-indescribable satisfaction in the shelter and warmth of this sturdy, comfortable home, which is heated, at least partially, with family-gathered coal from nearby beaches. It is then that we enjoy the fragile beauty of frost-etched windows or the delicate corona of sunrise on snow tossed thousands of feet above the sheltering Kenai Mountains by the furious winds from the Gulf of Alaska.

Memories build each year, and I can conjure all sorts of mind treasures from my time here: snow sparkling like heaped diamonds under a full moon; a silver moon path across the quiet bay leading to great peaks and glaciers; blazing, colorful sunsets; wild mirages of upside-down mountains that are mirror images of the real ones we see each day. Streams full of splashing, spawning salmon. Wintering moose daily in the yard. Full pots of claw-waving king crabs.

For more than two decades I have heard the rumble of spume-tossing surf as great westerlies have roared across lower Cook Inlet into Kachemak Bay. I recall dozens of solitary walks on Kachemak's many beaches when I was accompanied only by my dog and the plaintive cries of gulls, the slap of waves, the sighing of clean wind. Nothing is more soothing.

Despite changes, Kachemak Bay is still the loveliest place I know.

The changes during the quarter-century since I wrote this 1977 article about Kachemak Bay and its towns have been even greater than those that occurred during the

three decades after 1947, when I first saw the bay. There are now even more residents (four thousand within Homer city limits, and at least that many more in surrounding areas), more visitors, more roads, more urban sprawl, and some new problems.

Spruce bark beetles have destroyed much of the spruce forest that surrounds the bay. There are now huge patches of reddish brown, dead spruce trees. The king crabs are all but gone from the bay, and the commercial and personal fisheries for them have disappeared. The tons of shrimp once trawled from the clean waters are depleted. Other ocean types have replaced them; gray cod, once unheard of in the bay, are now common. But halibut and salmon are still abundant.

We no longer have to order everything from catalogs, for there are now well-stocked stores within a few blocks of my log home. Instead of one doctor, there are perhaps a dozen, with frequent visits from specialists, and two full-time surgeons. There are several dentists, instead of the occasional visit by old Doc Pollard with his foot-pedal drill.

I may be an old curmudgeon, but if I could turn the clock back to the mid-1950s when Homer was a village of about five hundred residents, I'd do it in a second—along with the gravel roads, the lack of a boat harbor, absence of a city water and sewer system, and lack of other amenities that are generally regarded as "progress."

There is much to be said for a slow pace of life, uncrowded living, low level of human strife (Homer had one state police officer in 1956; there are now ten city police officers plus two state troopers), and lightly traveled roads. Instead of the rural village I chose for a home, I now live in a lively, sprawling urban community, beset by traffic and visited by tens of thousands of tourists each summer.

I feel today about Kachemak Bay as I did back in 1977: despite the changes, it is still my choice for a home, and I expect to remain here for the rest of my days. But like most other longtime citizens of Homer, I think the old days were the best.

INDEX

ABOUT JIM REARDEN

A resident of Alaska for more than fifty years, Jim Rearden has written eighteen books and more than five hundred magazine articles, mostly about Alaska.

Recent books include *Alaska's Wolf Man,* which recounts the wilderness adventures of Frank Glaser; *Castner's Cutthroats,* a fact-based novel about the famed Alaska Scouts of World War II; *Arctic Bush Pilot,* a memoir of the Alaska flying career of James L. "Andy" Anderson; and *Shadows on the Koyukuk,* the life story of trapper, businessman, and public-service leader Sidney Huntington.

Rearden has served as a federal fishery patrol agent in Alaska, taught wildlife management at the University of Alaska Fairbanks, and was fisheries biologist in charge of commercial fisheries in Cook Inlet for ten years. He has also been a commercial fisherman and a registered big game guide. He served on the Alaska Board of Game for twelve years.

Rearden was outdoors editor for *Alaska* magazine for twenty years, and for twenty years was also a field editor for *Outdoor Life* magazine. He lives in Homer with his wife, Audrey, in a log house he built himself.

RECOMMENDATIONS
for readers seeking a greater understanding
of Alaska and its people:

ONE SECOND TO GLORY: The Alaska
Adventures of Iditarod Champion Dick Mackey,
Memoir by Dick Mackey, as told to Lew Freedman,
trade paperback, $14.95

OUR ALASKA: Personal Stories about Life in Alaska,
edited by Mike Doogan, trade paperback, $14.95

RIDING THE WILD SIDE OF DENALI,
by Miki & Julie Collins, trade paperback, $14.95

TALES OF ALASKA'S BUSH RAT GOVERNOR:
The Extraordinary Autobiography of Jay Hammond,
Wilderness Guide and Reluctant Politician,
trade paperback, $17.95

ARCTIC BUSH PILOT:
A Memoir, by James "Andy" Anderson
as told to Jim Rearden, trade paperback, $16.95

COLD RIVER SPIRITS: The Legacy of an Athabascan-
Irish Family from Alaska's Yukon River,
by Jan Harper-Haines, hardbound, $19.95

COLD STARRY NIGHT: An Alaska Memoir,
by Claire Fejes, trade paperback, $19.95

FATHER OF THE IDITAROD: The Joe Redington Story,
by Lew Freedman, trade paperback, $16.95

MOMENTS RIGHTLY PLACED: An Aleutian Memoir,
by Ray Hudson, trade paperback, $14.95

These titles can be found or special-ordered at your local
bookstore. A wide assortment of Alaska books also can
be ordered at the publisher's website,
www.EpicenterPress.com or by calling 1-800-950-6663.